irregular therapy

irregular therapy

STUMBLING INTO SELF-ACCEPTANCE, ONE RELATIONSHIP AT A TIME

RON WYN

Portland

Some of the names and identifying characteristics discussed in this book have been changed to protect the guilty and innocent alike.

This book reflects a personal journey into issues of identity and self-worth, transformation, growth, and discovery. It is not intended to serve as emotional or therapeutic advice related to individual situations. Nor is it intended to be a diagnosis, recommendation, or cure for any specific kind of problem.
The publisher and author specifically disclaim any liability resulting from the use or application of the information contained in this book. Always seek the advice of a licensed, qualified physician, therapist, or other competent professional regarding any mental-health symptom or medical condition.

Neither publisher nor author condone the use of mind-altering substances of any kind, participation in any illegal activity, or acting in any way that violates local, federal, or any applicable laws or regulations.

Wyn House
Portland

Published in 2011
Printed in the United States of America

Library of Congress Control Number: 2011901010

ISBN 978-0-9832810-4-7

To

My Wife—my unconditional friend and lover

My Son—my teacher

GRATITUDES

I am grateful to the people who have somehow been part of my journey. Really. This book could not have happened without you. To my father and mother, whom I dearly love as true friends and who did their best in my upbringing. Really. This book could not have happened without you. To my family and friends, who have been there for me, in one way or another. Really. This book could not have happened without you. To all the women with whom I was involved in deeper relationships. No, really. This book could not have happened without you. To all my masters and teachers, inner and outer, who have guided my every move thus far. Really. No, I mean, really. This book could not have happened without you. To the kind folks who helped me put this project together. Really. This book could not have happened without you. And last but not least, to me, of course, for sacrificing my privacy for the greater good, among many other things. Really. This book could not have happened without you.

The way to do is to be

—Lao Tse

CONTENTS

PREFACE Truth Be Told ... 17

ONE Long Live the King ... 19

TWO Mommy Dearest ... 27

THREE From Water to Wine...to Water ... 47

FOUR She's Not You ... 67

FIVE Ch-Ch-Changes ... 81

SIX The Devil in Disguise ... 99

SEVEN Variety ... 119

EIGHT Crazy Cara ... 145

NINE The Destroyer of Demons ... 157

TEN Liberation ... 169

ELEVEN The Leap that Never Was ... 179

TWELVE The Final Cut ... 189

THIRTEEN Pushed Out of the Nest ... 205

FOURTEEN Starting Over ... 223

FIFTEEN Shin Aleph Hey ... 241

POSTSCRIPT Fast-Forward ... 253

ABOUT THE AUTHOR ... 257

BEFORE YOU CONTINUE

Hi and welcome to my story. Before you continue, please take a moment to read this important message. As you go through the book, you will most probably notice my "not-so-peachy" attitude toward some people—especially women—who have crossed my path. Yet, while many of the understandably upsetting positions depicted herein can indeed be seen as damaging and offensive, this was surely not my intention. There is a reason for all this.

This book is primarily a catharsis, a deep emotional release. And, much like in a therapeutic environment, where one expunges inner demons by twisting towels, screaming, and cussing, I have made use of this medium to eradicate unwanted traces of culturally acquired garbage from my system. This meant allowing my sickly mental patterns, including the often insidious experience of male entitlement, to emerge and fully express themselves. In other words, my most sincere apologies, but I had to let whatever wanted to come up, to come up. No judgment. No censure.

With this in mind, as you come across the more provocative bits, please be sure to take two points into account. First, this work depicts a healing process and not a boastful description of my sexual exploits. Though the tone might seem self-indulgent at times, it is essentially a cautionary tale. It exposes not only root problems and issues, but also the positive consequences brought about by facing them head-on.

Second, and more importantly, this piece does not reflect my opinion on gender equality, sexuality, or any other issue that may have come up throughout the narrative. I would like to make crystal clear that I intend no harm to any woman in particular or to the female gender, and certainly don't condone any kind of misogyny or denigration of women. It is my firm belief that everyone—irrespective of age, ethnicity, gender, or sexual identity—deserves to be appreciated for their intrinsic worth. Everyone—regardless of religious preference, physical appearance, or socioeconomic status—is entitled to a life free of violence, insult, and abuse.

irregular therapy

PREFACE

Truth Be Told

Let me take you on a true journey. A man's journey through the rough seas of relationships. A journey that led him to realize that real change must come from within. A journey with themes so archetypical, so universal, that although it takes place mostly in exotic Brazil, it may as well have happened in your very own neighborhood.

Wait. Hold on. What a load of rubbish. Permission to speak freely...

Shortly before finishing this manuscript, I had it evaluated by a hotshot in the book business. He told me he found it easy reading and compelling. He told me the sex angle would bring lots of readers. He told me the book was nearly ready to go. But he also told me he had a problem with my preface. He told me it kind of wandered around and didn't really tell him what he could expect from the book or why he should read it. Shit.

You know, I've been working on this thing for a couple of years. I've reviewed it so many times I've almost memorized it. Yeah, you don't have to tell me. Such is a writer's life. But the fact is I'm completely saturated and can't wait to see it published. So when the guy suggested that I rewrite the damned preface, I almost fell off my chair.

But the hotshot fella's probably right. And after all, I didn't pay good money to teach my grandma to suck eggs. So here I go.

Let's see. Right. I suppose I could dish out the usual plethora of clichés found in prefaces and tell you this is a "coming-of-age book," a captivating truth-told sexual romp, an honest if not a bit single-minded story of a cure, and blah, blah, blah. Yawn. Boring.

I could possibly try to make you feel some sympathy from the start and say it took me many lost years to get my emotional cards in order or that despite the relentless fun and not too troubling approach, I saw a number of hard-earned lessons, over years, and changed accordingly to display the virtues learning those lessons brought. Well, these things are certainly true for me. But you might not see my story this way, nor do I think you will much care.

I could play shrewd, aim for the masses, and reveal that in spite of the bumps along the way (or maybe because of them), I've managed to find my soul mate and, with secret formula in hand, I can show you by example how to attract your own twin flame. Tacky, tacky, tacky.

Perhaps I could anticipate some criticism by posing as the conscientious writer and confessing that although my account may seem rather exploitative, especially from a woman's point of view, it couldn't be otherwise if it were to show my gradual emotional growth. Nah. Who am I to know what's on a woman's mind.

What if I appeal to your emotions by stating that through my troubled relationships, I've learned to respect and understand myself better, as well as others around me. Or that as a result of having had these experiences, I'm now able to see what was self-defeating and greedy and have been able to grow from and past it. Dear God. Too psychological.

Useless. I'm looking for something unique, something different, but the harder I try, the less comes to mind.

I hate to say it, but I feel I've run out of fuel. So much for telling you what you can expect from my book and why you should read it. Seems that this should be a simple enough task, but silly me. Trying to boldly write what no man has written before.

This is really getting on my nerves. And I'm going nowhere. Tell you what. If you don't mind, I'll just call it a day and you can go ahead and read the book. Deal?

ONE

Long Live the King

Born a poor, young country boy...hold it. Nothing so poetic. On November 9, 1965, I'm born into an upper-class family in Rio de Janeiro, Brazil. My birth isn't easy on my mom. She almost dies. As for me, after almost being choked to death by the umbilical cord before even getting a chance to live, I come out with a broken collarbone and have to stay in the hospital for a few days. Hmm. My relationship with Mommy doesn't begin on a very positive note.

After that minor mishap, I finally get to go home. Ah, home, sweet home. My parents have been expecting me for a very long time. After trying (bummer, a girl), and trying (crap, another girl), and trying (what the hell, still another girl) and trying (oops, born dead, but still a girl), they have finally managed to produce a baby boy—an heir to the throne, born and ready to be bred in a patriarchal, male-chauvinistic society. Great. I have it made.

Now, for the intros. My father, a prominent psychiatrist with very humble origins in a small town, has made it big in the city. My mother, an aspiring artist, comes from a rich and noble family of German ancestry. She divides her time among upper-class housewife duties, art school, and the beauty salon.

I have three older sisters. Liz, my oldest sibling, looks like my mommy—dark, straight, shiny hair and soft, silky white skin. She's kind of violent, though. Liz enjoys dragging my other two sisters around the house by their hair. Cynthia, my middle sister, the one with beautiful caramel eyes, is outgoing and always in a good mood. Finally, there's Veronica, my youngest sister, a cute, petite girl who studies the piano and likes to boss people around.

Our house is huge. My dad bought it from his father-in-law, who unfortunately passed away a few years before I was born. We have a nice yard and a swimming pool. My parents are constantly hosting dinners for the entire family, which is enormous. I have tons of uncles, aunts, and cousins. Yes, a pretty nice environment to begin a happy and successful life. And everyone's around me all the time. Spoiled, spoiled, spoiled. What else could a cute little boy like me ask for.

Right from the start, Mom and Dad decide my upbringing will be perfect—the perfect education, the perfect diet, the perfect guidelines. And from the beginning, I show my parents I can live up to their expectations. At two and a half, I'm the only child in the nursery who can actually tie shoelaces. My. What a genius.

May 10, 1968

Boohoo. My short reign's over. My brother was born a few days ago. Grrr. I don't like him from the start. My brother's not at all like me. He takes after Mom's side of the family. Blonde hair and green eyes. A little German greaseball. Whatever happened to all the attention I used to get. He has stolen my love. I see my mommy taking care of him. I see my mommy breastfeeding him. I see her smiling at him and holding him in her arms. I'm enraged. She has no more time for me. I don't understand. I'm confused. I'm jealous. I wish he were dead. I beg and I beg and I scream for attention. I'm ignored. I'm rejected. She loves him more than she loves me. In fact, she doesn't even like me anymore. I want to die. I'm lost. I'm sad. I'm also overreacting. What do you expect; I'm just a little kid.

I turn to my daddy in desperation. Hey, I've got to make do with what I have. He holds me in his arms. I feel nice and warm. I know I'm Daddy's boy. I inherited his dark wavy hair and deep, penetrating eyes. And I use them to send hate vibes to my brother on my mommy's lap. I'm really, I mean really, pissed off. Not good. Not good at all. Look at Daddy. He's witnessing the birth of a big-time neurosis.

Eventually I'm forced to settle for a new mommy. Sister Veronica gets the chance to take care of me. She's thrilled. She treats me like her own little doll. She sits me down and teaches me things. I memorize all the planets in the solar system. I know many state capitals by heart. I'm such a good student. I'll do pretty much anything to avoid being rejected again.

I study in my sisters' room, which is very cool. One of the walls has a large collage with strange pictures of spaceships and of a weird man with a painted face holding a snake. His name's Alice. I don't understand why he has a girl's name, but I kind of like him anyway.

Early Childhood Memory

We're on vacation in this place with hot springs. I'm in the swimming pool with Daddy. He's big and powerful. I touch his chest hairs. I like messing around with them. Daddy's smiling. He likes to have me close to him. He loves me very much.

My grandpas passed away before I was born. It would have been nice to have some of that pampering and spoiling only grandpas are able to provide, but I guess I'll have to do without it.

Both my grandmas are still alive, and I really enjoy being around them. Grandma Emma, my daddy's mom, is a wonderful little lady. She sings all day long. She still lives in the country. We meet up with my daddy's relatives when we're over at her place. They're a bucket of fun. My uncles and aunts are all very friendly. And they're all very loud. Especially when they drink.

Early Childhood Memory

I'm at my uncle's house. My daddy's brothers, sisters, and cousins are gathered together and they're chatting, eating, and laughing.

I'm sleepy. It's getting late. I don't want to leave the fun party. No problem. Daddy's here. He holds me in his arms. I rest my little head on his powerful chest and shoulders. I can feel his warmth. I can hear his voice resonating inside his body. Ah, what a soothing sound. I'm feeling great. I'll sleep very well tonight knowing that my daddy loves me.

It's 1969 and I'm enrolled at school. Big changes. New environment. New friends. New sensations. Inside and out. I sometimes feel a little funny below the belt. It's a nice tingling sensation that makes me want to move in a strange way while climbing poles in the playground. I've seen dogs do this on people's legs. I don't know what it is or why I do it, but I sure do like it. I wonder what it would feel like if I did this on someone's leg.

I also have a girlfriend. She often comes to my house and we play in my room. We have a fun game. We get on my bed and I lie on top of her. We kiss and I feel that weird little tingling again. Oh yeah. Nice.

I'm not a very faithful boyfriend, though. Hell, I don't even know what that means. I'll take on whatever or whoever makes me feel good between my legs.

Here I go again when my nice cousin Pam is over. I think she's gorgeous. Her cheeks are rosy. She makes me feel very, very warm inside. We play and play and play. We run around and then hide behind the couch. I start grabbing her all over. And she likes it. It's all innocent fun.

I'm one naughty little kid. One time, I'm showering in my sisters' bathroom when I have a bright idea. I'm going to climb up the window and show my wee-wee to the dog outside. I get to the window and stick it out, only to find one of Grandma Emma's young lady helpers staring at me in utter disbelief. Uh-oh. I'm embarrassed as can be and almost fall off my perch, but manage to get to the ground safely. That was scary, but kind of exciting.

Sometimes Mom drops me off at her mother's place. Grandma Ingrid lives in a small and smelly apartment, but I like it here. My grandma's very nice to me. Her calming blue eyes make me feel good. We play Scrabble and she cooks yummy German food. She has a large picture of this guy Jesus in her room.

Grandma Ingrid is into charity. She's also into this weird soul connection thing. She and her friends meet around a table in the dark and summon spirits. I don't understand any of this stuff. It used to give me the creeps, but I've gotten used to it by now.

I've become a very sexually active little thing. In fact, my friends and I now spend recess chasing girls around the schoolyard. I've become deeply infatuated with one of our preys. Her name is Heather. Beautiful Heather. Her skinny body and cute little face drive me out of my silly young mind. But unfortunately, she's not into me. She likes one of my friends. Oh Lordy Lord. For the second time in my short life, I've been rejected. Sure feels like my mom-and-brother ordeal all over again. I'm hurt. I feel sad. I feel inferior. I hate my rival. And I stop chasing Heather. I stop trying because I'm certain she'll never choose me over him. I just know it. And when I get home, I hate my brother even more. *Go to hell and drop dead*, is what I say.

A Traumatic Experience

Today Mommy has come to pick me up at school. What a drag. I don't want to leave. I want to stay and have some more fun. I'm playing with my magic sword. It's forged from the finest plastic. I'm Zorro. I'm King Arthur. I'm all-powerful. I'm having a ball. But my mommy has arrived and wants me to go with her. I try to escape her evil claws. She chases me around the parking lot. She finally catches me and beats me with my own magic sword. There goes my power. I'm afraid of my mommy. I have a feeling I'll never forget this incident.

By late 1971, I'm a celebrity at school. I've just won a high-jump competition. I'm a sports star. Everyone wants to know who I am. Everyone's impressed. They say my future is bright. They take many pictures of me. I feel good about myself. And my mommy and daddy rejoice at their perfect child.

At home, my mommy's very strict. She forces us to eat vegetables. She makes us go to bed early. It's good for our health, she says. But she exaggerates a bit. If there's something worth watching as a family on late-night TV, she makes us take an afternoon nap so we can stay up late. I hate naps. I have a hard time falling asleep during the day. So I fake my nap. But Mommy comes by constantly to see if our closed eyes are blinking and we're really sleeping. Damn. Big Brother's on my tail.

Although I'm not officially Catholic, Mommy prays with us every evening before bed. I like that. It makes me peaceful. And I feel closer to my mommy.

I'm feeling naughtier than ever. I constantly climb up to the roof to watch the neighbor girl. She's a bit older than me, but I don't care. I still think she's hot. Whatever that means.

One day, I grab a pencil and some paper. I write the neighbor girl a dirty note. I tell her I want her. I fold the little note into a paper airplane. I throw the airplane into her room. I hide. I'm embarrassed. I'm terrified. But I'm also very excited. I'm tingling all over. I climb down and run inside, wondering if she got my note. Well, I don't think I'll follow up on this.

Early Childhood Memory

It's early evening and Mommy wants to clean my belly button and my ears. She does that sometimes and I like it. I get to lie still and feel the cool sensation of the alcohol on the cotton swab while she cleans me up. And it's nice to be close to my mommy every once in a while.

The year is 1972. My parents decide my school isn't good enough for me. Too many days off, they say. I'm terribly sad. I love school and my friends, but there's not much a six-year-old can do about his mighty parents' decisions, so I'm forced to play along.

I'm being transferred to an American school, a place for children of expatriates, diplomats, and wealthy folks. It's right across the street from the clinic run by my daddy, so at least I feel safe. I can always run to him if anything goes wrong.

Upon hearing the news, a good friend of mine, Marcus, begs his parents to transfer him to the American school. They think it's a good idea. Their son will learn English and broaden his horizons. I think this is great because I won't have to face the new situation alone.

Not My Brother's Keeper

I've been angry with my brother since he took over my reign. Bastard. I'll never forgive him for stealing my mommy from me.

One day, I'm playing in the yard. I'm Batman. I'm Robin. I'm Superman. I decide to climb the little house where the electricity box is stored. I have an umbrella in my hands. I'm going to jump down six feet and the umbrella's going to be my parachute. Sweet. Just like the Penguin.

The umbrella barely slows down my fall, but I make it safely to the ground. This is fun. I do it a few more times. Then along comes my stupid brother. He wants to do the same. He really annoys me. He is always trying to copy me. He climbs on the house. He jumps. Oops. Not really. He trips and falls and breaks his arm. Hate to say it, but I get a kick out of the entire thing.

The American school is awesome. Marcus and I soon make many friends. We can do pretty much whatever we want. We yell and climb on tables. The teachers are very nice. But I'm afraid of our headmaster. He's tall and bald and mean-looking. He wears those large, shiny black Marine's dress shoes. I sure hope I don't get in trouble and have to go see him in his office.

I know very little English, but that doesn't really matter. I'm learning quickly and will soon be able to communicate with my foreign friends.

Strangely enough, I'm starting to lose that very strong sexual thing. Girls, gross. I do have a female admirer, though. Her name is Yvonne and she's completely in love with me. Her intense Italian dark brown eyes follow my every move at school. (you can tell I have a thing for eyes.) Although we still grab girls and pull down their bikinis at pool parties like little chauvinistic monsters, we boys do these things mainly to be mean and I don't want to have anything to do with Yvonne. I just want to hang out with my buddies and wreak havoc. We organize ourselves into gangs and have fun throwing rocks at each other during recess.

At home, I've become a loner. I love going up to the attic and from there onto the roof, where I lie down and gaze at the beautiful blue sky. No one can follow me here. I'm free. And when my mother grounds me in my room, I have a secret escape route. There's an opening above my bed that leads to freedom. Like the little monkey I am, I climb towards the attic and off to the roof I go. Ha, ha, ha.

TWO

Mommy Dearest

By my seventh birthday, I begin to notice things are not going too well between my parents. The atmosphere at home has become very tense and uncomfortable.

A Traumatic Experience

Today Daddy and Mommy openly argue in my presence. They are fighting about money. We are wealthy, but I think this is just an excuse for them to express hostile feelings towards each other. Mommy wants cash for groceries. Usually quiet and polite, my daddy is now visibly upset. And I'm just sitting here, watching the entire thing and they don't seem to care. At all. I'm astonished. I'm afraid. I guess they're just too upset with each other to even consider what this might be doing to me.

After a while he finally settles and throws a few bills at her. What does a seven-year-old take from all this. The beginning of a bad relationship with money and women, that's what.

February 1973
We are spending the holidays at Dad's hometown and my parents are at a party. My daddy has a jealous fit. What's the big fuss all about. Oh. He thinks Mommy is flirting with a guy. He's very annoyed and goes home early, leaving us all at my grandma's.

When we get home from our trip, my daddy is nowhere to be found. All his stuff is gone. My mommy and my sisters throw tantrums. My brother and I don't know what to do or think. We don't really understand what's going on. And I'm just plain sad because I think I've lost my daddy. Well, time for some tough growing up.

All hell has broken loose. My parents are now engaged in a full-blown separation war. While my dad remains quiet and refrains from speaking about the situation, all Mom does is bad-mouth him. She's always babbling about how he left us, how he doesn't support us, and how he has done all kinds of bad things. She has also placed a large load on my shoulders. She tells me I'm now the man of the house.

I'm being torn apart. On the one hand, I don't want to see my mom cry and suffer. On the other hand, I simply cannot see Dad as a horrible person. He now picks up my brother and me every Saturday so we can spend time with him. He's great. He takes us places. In the afternoon, he drops us off, and I feel terrible to be back home and have to hear my mom whining all the time.

My awful situation at home is reflected in my school environment. Although it's not at all my nature, I've been fighting quite a bit. I guess I'm venting anger in order not to explode. I'm angry with my dad for having left me alone to take care of my mom. I'm angry with my mom for having caused this and for being such a bitch lately. And I'm still very angry with my brother. I'm one tough little ball of anger.

My parents' court hearings begin in July. Fortunately, my brother and I are spared the horror show. Mom wants to involve us, but we're too young. My sisters are forced to go and make depositions against my dad. My mom's trying to make herself a victim. She wants everybody to feel sorry for her. She paints the picture of a poor homemaker, stepped on by her ruthless husband, who left her alone to bring up five kids. Big, big chaos.

By November 1973, Mom's having a hard time maintaining our house and blames Dad for it. She says he doesn't give us money. I find that strange, because my dad's not at all a stingy person.

So now I begin to live a double life. At home, I live with my poor victimized mother and her increasingly hard times. Then there's this other world where my dad fully supports me and I go to the most expensive school in town. And I'd rather live in the second world.

At school, I've become some sort of kleptomaniac. I sneak into the teachers' room after school to steal pencils, pens, and staples. The danger and thrill of doing something wrong and taking something away from someone gives me an adrenaline rush. And it makes me feel better in some creepy way.

Mom is desperate. She feels she has no one to support her. It's not long before she follows her mother's footsteps and starts looking for answers among fortune-tellers and religious temples. And of course she forces us to come along.

I really hate these temples. They're in shady, dirty neighborhoods and filled with weird people. The religious "sessions" are generally carried out at night. The people chanting weird songs and channeling spirits scare the hell out of me. This is much more hard-core than Grandma's séances. And what's worse, sometimes my mom even holds sessions in our own house. I want my daddy.

Hocus Pocus

We are at a temple and my mom has been told that I must engage in some sort of ceremony to please my spiritual guide. And guess what. I'll have to sleep in this stupid place, not shower for an entire day, and follow a specific diet. I don't want to do it. I want to be with my friends and my dad and run away from all this crazy stuff. But she forces me to stay. I spend the night on a dirty cloth with candles and all kinds of bizarre objects around me. Super.

It's now early 1975 and our situation at home has been deteriorating by the day. My mom's fully into her poverty trip and is trying to drag us along. She refuses to accept alimony from my father. But strangely enough, she still gets her hair done at her expensive hairdresser whenever she can, even if it means we're having soup dinners for the rest of the month. And then she blames my dad and the fact that he doesn't give us money. What a load of crap.

Then one day, Mom drops a bombshell: I'll have to leave my beloved American school because she can no longer afford it. She says Dad hasn't been giving her money for school. I am sick of this. It's always my dad's fault.

One of my teachers has noticed that I am different. I tell her I'm sad because I'll probably have to leave school by the end of the year. She feels bad for me and tries to give me support whenever she can. And I'm grateful for her support. I could really use a positive female image right about now.

In July, I begin taking entrance exams for two other schools. The exams aren't hard, but I don't do well because I don't want to leave my school and will boycott my transfer as much as I can.

Then, just when I think my cause is lost, my prayers are answered. My dad has suddenly decided to take direct charge of school payments and I'll no longer have to leave. The reason for his change of heart is not really clear, but after that incident, Dad stops giving my mom child support money. Instead, he takes on direct responsibility and pays for our bills, health, clothes, food, and education himself.

After a couple of months and a few more awkward situations, my parents are legally separated. Mother has been trying to make us read the court proceedings and the entire lawsuit. She wants us to see what terrible things my father has done to her. What is she doing. I am only nine. And this is none of my business. I don't ever want to read any of this stuff. But I can see she's suffering a lot with the separation. I feel sorry for her, and many times even feel guilty for not supporting her as much as I think I should.

Because my dad and mom now avoid each other as much as possible, they start using me as a communication channel, especially when it comes to money. I'm the one who has to take our utility bills to Dad and collect his check, which later I give to my mom. Damn.

So my mom's in a bad mood because she's powerless without money. My dad's in a bad mood because of the constant demands. And I'm obviously making harmful connections about money in my mind.

One good thing has come out of my parents' separation process, though. Mom seems to have become quite friendly with her lawyer, George. He's also separated and has four kids. We go to his house and do things together sometimes. I sure do hope she finds another man to love and leaves us all alone.

A Recurring Fantasy

I'm an all-powerful being. I make use of my powers to stop the world and all the people in it. Time has stood still. I then decide to bring the girls of my choosing back to life. One by one, I wake them up and we do naughty sexual things. I can't tell exactly what I'm doing to them, but it doesn't matter. I feel strong. I feel powerful. I feel fulfilled. Whoa.

November 1975

I think I like women again. It's about time. Whatever happened to the latency phase. Oh, well. I'm in love with a very cute girl at school. I want to approach her, but by now my parents have kind of hammered my self-esteem to the ground and I'm very insecure and shy around women.

One day, my crush throws a birthday party and invites all her friends. At the party, I really want to talk to her, get close to her, but completely lack the courage. After a while, I notice she's holding hands with a good friend of mine. I'm stunned. I feel terrible.

I feel betrayed. I feel rejected. I feel an intense pain in my heart. This stupid rival thing is starting to repeat itself every once in a while, and there's nothing I can do about it.

By mid-1976, my mom finds yet another way to rock our world. Unfortunately, she can't escape her victim thing. Now she tells us that we can no longer afford to live in our house. She also says that the neighborhood's not what it used to be and that it's not adequate for a separated woman to bring up her five children alone. And as usual, my dad doesn't get involved in her decision. I resent him for this because it involves us all.

But I know what he's trying to avoid: contact with my mom. And we're the ones getting screwed for it. Too bad. No more roof trips. No more swimming pool. No more friends over. I'm sad. I truly love my home. It is the only place I have ever lived.

And to top it all, my dad has started seeing another woman. A psychologist. Don't know why, but I have a feeling they'll soon get married. The lady has three daughters about my sisters' age. Although my mom's still flirting with her lawyer, she makes a big fuss about the news, and my sisters feel rejected in a big way. But my brother and I aren't really affected by this and continue to see our dad every Saturday.

We move to a rented apartment. It's much smaller than our house. But it's nice. And it's not long before my older sister gets married and leaves. Good for her.

I'm now a sixth grader. My teenage years are about to begin, and the parties and social gatherings take up much of my free time. Yvonne still likes me. I now feel I have enough courage to handle a woman, but she's too easy. My struggle and rejection patterns simply don't respond, and I have no interest in her whatsoever.

Middle school's a big change for me. We can now cross the feared yellow line every once in a while to have classes in the high school area. Ooh. Now isn't that special. I feel important and grown up.

My mom has found a new job in a private jet company. We're doing okay, especially because she has been complaining less and less about my dad. We still see lawyer George around, but I think their relationship is going nowhere. I guess Mom's afraid of getting hurt once again.

The year 1977 brings about even more changes. I feel as if I'm in a roller coaster, but the biggest drop has yet to come. My mom no longer works for the jet company. She has managed to get a new job and now writes a column for a fashion magazine.

We aren't going to stay at our apartment much longer. Our old house has finally been sold. Mom gets half the money and the other half is divided among the five of us. Our money is deposited in a savings account, to be withdrawn when we come of age.

Mother takes her share and purchases some land in a faraway and brand-new neighborhood. The lot is not too big, but it's nice. She intends to build a house soon. The neighborhood's pretty deserted, but we figure we'll be safe because we are next door to a very large furniture store and a tennis club. Security guards roam around the vicinity and a bunch of luxurious houses are being built in the area.

Dad offers financial help to build our house, but guess what. My mom refuses. She wants to do it all by herself. She wants to boast to everyone about it. But of course, she has very little money left, so I'm pretty sure we are going to have to settle for a very small and uncomfortable house.

New Sensations

Mom's lawyer, George, has invited us to his beach house for the weekend. In the evening, all the boys are in one room sharing bunk beds. There's an older boy with us. He's telling us about a new thing called masturbation. Hmm. He tells us that when we masturbate, a white liquid's supposed to come out of our penises.

The next day, I give it a try. Nice. This masturbation thing reminds me of the pole-climbing practices in my old school. But wait. What's going on. Where's that white liquid the guy spoke of. Maybe I didn't do it right. So I try it again. And again. And again. Still no white liquid. Damn. My penis must be broken.

It is now July and our apartment's rental contract has expired, but our house isn't ready yet. We're going to have to move anyway. Mother has plans. She scatters us all over the place. At first, my brother and I stay at George's apartment. It's okay, but his home's far from school and his youngest son's a pain in the ass. And we hate being in someone else's house.

After a few months, we move again. This time, my mom has met a long-time school friend, who has gladly offered to have us stay with her. She and her husband live in a small house in our new neighborhood. I don't like these people. Not at all. They look like they've come straight out of a B-grade horror movie, kind of like bad copies of Uncle Fester and that ugly-ass old lady in the *Addams Family*.

Everything's fine during the first couple of weeks. Then the woman's stupid husband starts freaking out. He obviously doesn't want us here. He's rude and gives us dirty looks and yells at us for no reason. It isn't long before we get kicked out. Quite literally. Shit. (Yep, that's right. I now cuss.) I'm scared. I feel unsupported. Where's my dad. Why can't I stay at his place.

Luckily, our house is finally ready. But it's a piece of crap. It's too small. I knew it. We have no wall around the property, and that's unfortunate because we're exposed to all kinds of hazards, including huge rats cruising around the adjacent lot. Our home looks like a warehouse, with its single rectangular body and fiber cement corrugated sheets for a roof. In addition, the front's completely open, like a garage. The roller shutter door used as our main entrance is made up of bars that allow anyone to see inside our house and make us feel completely exposed. Our electricity is borrowed from the furniture store's enormous generator, which is literally stuck to our back wall.

Ah, the generator. It starts running very early in the morning. The house shakes all day long. The damned thing's so loud we can barely hear each other speaking. And what's worse, it doesn't stop until ten o'clock in the evening. That's when our lights go out. That's our curfew.

I'm so embarrassed of this place. While all my friends from the American school live in huge houses and nice apartments, I get to live in this hellhole. I'm pissed at my mom. I think she's very irresponsible.

By now Mom's no longer working at the magazine. She's into painting T-shirts. Batik and that kind of stuff. So on weekends, in addition to taking turns manually pumping water from the well in the property (as you might expect, we have no street water), we get to help her with her T-shirt business. What a great way to live.

We're still adapting to our new and exciting life. We finally have a wall around the property. I spend my weekend afternoons up on the roof, shooting at rats on the lot next door with my BB gun. Just like in my childhood, the roof's pretty much the only place I feel free. There's no way my mom can get up here.

I've started working in the evenings. I'm a ball boy at the tennis club next door. I hate my job. I'm embarrassed. None of my rich friends work. But on a positive note, I make some money, get to meet many nice and new people and learn to play tennis. Oh, and I no longer have to take bucket baths at home. I now get to use the facility's nice warm electric shower.

I've been masturbating quite a bit. I'm finally discharging that white and sticky thing from my penis. Hey, it doesn't seem to be broken after all.

I think of women all day long. Any tiny stimulus is enough to give me a hard-on that lasts for hours. I fantasize with women at school. I fantasize with women on the streets. I even fantasize with my sister. The beaten bathroom door at my house has a nice crack that allows me to watch her taking showers. Dirty bastard.

One of my friends from school lives in my neighborhood. Jack is an American kid who's always doing tricks on his cool mountain bike. Jack and I are bad news in the area. We often meet up with other evil spirits and do all sorts of nasty things. Like little twelve-year-old degenerates, we walk around nearby properties looking for things to rip off and vandalize.

In the evenings, we hang out in house construction projects, drink cheap wine, and smoke cheap cigarettes. We also like the rush of going to the supermarket and stealing things. In fact, we do get caught a couple of times, but there are no consequences. I suspect my mom would have killed me if she ever knew.

At school, during recess (bad things always happen during recess), we hide under the gym to smoke cigarettes. I also try this thing marijuana a couple of times, but don't feel a thing.

Jack's sister Betty is a couple of years younger than we are. I think she's cute, especially when I see her around her house in her tight swimsuit. But aside from the fact that I get to touch her butt when we play tag in the swimming pool, I don't give her much attention. That is, until the day someone tells me Betty has a crush on me. I immediately fall in love with her. Immediately.

She Loves Me, She Loves Me Not

A few of us are gathered together at a friend's house. Betty and I start getting friendly. We hold hands. We even kiss briefly. I can't even begin to explain my exhilaration.

Then, the following day, she gives me the boot for no reason. Maybe she's afraid. Maybe her mom thinks she's too young to be dating. I have no idea. The fact is that I'm now very depressed. I intensify my wine drinking and start smoking more and more cigarettes. I've found this helps me ease the pain in my young heart.

Lonely Wolf

I'm drunk. I'm bummed. I've been rejected big-time. The more I think about Betty, the sadder I feel. I'm at a nearby beach. I'm all alone. The beautiful full moon reflects off the clear ocean waters. The white sand around me glows under the starless sky. What a magical moment. But my heart hurts like never before. I call out Betty's name in the darkness. I feel like a lonely wolf crying out to the moon. Aye. This will do to hook a guy on smokes.

By late 1978, my kleptomaniac behavior has expanded to include my father. Whenever I'm at the clinic to see him, I steal small amounts of cash from his wallet. He's not the controlled type and never keeps track of his dough. I think I might be mistaking my daddy's love for his money.

Then one day, he notices some of his cash is missing. Oh shit. He questions me about it. I vehemently deny having taken any money from his wallet. Liar, liar. He asks me if I'm sure. I swear to him it wasn't me. I'm so afraid of telling him the truth. He's forced to make a big scene at the clinic. You just can't steal from the director. The situation becomes extremely uncomfortable. It's an unspoken fact. Everyone knows I took the money, but no one dares say it, because my dad's the boss. After a while things quiet down, but I feel very bad.

Playmates

My dad sometimes takes us to his private office during weekends. This week I discover his *Playboy* magazine stash and I'm delighted.

Without his knowledge, I take a good look at the magazines. Oh yeah. Masturbation material for sure. I want to take some magazines home, but dare not steal any; enough of that. So I retain the naked women images in my mind and discharge all the contained energy later during my two-hour-long shower.

I always look forward to vacation time. I often get sent away to other people's houses and can forget about my problems at home for a while. Now I'm off to visit family friends in another town. I'm excited because it's the first time I'm on a plane alone. I still have strong feelings for Betty, so this might be a good opportunity to forget her.

Will and Martha have been friends with my mom's family for ages and they have eleven kids. Stan, Art, and Amy are nearly my age. Oh, then there is Val, their cousin, who's always around. We hang out and do all sorts of crazy stuff, basically acting like normal teenagers.

I truly love it here. No one bothers me. And my routine is pretty awesome. I get up in the morning and work out with some cement weights I found in the back of the house. After breakfast, I go to work with Stan and Art at the small family shop adjacent to their home, where we spend the rest of the day munching on ice cream and listening to Stan boast about his sexual adventures (I'm pretty sure most of it is bullshit).

In the evening, I hang out with Amy and Val. We watch TV, tease and grab each other. Yummy. Two brunettes at my service. I have a feeling Amy's starting to like me. She's pretty and all, but I don't have feelings for her. Easy meat is not my thing. Now Val, she's an entirely different story. I can tell she enjoys the teasing game. She's playing hard to get. And she's driving me crazy. I'm hot for her newly formed breasts. I'm hot for her perfect legs. I'm hot for her moist, thick lips. But I'm also terribly afraid of rejection and end up doing nothing to conquer the lady.

On weekends Stan, Art, and I go to the neighborhood square. We get to see lots of girls. We drink and smoke. I'm a very shy kid and really don't look forward to going out in public, but for some reason, I go out anyway and never stay at home. Peer pressure, I guess.

One evening, I notice a most beautiful girl. I'm struck by the cute freckles all over her face. Very exotic. Someone tells me her name's Francine. She's checking me out as well. And boom. That's all it takes. I'm immediately in love with Francine. Forget Val. Forget Amy. Forget Betty. I now want Francine. Badly. I'm truly amazed at how fast I can transfer such intense feelings from one girl to another.

For the next couple of weeks, I go to the square with the sole purpose of admiring my new crush from a distance. I'm terrified to approach the girl. We exchange a couple of looks, but I remain on my platonic thing.

Unfortunately, before I know it my vacation is over. Francine is lost forever. So is Val. I'm devastated, but also relieved because my feelings have been diluted. I don't know which girl to grieve for. Great consolation.

A few months after my vacation, my heart confusingly aches for Val and Francine. Still. Then one day, I notice this girl at school. Her innocent-looking figure and sweet voice attract the heck out of me. Her name is Kathy and I think I might be falling for her.

I'm suddenly in love with Kathy, but I don't think she even knows it. Once again, I'm too shy to even tell her or anyone else. A couple of months go by and now we're off to a sports event. We are all very excited. A bunch of kids on a bus. Barely any adults. Kathy is here, too. Shoot. I just hate myself. I can't get around to telling her how much I like her. Well, the entire meeting goes by and I don't make a single move.

On the way back, one of my friends ends up making out with her. I'm completely heartbroken. But I'm not mad at him. I can't be. My lack of initiative is so obvious to me that I know it's really my fault. But once again my rival has defeated me. I begin to notice that this shitty love triangle situation is not a new thing.

One of the bad things about my school is that people are always leaving. You know how it is, expats living abroad. So, as the semester comes to an end, many of my friends are going away, and that includes Kathy.

By now the girl's obviously aware I'm madly in love with her. I guess she can tell from all my drooling. We start hanging out, but it's really too late.

Broken Heart

I have come to see Kathy in her hotel. She's leaving for good. My heart's completely broken. She's the love of my short life. I'll most probably never see her again. And we didn't even get to kiss once. Wow. How could I have been so shy. How could I have been such a wimpy loser.

Soon it's time to go. We hug and wave goodbye. I'm in the elevator. The door starts closing and her image is closing with it. I feel the exact same pain I felt when rejected by Betty. I want to howl to the moon, but there's no moon in the elevator and people would think I was crazy. So I go home utterly depressed. Damn. I think I need someone new to transfer my feelings to.

It's August 1979. I'm still badly hurt and school seems empty with so many friends gone. But I'm excited I'm finally in high school.

I now hang out with some crazy folks, Craig and Elsa. One day, Craig brings some of those tiny liquor bottles they serve at airplanes to school. After class, the three of us are in the smoking area having some smokes and taking sips of whisky. Suddenly, we hear footsteps. We're terrified. In an attempt to hide the bottle he has in his hands, Craig carelessly places it near the foot of the bench we are sitting on. Then along comes crabby Mrs. Stamford, head of student activities.

The screw-up timing is just perfect. Just as Mrs. Stamford walks by us, the bottle tips over and she sees it. We are doomed. She takes us to her gloomy office. We somehow convince the old hag Elsa wasn't involved. So Craig and I take full blame and get suspended for two weeks.

Oh, boy. You can imagine my mom's reaction. She gives me a whole lot of shit. She tells me I'm no good. She tells me I'm irresponsible and immature. Then comes the punishment (as if I weren't feeling bad enough already). She grounds me. She forces me to get up at six in the morning every day. I can't speak with any of my friends. Crap. No sympathy whatsoever. What the hell. I'm a teenager after all. I don't think Craig's parents are being so hard on him. And they are German.

You might think things would have quieted down for a while after that incident, but think again. About a month later, my dill-hole brother sees me smoking at school. And of course, he tells my mom. Once again she busts my chops. I deny the entire thing. This time around, Mom's not so hard on me, but she warns me that the drinking episode was enough and that if she ever catches me smoking pot, she'll kill me. Oops. Too late.

I'm now fourteen and this is the most difficult time of my life yet. I absolutely need some guidance. I feel abandoned. Although I see my dad pretty often, he's not really present enough to give me emotional support and orientation. And my poor mom can't help me out either because she's overly stressed. She yells all the time. She plays the victim. I have taken up cigarettes and drinking to cope with my hardships. Welcome to teenage life.

Neurotic Fantasy

I don't know why, but I feel like going to the movies alone. The film playing is called *Small Change*. It's a French film. It's probably very boring. But I go anyway. By the time I leave the theater I'm madly in love with the little girl in the film. I have to come back and watch it again. And again. And again. And again. And again. I want to run away. I want to go to France. What a crazy fuck. I am really needy.

Tenth grade has started and I now have a crush on my French teacher. She likes me, and we get along fine, but I don't think she has the slightest idea of what I dream of doing to her.

At home, in the evenings, I hang out with the security guard who works at the phone company facility across the street. He's cool and tells me about his sexual adventures. Sometimes I even see some women coming by to see him. This guy's my hero. He reminds me of my vacation buddy Stan. Yep. I know this is cheap entertainment. But it sure is better than staying at home and doing nothing.

On weekends, I get together with my neighborhood friends. We drink and smoke. We spend most evenings checking out porno magazines and watching women taking showers through the keyhole.

It's soccer season and I barely manage to make the team. But I'm happy because I'm only a sophomore and competition is fierce. The older kids on the team mock me and put me down, but I don't care. All I care about is that now I'm officially a jock. And I get even closer to Elsa, who's on the volleyball team. Then one day, someone tells me Elsa likes me. Oh, crap. Here I go again. Although I'm not at all physically attracted to her, I immediately fall in love with the girl.

Unbelievably, Kathy's ghost had still been haunting me, but suddenly, all I can think of is Elsa. Despite my shyness, I somehow manage to approach her and after a few days, we start dating. Sweetness. Elsa is my first official girlfriend since my five-year-old Don Juan days.

Police Business

Elsa and I go out on weekends and I start having my first sexual experiences—that is, if you call getting to second base a sexual experience. This means coming home late at night more often.

One evening I come back late and find my mom sitting on our old rocking chair in front of the house. She's crying. She sees me and is hysterical. She has called the police. Where have I been. It's very late. She's worried sick. I tell her what the heck. I've just turned fifteen and know my way around town. I remind her she was the one who had me ride a public bus to school alone when I was nine to encourage me and teach me some independence. And now this. I am confused. Our relationship really sucks.

I'm a jealous guy. I'm always on the lookout for rivals. I'm afraid I will be rejected. I'm afraid someone better than me is going to come along and steal my girlfriend. And of course, my fears soon come true.

Meet my rival: Elsa's former boyfriend. As soon as I find out about him, I know I'm doomed. I'm scared to death Elsa is going to leave me for him. I become a royal pain in the ass. I'm constantly suspicious. I'm needy. I'm submissive. Shit. I can't stand myself. And neither can Elsa. She soon dumps me for her ex. I'm completely shattered. I'm like a little puppy begging for love.

Unbelievable. I have become Elsa's servant. I do everything for her—favors, homework, anything—in the hope she'll return to me. But I have the feeling this is only making things worse. I see she has lost all interest in me. Figures. I'm too easy.

End of the Rope

One afternoon, I'm alone in my room. I'm feeling very depressed. I have been rejected once again. And what is it with this rival business. I think I've seen this movie too many times already.

The pain in my heart is so strong that for the first time in my life I contemplate killing myself. Maybe that will end my suffering. Maybe that is the answer.

Fortunately, I'm too depressed to take any action. I just sit on my bed for a while and wait until the horrible feeling goes away. Whew. That was close.

But not everything is lost. Volatility's still the name of the game. After all, Elsa does have a couple of cousins.

Mandy is fourteen and her bod knocks me off my feet. I'd love to do unspeakable things to her, but she's too shy, even for my standards, and won't allow me to get near her with a ten-foot pole.

So I turn to Elsa's other cousin, Lindsey, a beautiful blonde with short hair and seductive green eyes. We start hanging out at her house. We go to the movies. We get really close. But we are only friends.

After a while, I start to have feelings for Lindsey, but I'm just too shy to approach her and hate myself for it. I wish she could be my girlfriend. But I don't have the courage to tell her I like her and we end up drifting apart. Oh, well. At least my feelings for Elsa are gone.

A few months later, I meet up with Lindsey again and mention the crush I had on her. To my surprise, she tells me I should have told her about it. She kind of liked me, too. But now she has a new boyfriend. I feel like a bonehead. I feel like banging my bonehead on the wall. Why am I such an incompetent fool. Regret, regret, regret.

July 1981

Both my sisters have moved out. Cynthia has gotten married and Veronica shares an apartment with her very sexy friend, Marcia. I sometimes sleep over at my sister's apartment. I dream of having sex with Marcia. I want her so badly that I almost jump her a couple of times when we are alone, but I'm terribly afraid she will freak out and tell my sister, so I back off. Masturbation time…

I'm now a junior at school and have developed another foolish platonic relationship. The girl's name is Patricia and she's a senior. We have literature class together. I think she's amazing. She's also kind of quiet. My feelings for her have been growing for a while. Maybe I'll have the courage to say something to her. Then again, maybe not. I'm so sick of being shy.

On her birthday, Patricia throws a party at a disco and I'm invited. I'm very excited, but also very nervous. I get to the party and she's there to greet me. She looks gorgeous on her very sexy black dress. I'm salivating over her partially covered breasts and deliciously tanned legs. Many of my friends are here. My French teacher's also here. My legs tremble. I have to sit down. There is no way I'll have the guts to say something to this girl. She's going to reject me, for sure.

I watch Patricia from a distance. I'm delirious. She looks like Helen of Troy or something. She looks over sometimes, but I deny to myself she might be interested in me. I'm depressed. My French teacher comes over to my table and asks me what's wrong. She tells me to go dance and have fun. I just can't. I'm confused. I'm scared. What if I talk to Patricia and she blows me off. What if she doesn't. What if she likes me. If I don't talk to her I'll never know, now will I. Well, I guess I'll never know.

THREE

From Water to Wine...to Water

Things really start to change in my senior year. I'm now the school jock. Again. In October 1982, our school hosts an athletic competition. Some supernatural power has taken me over and I'm playing great soccer. Just in time for my dad to finally come around and see his son's success.

But above all, I'm very excited to see that my newly acquired status seems to attract girls. And so one day, after a game, a friend tells me my classmate Jill has a crush on me. Bam. I'm immediately interested in Jill.

A couple of days later, a bunch of friends are out partying. Jill and I get very friendly right from the start and by the end of the night, we can't keep our hands off each other. I'm thrilled. I have a new girlfriend.

Goddess

After dropping Jill off at her apartment, I'm driving home. I feel awesome. I don't think I've ever felt this way. Everything's great. My body feels warm, light. I'm in utter bliss. Jill's image comes to mind. She's a goddess on a pedestal. Her long, dark-brown hair waves in the wind. Her naked body shows through her transparent Roman toga. The red sun sets in the background. Cheesy. I'm drowning in a sea of ecstasy. Crap. It hasn't even been a day and I'm completely in love with this girl. She's all I can think about.

Jill and I get along very well. We hang out at school all the time and go out on weekends. My feelings become stronger by the day. Soon I want to marry the girl. She has become my property.

Half-Ass Solution

Even though I badly want to have sex with Jill, she's holding off. She wants to preserve her virginity for her future husband. I respect that, but my sexual energy's on the rise. I insist and insist, and she agrees to have anal sex. Not exactly what I had hoped for, but I guess it'll do.

We're in her living room late one night. We're having a great time on her couch. We are making out. I'm feeling her up. Then she kneels in front of me, unbuckles my jeans and gives me a long blowjob. I close my eyes and slip into the sensation. Can't believe I'm finally having a real sexual experience. We then move to the carpet. She takes off her pants, gets down on her fours, and I lose my virginity. Well, sort of.

Unfortunately, it doesn't take long before our relationship drifts into an unhealthy routine. We argue quite a bit. I still feel I have to win Jill over. She is not entirely under my spell. I'm one jealous motherfucker. And then there's my rival. Of course. Jill has a cousin in the States, whom she speaks of very fondly. Her friends even joke around saying she has a crush on him. She carries his picture around and is always saying how handsome the fucker is. And that greatly annoys me, but I guess it satisfies my pattern and makes my feelings for Jill remain strong.

Soon everything changes, though. I find out I can control my relationship through sex. I have very quickly perfected my skills and learned that the way to power lies in providing my lady with plenty of pleasure. And that includes giving her awesome oral sex. Ha, ha. Jill is in the palm of my hand. But what I can't see is that this is a double-edged sword. Once I gain control, I get the power but no longer have the girl to win over and lose all interest. And what's more, fame and fortune have made me bolder. I'm thinking maybe Jill is not the only girl in the world.

Mistaken Identity

During a holiday at a friend's beach house, everyone's having fun but I'm bored. I've had it with my girlfriend and long for new and exciting experiences.

A couple of days into our stay, it becomes obvious that one of my long-time friends is very attracted to me. Oh, yeah. This is what I had been waiting for. No need to think twice. I break up with Jill on the spot. She's in shock.

But not for long. Jill's one clever cookie. Instead of getting all girly desperate, she starts flirting with one of my friends. Boy, and does that tick me off. I thought I was over her, but I was wrong. I still think Jill's mine. I'm with the other girl, but she doesn't interest me any longer. I want my girlfriend back.

On the last day of our trip I'm watching the sunset at the pier. Most of our friends have gone home. I feel miserable. I want Jill badly, but now I got another girl involved and I don't want to hurt her feelings. And then there is my friend. He is sort of shy and naïve and I feel sorry for him. Poor little hypocrite me. But my pattern's stronger. Once again I have something to fight for and I must win Jill over.

My new pseudo-girlfriend walks to the pier and sits by my side. I tell her I want to break up. She's devastated and dashes off. I feel bad, but I'm also sort of relieved. Now all I have to do is ask Jill to take me back.

Back home the next day I waste no time and head for Jill's home. I'm excited. I'm scared. Many things are going through my mind. What if she doesn't want me. What if she wants revenge. What about the other girl.

I get to her apartment and hesitantly ring the doorbell. Jill answers the door. She's smiling. She had been waiting for me. She knew this was going to happen. We speak for a while. I apologize.

I tell her I missed her. I tell her she's the woman for me. I beg her to take me back. And she does. In a flash. To hell with my friend. To hell with the other girl. I'm instantly on cloud nine.

Naturally, it only takes a couple of weeks for our relationship to return to its old patterns. And things are even worse for me—I have now acquired a bad reputation at school because of what I did to my feeble friends.

One month later, we travel to a nearby town for our senior trip. Oh, yeah. We're in for some great times. I'm kind of fed up with Jill, but by now our relationship has become a habitual thing and we just keep going automatically.

In the first evening, we're all drinking and wreaking havoc in the small town hotel. I'm very horny. I want to have sex with Jill. Proper sex. I'm no longer satisfied with the anal thing. Maybe tonight she'll put out.

We're naked in her room fooling around, but Jill won't make me a happy man. Eventually I lose my patience. She tells me she wants to go to sleep. Fine. I leave her in the room and go meet my crazy friends to party some more. Among them is Donna, who's looking mighty hot tonight. She's Jill's good friend, but doesn't seem to mind much when I make advances. We end up making out and I don't feel guilty at all for having cheated on Jill. The way I see it, she had it coming to her.

At home, I haven't been getting along with my mother at all. One day, my dad, Jill, and I are in his car, just outside my house, waiting for my brother. Suddenly Mom comes out of the house. She's hysterical. She's yelling at me. She has a letter in her hands. The letter says we broke into our school and trashed it. Oh, so that's what the big fuss is about. Silly woman. I tell her to calm down. I have an explanation for that. I tell her this is a school tradition. Well, kind of.

As seniors, we are allowed into school earlier on our last day to decorate the surroundings. But what I didn't tell her was that our class wanted to make a strong statement and graduate with a bang. And we might have exaggerated a bit.

We arrived about two hours before we were expected and trashed the entire school. We yelled names at the jerk headmaster when he got there. He's now very, very pissed and doesn't want to let us graduate. And that's what this letter is about. Hey, no big deal. We are just teenagers having fun.

But all my mother cares about is that I did something wrong. I have broken rules. And now she's embarrassing me in front of my girlfriend. She's also yelling at my dad and wants him to do something about the situation. He reprimands me on the spot. I tell them it's a shame they are so unsupportive of their son. Most of my friends' parents understand and are okay with what we did. But not my folks. No, sir. They only care for what's right. They think that giving me shit is more important than supporting my sorry ass. Never mind love. Never mind understanding. Boy, do I feel like crap.

Despite our little adventure at school, the headmaster has allowed us to graduate and I'm ready to go to college. I was accepted to a few schools and chose to go to the University of Connecticut. Yep, that's also where Jill is going. I'm using the money I got from the sale of our old house to pay for the first year of college. Then I hope my dad will take over. Jill has already left for the States and will meet me in about a month. I'm a bit worried about her cousin issue, but there's really nothing I can do about it. So I just try to relax and enjoy my last few weeks in Brazil.

Cheating Spree

One night, five of us go out drinking and then drive to Donna's house. Donna and I are making out on her bed and being very naughty. My fingers are very active tonight (if you know what I mean). She's quietly moaning and really turning me on. I'm dying to have sex with the girl. At some point, after she's completely wet, I try to take her jeans off, but she won't let me. I insist but it's definitely a no-go. Slut. What's her problem. Oh, well. Guess I'll have to settle for smelly hands and some masturbation later. But the last person I'm thinking of is Jill.

Then, on another night, a bunch of drunk friends are out at a disco. I have become unstoppable. I have my eyes on another of Jill's friends. I approach her and try to kiss her but she pushes me away. What about Jill, she says. Forget about Jill, I say. And so she does. We make out all night long.

It's finally time to leave for school. I have to arrive earlier because of soccer practice. I'm very happy to be on the team, which is one of the best in the country. Also, I can't wait to see my girlfriend. Nice. I see a pretty promising future ahead of me.

Complete Disaster

Although I've been brought up as an American, this is really my first time in the States and I'm thrilled. New environment, new people, new life. I'm also a bit scared because I'm alone, but I figure I won't have a problem with that for long. I'll soon be with my sweet girl.

I still have a couple of days before I can move into my dorm room, so I'm staying at a motel near the university. I check into my room and immediately call Jill. Hope she misses me as much as I miss her. I wonder when she'll be arriving. Can't wait to hold her in my arms.

She answers the phone after a couple of rings. I warmly greet her. Jill seems unusually cold. She says she has something to tell me. Oh, shit. Oh, no. She goes straight to the point and breaks up with me. I get the greatest shock of my life.

I ask her why. She gives me some bullshit reason but I can barely hear her. My ears are buzzing. I'm shivering all over. I try to talk to her. I insist, but it's no use. I hang up the phone and don't know what to do. I'm dizzy. I'm heartbroken. I'm desperate. It's not like it's the first time this has happened, but I feel as if it were, just the same. My heart's bleeding. I feel some serious pain. But somehow I have to get on with my life. I've got to go to soccer practice and school starts in a few days.

Three weeks later, I still feel like shit, but things have begun to improve. I've met a bunch of hell-raising guys. We drink a whole lot and jam pennies in people's doors to lock them in their own rooms. Were it not for Jill, I'd be having the time of my life.

I'm a very impulsive young man. The way I see things, since Jill doesn't want me, there's nothing else here for me. I want to go someplace else. I don't care that I have made the soccer team. I don't care that I have made lots of friends. What a hassle. My life is completely driven by relationships.

Craig, my old high school drinking buddy, goes to college in Minnesota, where he seems to be having a ball. I soon start making plans to transfer out of Connecticut. He also introduces me to a girl named Betsy. We start exchanging letters. She sends me her picture. Hmm. She looks pretty cute. She has short brown hair and big sky-blue eyes. I find a bit of relief and something to look forward to.

More relief comes my way when my UConn friends introduce me to all kinds of drugs. After my I-don't-feel-a-thing marijuana initiation in high school, I smoke pot and finally get high. I also try opium, cocaine, acid, and mushrooms. Even though I have internalized my parents' strict moral values and feel sort of guilty, it sure beats sitting in my room looking out the window and crying to tawdry Pat Benatar songs on the radio.

And speaking of radio, my friends also introduce me to all kinds of good music. I've found that my pain has suddenly subsided quite a bit and dive into the psychedelic music scene.

Acid Trip

It's Friday. My good friend Mark has asked me if I want to take some LSD. Hell, yeah. Anything to ease my pain. After class, I drop by Mark's room. My friend greets me with some weird little stamps. We each take one and a half and wait. Good music on the turntable. We start doing bong shots and drinking a little. After about a half hour, the Jimi Hendrix picture on Mark's wall comes alive and starts jamming. Whoa. This is sweet.

We get bored after a while and decide to go to the co-op for some food. The ground below my feet is soft. I feel as if I'm walking on foam. Everything's incredibly detailed. We get to the store and the vivid colors of the candy on the shelves hypnotize me. Mark tells me to stop acting like a fool. We buy lots of chips and chocolate and float back to his room. We then listen to good music for a few more hours until we come down. I go to my room and sleep for an eternity.

Next day. I get up pretty late. That acid last night royally kicked my ass. I can still feel the effects of my trip. My vision is blurred and I see trails. I'm freaking starving, but have run out of money, because I've been ordering out every day since I got here. I hate cafeteria food. And I also don't want to bother my father for cash. I don't want to hear all kinds of shit about how life is hard and how money doesn't grow on trees. So I might as well try to eat at the cafeteria and if that doesn't work, well, I'll just get high again.

November 1983

My transfer has been accepted. I am going to Macalester College in St. Paul. But now I'm sad. I've made friends in Connecticut. I play soccer here. I'm getting used to this place. I'm actually having a good time. I don't know if I want to transfer, but now it's too late. I might as well take advantage of the month and a half until winter break.

I also get news from my father. He has some business in Canada at the end of the year, and he and my brother are coming to pick me up. We're spending the New Year in New York City. My mother has also decided to come (not with my father, of course) and she's traveling to Minnesota with me—a very busy holiday season indeed.

December 23, 1983

Last day at UConn. I don't want to leave. I'm very depressed. I'm such a moron. Why do I have to be so impulsive. Well, now it's no use crying over spilled milk. Mark gives me a few Quaaludes as a going-away present. At noon, my father and brother arrive to pick me up. We pack my stuff and take off for NYC.

My father's being a stingy asshole. We're staying at the YMCA. My brother and I are outraged. The old man has money, but he's on some kind of poverty trip. The YMCA is a dump. The rooms have no private bathrooms. The walls are cracked. I also see some unwanted insects. Even my dad's sort of shocked. Eventually he agrees to upgrade. We spend the night at the filthy place and the next day we find a better place to stay. After all, we'll be here for an entire week.

We get a good deal at the Lexington Hotel, but we're still eating cheap deli food, pizza, and pretzels. I'm so spoiled.

I find this situation appalling, especially because my father is the kind of guy who always eats in fancy restaurants. But overall, we manage to have fun. We walk a lot and see many things. We go to all the free attractions in the city.

After a crappy Christmas, my father and brother are leaving. And my mother has just arrived. She'll be staying for one week. Funny how she's supposed to be the poor and stingy one, but this time the roles are reversed. I'm pleased to see she has also booked a room at the Lexington. On our first night out she takes me to a nice Indian cuisine restaurant.

My mother starts getting on my nerves. She doesn't speak any English, but won't let me deal with anyone either. She has no respect for me whatsoever. Instead of just being quiet and waiting for me to speak, she mimics and emits strange sounds to make herself understood. I feel embarrassed. I wish she would go away. At least in the evening, we go to another fancy restaurant.

Fortunately, the week flies by and soon it's time for us to go to Minnesota...by bus. Why the heck aren't we flying. I think my parents are out of their minds—the plane ticket costs the same as the stupid bus ticket.

The bus stinks and is full of weird people. I have Mom sit on one of the front seats while I stay in the back to smoke and to get away from her for a while. There's this guy who's playing poker and winning quarters off some people. I'm bored. I look out the window and all I can see are endless snow-covered cornfields.

After a two-day trip we are finally in St. Paul. At Macalester, I get to stay in high school buddy Craig's room until school starts and I am settled into my own place. In the evening, it's time for my mom to leave. Overall, this has been a nice experience. But now I'm all alone again. Time for those Quaaludes.

Interim

Today I'm thinking about my first six months in the States. Boy. I've changed quite a bit. I'm not as stuck up as I used to be. This is certainly due to my intake of drugs. This was one good thing about drugs. They opened my mind to new perspectives.

Macalester's pretty much deserted except for a few folks who have stayed for interim classes. Betsy is not here, but I get to meet two girls who live in the dorm.

Sue and Marcy are not attractive at all, but I don't care; I'm desperate for a woman. They are both nice to me and I'll not reject them if the opportunity comes up.

In fact, this very same evening, Sue knocks on my door. She has brought some booze. We talk for a while and then I'm drunk enough to make a move. We make out and I even try to have sex with her, but she does not allow me to get too far. And to tell you the truth, I'm not really sure I want to either.

The next day, I sort of regret what happened. Damn. If my friends find out I made out with Sue, they'll make fun of me for the rest of my life. Fuck it. They'll never know.

In the evening it's Marcy's turn. We drink and I even get to second base with her. Later I feel ashamed and think to myself, *I'd rather be alone than to have to deal with fat, ugly chicks.* Damn. I'm such a prejudiced bastard.

School soon starts and I get to meet Betsy in person. What a disappointment. She's not at all what I had pictured. I guess I'll be looking elsewhere for a good time. But although nothing really happens between us, I internally acknowledge Betsy for helping me feel better when I was down.

My advisor finds me a place in another dorm. Despite having a nice double room and no roommate, I seldom sleep there and usually crash on the bean bag at Craig's because that's where the action is. And I'm usually too fucked up to walk back to my room anyway. I'm also freaked out about the co-ed bathrooms on my floor. I've never seen that before and the sheer thought of being in the bathroom while a chick takes a dump sort of scares me.

Close Call

Drunken Sue has been roaming the dorm halls in a towel. She's screaming for sex in Spanish. *Quiero singar. Quiero singar.* We lock the door and turn out the lights. She bangs on our door and calls us *maricones.* We make a big joke out of the whole thing. She goes away to bother someone else. Boy, I'm sure glad she never mentioned anything about our little thing.

May 1984
I've met a pretty nice girl. Her name is Vera and she goes to an all-girl college nearby. I'm really turned on by her Scandinavian looks. Fair skin, slim, blonde, blue eyes. Unfortunately for me, she's Craig's girlfriend.

Vera usually comes over with a friend, who's kind of skanky. The girl has a pretty bad reputation but I don't care. I want them both. I want sex really badly. I'm climbing up the walls.

I'm a Man

My first semester at Macalester seems to fly by and soon it's summer vacation time. Everyone's getting the heck out of here. Craig has just left for Brazil and I'll be traveling there myself in a couple of weeks.

But before I leave, Vera comes by to see me. We take some Quaaludes. We get friendly. And we make out. I don't feel bad for my friend. Not at all. He treats his girlfriend like shit.

I, on the other hand, am starting to like her. Vera invites me to her house in Wisconsin for the weekend along with two of her friends. Hey, why not.

Vera's parents aren't home and the four of us have the house all to ourselves. How convenient. While Vera's friends are in the kitchen getting plastered, we head straight for her bedroom. We take each other's clothes off. I'm almost too drunk to realize I'm finally, finally about to have proper sex. I'm amazed at myself. I'm acting like a pro. The booze has completely loosened me up. I whisper sweet nothings in Vera's ear while running my fingers down her perfect body. I can feel she has goose bumps all over. She then wraps her arms around my neck as I lay her down on her soft bed. She pulls me towards her. Vera has obviously done this before. She directs my incredibly hard penis into her vagina and I instinctively start moving on top of her. It feels natural. It feels warm. It feels great. I'm now officially a man.

Vera and I are very compatible. We enjoy the same music, we love to get high, and we love to have sex.

Okay, I think I have a new girlfriend. And the funny thing is that I'm the one posing as a rival and winning the girl over for a change. Let's see what my friend Craig thinks of this.

A few weeks later, I am home. Crap. I don't think I even want to be here. I miss Vera already. I can't wait to get back. But now that I'm here I might as well enjoy myself.

One of my friends throws a party and Jill is here. Surprise. At first it seems pretty awkward, but we soon feel comfortable with each other again. In fact, we get along like never before. But we are both somewhat scared and nothing really happens. That's it. I think this is really the end for Jill and me. No, I mean really.

Meanwhile, Vera officially breaks up with Craig. He is mad at me for a few days, but soon forgets the entire thing. He never really cared for her anyway.

My feelings for Vera have been growing exponentially. I manage to book my ticket back to the States almost a month early. Right before I leave, though, my mother comes up with a doozie.

She tells me she's going to petition to have the local government issue her a poverty certificate. What the hell is this woman trying to do. She wants everybody to see she's a big victim. And her tactic sure is working on me. I feel so guilty. I make sure I buy her some food when I go because I think she might starve.

Oh, I almost forgot. As a going-away present my sweet mom also tells me she's going to sue my dad for not having paid child support. Say what. Although he has never formally deposited any money in an account, my dad has fully supported us throughout the years. I'm well aware of that. But she's trying to take advantage of the fact that he has no official proof. It kills me that she now wants me to sign some paper stating that he has never given me money. What a load of crap. I tell her she is crazy. I'm not going to sign the stupid paper. She's very mad at me. Hey, fuck her. When will these people leave us alone.

Anyway, I take off and forget the entire thing. Vera picks me up at the Twin Cities airport and we just can't keep our hands off each other. We get to her house and I finally meet her parents, who seem to like me. They've allowed me to stay in their basement until school starts. Oh, yeah. In the evenings Vera sneaks downstairs for lots of sex.

By now, money has become a major problem for me because I'm away from my father and cannot engage him in the old money-love relationship. I also hate the fact that I have to write and beg for dough, so I just don't do it. And I don't know how the hell to make money on my own, either. But somehow I do manage to get a job as a janitor at the college's science building. It doesn't pay much, but at least I have my own source of income for cigarettes and McDonald's burgers and drugs.

Vera and I are around each other a lot. I spend many nights over at the all-girl school, and in the morning, I have to sneak out because boys aren't allowed in the building past curfew.

One evening, I'm at Vera's and the fire alarm goes off. Shit. What am I going to do. If I leave the building I'll get caught and get kicked out. If I stay I run the risk of roasting on a fire. I take my chances and hide under the bed. Luckily it's only a fire drill.

Although our relationship is moving along smoothly, I feel I'm trying very hard to activate my old rival pattern. I just can't help it. Fortunately, I can't seem to find anyone to play the role. Vera does have an ex-boyfriend, but he lives far away and seems too mentally challenged, even for my pattern. Furthermore, I've managed to keep Vera on a short leash by giving her lots of great sex. I have the power and it feels good.

September 1985
I'm back after another eventless summer in Brazil. My power trip is fully active, routine has settled into my life, and I start craving for someone new. I resent the fact that time is passing me by and I haven't made friends, and I blame my relationship for this.

Vera and I can't understand each other any longer. A strange uneasiness has been building up for a while. All I need is a good excuse to break off the entire thing.

November 23, 1985
Vera and I have been drifting apart more and more. It's late. I'm in my room and get a call from her. I can tell she's really drunk. She says she's at some guy's house and wants me to pick her up. I can barely understand what she's saying, but it seems as if she has made out with the guy, but now he's trying to have sex with her and she's trying to get away. I'm enraged. The bitch is cheating on me. I've had it with this situation. I go over to Sue's room and beg her to drive me to the guy's house. I get there and Vera's at the door and so's the guy. He's only like four feet tall. Not worth beating the shit out of. She gets into the car. She's drooling and babbling. I just tell her to shut up and we drive her to her dorm. I'm very embarrassed. I'm truly fed up.

December 29, 1985
I've decided to break up with Vera. She's away in Florida with her parents for winter break. I write her a letter and end the whole thing. The cheating episode was just too much for me. I tell her not to bother coming to see me and to have a good life. I'm a little scared, now that I'm alone. But I'm also proud of myself. For the first time in my life, I'm the one rejecting a woman. I must have learned something. Well, I'd better get out and get to know some new folks.

The year 1986 has barely begun and already I've been making up for lost time. I'm meeting many new people. I do drugs with my buddies and play pool and go out to eat the seven-man breakfast at Perkins at three o'clock in the morning after the bong-a-thon.

Naturally, I've also noticed a beautiful girl who works at the student union. Her name's Jen. As we get to know each other, she shows no special interest, but you never know. I think I'll hang around her for a while and see what might happen.

It's been a while since I've had sex and I'm horny. I decide to invite a friend over to snort some coke. Although I think she's kind of gross, I'm high as a kite and will screw anything in sight. Oops. I've surely heard this one before.

She comes over, we talk for five minutes, do some lines, have sex, and then she leaves. I'm satisfied.

Three days later, I notice a weird liquid coming out of my penis. It also burns when I piss. I go to the university physician for some exams. They are terrible. The fucking doctor sticks a wire up my dick. It hurts like hell. Apparently I have *Chlamydia*. Damn. Next time I have to remember to wear some protection. But hey, this is the '80s and people don't wear condoms.

I'm feeling great. I now know quite a few people. Hey, I can even say I'm a reasonably popular guy. I walk around like a politician, waving left and right. I have no girlfriend, and I guess that's okay. I do miss the sex, though, and feel I'm not getting enough. I go to weekend parties at the student union, but since I'm so high and drunk I feel very shy and don't pick up anyone.

But today a few of us are taking mushrooms and we're in the lounge right next to my room. My student-union crush Jen's here. She's wearing a very short skirt and I just can't keep my eyes off her great legs. But another guy's also making moves on my prey. Competition. Initially I don't think I stand a chance. But despite my best efforts to sabotage my own happiness, Jen's interested in me and we end up in my room. This is the first time I've had sex while tripping on mushrooms. From what I can remember, it was great. And what's better, I have once again overpowered my rival.

A couple of days after I have sex with Jen, though, I notice a few sores on her face. I find out she has herpes. I'm grossed out and worried that I might have caught it. Now she wants more sex, but I won't dare touch her. Cheap excuse. In reality, I got what I wanted and lost all interest in the woman. Time to move on.

June 1986

I arrive in Brazil for yet another summer vacation. I find out that Dad is separated from his wife, the one with the three daughters, and my sisters are trying to have him get back with my mom. I think this is ridiculous, but then again, it's none of my business. What is my business is that his single status means that he's willing to give me some more cash for college. Yes. This is my father. When he's in a good mood, he dishes out lots of money.

By now I have a few scholarships at school, but I feel that if things continue this way, I'll still leave college with a debt. This scares the hell out of me. I've never had a debt in my life and the thought of owing money to others is simply appalling.

Well, I know this is not entirely my dad's fault. I've had a few jobs and could have saved some money, but I'm too stoned and depressed most of the time to even think of anything of the sort.

Senior year. Vera has been coming around for sex. Lots of it. I like this because we get along great and don't involve ourselves in commitments. I guess I'm learning how to detach a bit more. But I'm still on the lookout for a girlfriend. Loose sex is by no means enough to feed my hungry patterns.

One day, a friend introduces me to a woman named Carol. She's a beautiful and provocative brunette. And I'm completely paralyzed. I look like a shy little nerd. I'm petrified to even talk to her.

I don't know what to say. But I somehow manage to ask the girl on a date. And what do you know. She says yes.

I take Carol to a nice restaurant for dinner. It bothers me that I'm having a hard time bringing forth my personality. But we're able to have a decent conversation. Carol is a dancer. She's even part of a show. All right. Dancers are flexible. Before I take her home, we make out and set up another date. I think I have a new girlfriend. I'm thrilled, but I'm also scared. I just can't be myself around this woman.

A few days later, Carol and I have sex in my room. She takes full advantage of her dancing skills. I Love her acrobatic moves. Legs up, legs down, doggie style, wheelbarrow, we do it all. Now during sex I have no problem whatsoever being who I am, and I can tell Carol liked it very much. I'm starting to loosen up a little, but I still feel submissive and afraid she will eventually find someone else.

The weeks go by and we get closer. Although we had sex a few more times, I'm still uncomfortable around her. I don't know why.

Then one day we go out for a few beers with one of her friend dancers, who has brought along a guy named Jim. To my utter despair, Jim is funny and loose. He also seems very confident. I'm getting scared, because I sense this may well be a rival. I can tell Carol is delighted to have him around. Oh, shit.

And of course my gloomy prediction comes true. A couple of days later, Carol wants to speak with me. I already know what she wants. Break up time. Yes. She has fallen for fucking Jim. I'm living my personal nightmare once again.

Emotional Hell

I'm looking out the window at the third floor lounge. Everything seems gray. I'm completely down. I want to jump off the building. My heart's completely broken. Again. It's like a very bad case of heartburn. My chest is compressed. My head is swollen. Crap. I know this damned feeling too well. Betty, Kathy, Elsa, Jill, and now Carol. When is this ever going to stop. Hey, at least college will be over in a couple of months and I'll be away from here.

April 1987
I'm counting the days until I leave this place. All I do is hang out and do drugs with my friends. My grades suck. For the first time ever, I get a D in a class and I'm pretty sure I'll have to drop another. I also owe the college a lot of money. I just want to go.

The Final Blow

Graduation day. All my friends are dressed up in their beautiful black gowns and lined up to receive their diplomas. And I'm here, standing on a corner, in jeans and a T-shirt, just watching the ceremony. The college won't let me graduate because of my debt and missing credits. This hurts.

After the festivities, I pack up my things and get ready to go for good. I leave half of my stuff at college storage, thinking I might be back some time to work and pay my debt, but somehow I know I won't.

FOUR

She's Not You

Back in Brazil from my college experience. I feel completely exhausted. I have no idea of what I'm going to do next. I feel I want to rest for a long time. But my mom won't give me a break. Shit. I can't stand this any longer. Now she blames my dad for my failure to graduate and is dying to get him back. She wants to force him to pay for my school. I tell her it's none of her business, but she doesn't listen to me. All she really wants is to give him hell. I've just about had it with this situation and want to move out of her place.

I speak with my father and he suggests I go live in his office, a two-story house in the neighborhood where I was born. There's a huge empty room on the second floor, and this will be my new home. I'm delighted. I'll have more independence and hopefully free myself from my mother's talons.

You might think I would have had it for a while with the relationship thing, but I soon attract more trouble. I just can't help it. My childhood friend Marcus and his girlfriend have arranged a blind date for me. The chick's name is Monica.

My first impression of Monica is not that great. She's cute, but too short and skinny. I'm not very psyched, but what the hell. Let's see where this leads me. The night wears on and we get to know each other a little more. Like Marcus's girlfriend, Monica's a psychology major. She's a bit younger than I am. She's into ballet. Hmm. Another dancer.

After dinner we all drive to Marcus's apartment. Marcus and his girlfriend are in the other room. Monica and I are alone. We talk for a while and then I think it's about time I make my move. I ask Monica if I can kiss her and she's delighted to say no. Bitch. Why did I even ask in the first place. I want to tell her to fuck off but I control myself. We just remain here for the rest of the night watching TV and waiting for Marcus and his woman to finish their thing. Then they take us home and we agree to meet some other time. Maybe.

About a week later, one of my friends invites us all for a boat ride. But this time around I see Monica with different eyes. I decide to approach her once again, but if she gives me a hard time, I'll just tell her off and move on. I don't feel needy, not really.

Oops. Spoke too soon. On the boat, I notice this Dutch guy my friend brought along is hitting on Monica. I suddenly get very jealous. My patterns move in and I begin to feel submissive. I'm starting to think I'll probably lose this woman. Then I come to my senses. Or is it a defense pattern. I think to myself, *who cares. I barely know her.*

Monica seems to notice my lack of interest and immediately turns her attention to me. We end up having a superb time and agree to meet up later with Marcus and his girlfriend. And no Dutch asshole.

We are all back in Marcus's apartment, and this time Monica gives in. We make out and talk and cuddle together for hours and once again I have a new girlfriend.

Things are not going very well between my father and me. The problem is that he gives me cash when I need it, but forces me to do things in return. He's actually making me work for my money, but I can't see it that way. And neither can he. He makes me go do errands in the bank and I hate it. The lines are huge. And what really sucks is that he often gives me stupid predated checks from his patients, which means I have to return to the bank lines to cash them. I hate being dependent. Then there's the college debt issue. Macalester didn't grant me my diploma, and I'm completely lost. What am I going to do with my life. I guess I have really come to hate money, because it's the cause of such a bad relationship with my dad.

A few weeks into our relationship, Monica and I finally have sex. It's possibly the best sex I've ever had. Our bodies move together as if they were one. Our orgasms are incredible. I've never felt so relaxed before. I'm also smoking very little. About two or three cigarettes a day. Although Monica doesn't smoke or get high, she doesn't mind that I do. But the thing is, I just don't feel the need whenever I'm around her. And we're together all the time. As for rivals, none in sight. Could it be that I've gotten rid of my pattern. Things are running smoothly. Almost too good to be true...

Litter

We are at Marcus's girlfriend's house. One of her many dogs has a new litter. We are offered a dog and Monica wants one. I'm playing along. I've had a few dogs in my life and they are fun. I'm totally involved with the woman anyway and would never say no.

The puppies are half Great Dane, half Siberian Husky. But they're very cute nevertheless. We end up leaving not with one, but two, puppies. And guess what. There's no room for them in Monica's house. They're coming to stay with me.

And so my newly acquired freedom's suddenly gone. Fuck. This sucks. I now have to take care of two dogs that eat and sleep and shit all over my house. What was I thinking.

Although she no longer lives with me, my mom still wants to control my life. She's quick to team up with Monica and they're now demanding I do something about my stagnant situation. In a way they're right. I get up late and do nothing all day except take care of the fish tanks I have at home. In the afternoon, I go out with the dogs and in the evening, I get together with my friends, get high and go to sleep very late, only to start the same routine the next day.

After much insistence, I give in and go talk to my dad about my uncertain future. We agree that I have to start doing something productive. I tell him I want to go back to college. Maybe this time I can get a diploma. He's happy with my decision, especially because I tell him I want to study psychology.

I start going to night school right away. I need to get ready for college entrance exams. Night school is fun. My childhood friend Marcus is here with me. There are many cool people. After class we go to a local bar and drink, drink, drink. I'm tempted to hit on a few girls, but Monica's on my tail all the time.

November 12, 1987
I've done great in my exams and have been accepted at the Catholic university. Classes will start in a few weeks. Dad's still giving me a hard time about money. And what's worse, now he also has my college to pay for.

Financial Crisis

One day, after having begged and begged and not gotten the cash I wanted, I have a deep crisis in my father's office. We argue and then he leaves. I'm sitting on his leather armchair and can feel a dark cloud over my head. I feel a very strong depression set in. There's really nothing I can do about it, so I just sit around and feel my pain through. I've completely had it with this situation.

It's been a while since I started dating Monica and I'm beginning to lose interest in her. The old sexual power trip has kicked in. She's completely under my control and sex isn't so fun anymore.

Meanwhile, classes have started at the university. I feel I'm in paradise. My classes are mostly girls. I know there are many women who would like to have me, and this makes me feel cocky and fearless. But it's also harder to resist. And the funny thing is, the less I care about Monica, the more she cares about me.

Cheater

Tonight I'm out with a bunch of people. I'm very, very horny. I lay my eyes on an old school friend. I have my dad's car and offer to take her home at the end of the night. The liquor has loosened me up and I'm questioning my moral values. Why am I so stuck up. Why do I have to be so faithful.

We end up in my house. I waste no time in taking her clothes off and we have sex downstairs in my father's office and then in my bed upstairs.

While engaged in the old in-out routine, we notice a photo of Monica on my bedside table. She's staring at us. We feel intimidated. Oh, well. Not really. I just turn the stupid picture over and carry on with my pleasurable activities.

It doesn't take long before I start feeling incredibly guilty for having cheated on Monica. I'm also afraid someone's going to tell her what has happened. I'm getting paranoid. So, in a move of pure stupidity (or is it honesty), I decide the best thing to do is to tell her myself. She is incredibly pissed. And I guess things will never be the same from now on. In fact, I guess our relationship is over. I tell her I don't want to see her anymore. She is appalled. Who cares. I can have any girl I want at the university.

By mid-1988, I'm on top of the world. I feel great. I feel free. Except for my dogs, of course, which by now have grown into two monsters. I give Monica a call and tell her she has to take them away. She freaks out. She has no place for them. Tough. I've been taking care of these beasts for a while and now it's her turn. She's very sad. She had been using the dogs as an excuse to come and see me after we had broken up.

Nightmare

I wake up in the middle of the night after a terrible nightmare. I dreamed I was back in the States. I was in college alone and with no money at all. I was terrified. I was unsupported. These nightmares have been recurring for a while now. College experience, especially at the end, was really traumatic.

The days go by and I hear Monica is depressed. She has lost a lot of weight. She's sick. She doesn't eat. And all because of me. I'm beginning to think this woman is really in love with me.

Then one day, Monica comes over to my house. She wants to talk. She doesn't look so sick anymore. In fact, she looks yummy. She tells me she has given a lot of thought to our situation. She tells me she'll not hold herself back any longer and will do whatever she feels like. This means she wants sex. I'm not against that. Great. Just like Vera a while back, in the States. A fuck buddy. No strings attached. I can go for that.

Oh, boy. I'm unknowingly falling for Monica again. Our new relationship is great. I have no responsibilities whatsoever. I'm now fully aware that this girl really loves me. She's great. Sex is great. What more can I ask for.

Then my feelings grow to the point I want to tell her how I feel. Maybe it's time we get back together on a formal relationship. I call her and ask her to come over. I tell her I value her and

I've fallen in love with her again and want her back. Her reaction startles me. I don't really think she wants to go out with me anymore. She looks very scared. She asks me for some time to think. I'm worried.

Later on that week, she lets me know she no longer wants to see me for sex. Monica has officially rejected me. I have a strong feeling she'd been waiting for my attitude towards her to change so that she could free herself from me. Now the tables are turned. I want her and she doesn't want me.

But I'm not about to give up just yet. I insist. I come by her house often. But the more I approach her, the weaker I feel. The more fragile I feel, the stronger she gets and the more she rejects me. I think I know where this is going.

Then I hear Monica has found a new boyfriend. He's short and ugly and a jerk. I think she's trying to free herself from me as quickly as possible.

Time goes by and my feelings for Monica are still very strong. Her rejection has sent me in a downward spiral. I'm depressed. Sitting at home, I don't feel like doing anything. I just feel bad. Once again I can see a dark cloud in my mind. It's so dense I can almost touch it. I think I need some help.

Fortunately my cousin Tamara lives close by and she reads the Tarot. I haven't been in touch with that kind of stuff since my childhood days, but I'm desperate. I call her up. Tammy's happy to hear from me and will gladly see me. I go to her house and she gives me a reading. Things are not looking good. But I like the Tarot. I ask Tammy to teach me a few things about it. She recommends I buy a deck. She also tells me meditation might help. I've never tried meditation before. I'm willing to try pretty much anything to ease my pain.

I follow cousin Tamara's advice and buy a book with active meditation techniques. I find meditation isn't what I expected. Instead of just sitting around, the book instructs me to dance, move, shake, and yell. Weird, but this just may make me feel good. After all, I feel I have to shake this shit off my body anyway.

I also buy a Tarot deck. Tarot is cool, but I have a problem with it. I have a hard time being objective. All I can see is what's on my mind: tragedy, tragedy and more tragedy. This makes me feel worse. Fantastic.

I've also come across a book by this guy, J. Krishnamurti. He speaks of a strange kind of liberation. He speaks of freedom from the mind. Although I'm having a hard time understanding what the fucker's talking about, I'm somehow hypnotized by what he says. On the other hand, something about Krishnamurti really bothers me. He's too harsh and strict. He seems like my father. I eventually push it all to the back of my mind and forget about these ideas altogether.

It's now my turn to use the dogs to try to get closer to Monica. I call her up and tell her I want to visit them. She takes me to this woman's house where the dogs are being kept. We get there and I feel incredibly bad. I feel sad. Why did I give up my dogs. I tell Monica I want them back. Well, at least one of them. And guess what. Since I can't have Monica, I end up taking the bitch back home.

I have no interest whatsoever in any woman except Monica. I'm trying to find ways to be in touch with her. So I become good buddies with one of her friends, Linda. We start hanging out a lot. Linda also enjoys the Tarot, and I make her read the cards to me all the time. She's also into this other oracle called I-Ching. I like the I-Ching. It's easy. All I have to do is toss three coins a few times and record the head-tail sequences. I then get a figure and read its meaning in a book.

It's not long before I hear Monica's getting married. I'm incredibly sad. The pain is so great I think of killing myself. Again. My pattern's eating me alive.

Black Christmas

Everybody's at my sister's for Christmas. Plenty of presents, food and fun. But I'm feeling like shit. I want to go home. I can barely make conversation. At some point, I excuse myself and go to the bathroom. I lock the door and cry and cry and cry like a baby. My God. What's happening to me. I'm in really bad shape. Monica's lost forever and I'm desperate.

After a while, I wash my face and go back to the party. I don't think anybody notices I'm not okay. I stay here a little longer, but soon take off and go lick my wounds at home.

I call my father and ask him to help me get rid of my dog. I love her dearly, but cannot see her and not think of Monica. We take the bitch over to my dad's clinic. She can stay there for a little while, but we're going to have to find a place for her. We get there and the caretaker's immediately struck by her beauty. She really is a beautiful dog. We tell him we have to give her away and he's more than happy to take her home. I'm saddened to see my bitch go, but on the other hand, I'm relieved my ordeal is finally over. And I'm also relieved she's getting a great home.

By now, Linda and I have become inseparable. And I really don't know what to make of our relationship. I'm somewhat attracted to her, but I think she only wants me as a friend. Well, we might as well leave it at that for now.

Quasi Orgasm, Part One

Today Linda and I and one of her friends, Daisy, are going to the movies. I know Daisy. She's hot. She looks like Monica. I could get into bed with her in no time. No questions asked.

Linda and Daisy come to my house before the film. Sparks are flying between Daisy and me and Linda notices. She's jealous. I want to have sex with Daisy, but Linda's between us. To my surprise, she doesn't leave us alone for a moment.

At the movie theater, she wants to sit between us. Daisy and I exchange places. I have an incredible hard-on. While she slips in front of me, my hard penis finds her buttocks and for a moment, slides in between her ass cheeks. I almost have an orgasm right here and now. I don't think I'll ever forget this feeling. .

After the movie episode, I'm thinking Linda likes me. The male chauvinist inside says I should do her. She's a bit chubby, but a gorgeous woman nevertheless. Her long, black hair falling to the waist and beach-tanned skin really accent her figure and make her very attractive indeed.

I borrow a friend's mountain cottage and invite Linda over for the weekend. Just the two of us. And, much to my delight, she agrees.

On the first evening, we're drinking wine and chatting by the fireplace. After a while I decide to make my move and we start making out. I then go on to second base. So far so good. I'm thoroughly enjoying her firm breasts in my mouth. I move on to the next logical stage. I try to take off the rest of her clothes, but she doesn't let me. Piss me off. I don't feel like insisting and we go back to making out. I pretend everything's okay but now have all sorts of nasty thoughts in my mind. Who does she think she is. I don't need this shit. What's she doing here anyway. Blah, blah...

We just cuddle for the rest of the night. And since we're not here to have sex, we end up getting bored and leave the next day. I don't think I want to see this woman anymore.

A couple of months have elapsed and I'm still hurting for Monica. I'm so desperate I've asked my mother for help. Now that's how desperate I am. We go to her favorite religious temple to ask the spirits for guidance.

At the temple, I'm told my life was supposed to be really easy. Right. Apparently, things haven't happened the way they should because of that ceremony done years ago, which connected me to the wrong spiritual guide and has been causing me trouble ever since. Damn. How's that even possible.

I look at my mother and she's feeling as guilty as sin. And I'm one dumb fuck for coming back to this dump and not having learned my lesson.

Now the effects of the previous work must be undone. And what's more, the guy at the temple wants me to do another ceremony to connect me to the right guide. Not a fat chance. I tell him fine, I'm willing to wipe out the wrong guide, but there's no way I'm going to commit myself to anything else. He insists, but in the spirit of the '80s, I just say no.

A week later the three of us drive to a waterfall. It's raining so hard we can barely see our way. I am near the water while the guy chants and spreads a smelly yellow paste on my forehead, wrists, and ankles. My mom's watching. We then go to a deserted road, where I throw some beans up in the air and he breaks a bottle of beer. We also leave behind a big potato with toothpicks stuck into it. That's it. Now let's see what happens.

Incredible. I hate to admit it, but the spiritual mumbo jumbo worked. It's only been a couple of days since my ceremony at the waterfall. After almost two years of bumming around, I get a call from my old high school asking me if I want to have some private students. I'm excited at the possibility of earning quite a bit of money teaching rich kids. I know the school, I know the textbooks, I know their style. Piece of cake. Why hadn't I thought of that before. That same evening, I pick up my brother-in-law's guitar and start strumming. And I like it. I think I might be doing some more of this. As for Monica, I still have strong feelings for her, but they have definitely diminished. I'm ready to go out and hunt for some other women.

And so my routine has instantly changed. I go to college in the morning, and in the afternoon I have my private lessons. Sweet. I'm finally earning my own money. My dad will have to find another bozo to stand in bank lines. Although he still pays for food, clothes, and everything else, things are definitely looking up.

I have been playing the guitar quite a bit. I'm sure glad I've picked up a good habit for once. I also love singing. I get incredibly high every night, sing and play until my fingers hurt like hell. Hey. Who knows. This could become a long-term thing.

Little by little, I'm loosening up. The psychology classes are helping me become more aware of my needs and patterns. I no longer feel I have to marry the first woman who comes along. I can have affairs and don't have to make commitments.

One afternoon, I invite one of my college friends to dinner at my house. Guess what I'm up to. She's kind of cute, and has one hell of a body. And I can tell she's really into me.

We get to my home, sweet home and after some small talk, start making out. Forget dinner. We both know this is not what we're here for. Soon we're having sex on my couch. We engage in all sorts of Kama Sutra positions. She's constantly telling me how she loves and wants my big...foot. And I feel great. Not only due to the compliments, but also because I haven't had sex in a while. That was easy. Hmm. Too easy. I guess this means I'm in control and will lose all interest in the poor woman.

In fact, the very next day, I try to avoid her as much as I can. My friend (or should I say former friend) is mad at me because she thinks I have used her. But I really can't help it. I got what I wanted and I no longer feel any attraction.

What the Hell

I wake up scared in the middle of the night. I've just had one of those recurring nightmares. Once again, I dreamed I was back in the States with no money or support and was under a lot of stress. I'm sure glad it was only a dream. Shit. It's been two years and I still have to deal with this.

Temptation, Part One

I've become a very busy man. In addition to college and private tutoring, I'm my Behavioral Psychology professor's assistant. We get along well. She even lets me have the key to the lab. And I'm starting to have funny ideas.

I'm teaching one of my students in the lab. She's young. She's sensual. She's also very attracted to me. I'm at the board writing something. She gets up from her chair and squeezes into the very narrow space between the board and me. She then turns her back to me and starts writing, wiggling her very nice ass. I feel like doing her. But I do have moral values after all. She's a minor and I'm here as a teacher. After class, I can tell she's somewhat disappointed. And I'm trembling all over. I need to go home and take a long, cold shower.

Temptation, Part Two

One evening I get a call from my former high school. They want me to come and substitute for a math teacher. Hey, why not. It'll be nice to teach an entire class for a change.

As soon as I get to my class the following day, I notice a most beautiful girl. Her name is Clara. Clara smiles at me all the time. I'm impressed at how gorgeous she is. I want her badly, but have to control myself. She's only seventeen and I'm at work.

A few days later, I'm asked to substitute for the same teacher again. Clara's all smiles. I'm overly nice to her. Of course. I want to do her. And I can tell she likes me. But I must be strong and resist. The good thing is that now I have a new ally. I can go home and get very high and play the guitar. I feel great and it calms me down. I'm so happy I've started playing.

Up from the Skies

We get the startling news that a boat full of marijuana was intercepted along the coast, but before the dope was seized, some very kind people dumped most of the cargo overboard. The weed was stuffed into many, many tin cans, each holding about three pounds. And the cans washed away on the Rio de Janeiro shores, like gifts from God.

And luckily we manage to get a piece of the action. We buy a can from a fisherman and bring it over to my house. We're all very excited. We use a can opener to open it and a baseball bat to push the stuff through the open end of the can. Most of the pot is staying with me. I buy about one pound for myself and keep one pound a friend has bought, because he can't take it home.

I can't wait to try out the marijuana, which local people have lovingly nicknamed "Mike Tyson." And I soon find out why. The high is so intense I trip for several hours on a small joint. Wow. A true knockout. I have a feeling the rest of the year's going to be one big blur.

FIVE

Ch-Ch-Changes

I'm now fully aware that I must make some internal changes if I'm ever going to see improvements in my life. And by that I mean I must shock my system a little. I'm getting funny ideas from the Carlos Castaneda books I've been reading lately and am in the mood for lonely adventures and new experiences.

One day I get up and suddenly feel the need to go on a quest. For a while now, I've been very much afraid of going into the forest. I feel a creepy presence, as if something is out there to get me. Maybe Mother Nature. Maybe just the Mother. I have a four-day holiday ahead of me and decide to spend some time alone in the darkness of the jungle trying to conquer this fear.

February 18, 1990
After an intense adventure, which I'll surely tell you about some other time, I'm back home. And I feel stronger. I feel much more comfortable with myself. I feel fearless.

Boogeyman

I wake up in the middle of the night after a terrible nightmare. Ouch. I dreamed I was sleeping in my own bed, when a strange noise woke me up. The door to my room was wide open and everything was pitch black. I could barely see the stairs that lead to Dad's office. I sat up and could suddenly hear this horrific growl coming from downstairs. I knew it was a horrible monster. It was out to get me. I was terrified. And then I wake up to real life. But it's only around two in the morning and I find myself sitting on the same bed, in the exact same situation. Shit. Fear completely takes over. I can almost hear the monster's growl. And, worst of all, my bedroom door's closed and I can't see the stairs. I curl up in bed and shiver for a long time until I finally go back to sleep. I thought I was through with this kid stuff.

I've met a new friend in literature class. Her name is Tina. I don't feel any sexual attraction to her. But we get along and hang out at school. It's nice to also have girls as friends. They help me understand female nature outside a neurotic environment.

Sausage Talk

I'm once again in the mood for adventures. And lucky me, there's another long holiday coming up. This time, I need to get away from home for a while. I've got to do it. The farther, the better.

I decide to hop on a bus and head south. I don't really want to make any plans. I'll follow my intuition and play along as I go.

I have a bright idea. I'm first going to see my former high school girlfriend Elsa and her sisters, who soon after graduation moved south. I'll spend a few days there and then move on to who knows where.

I'm in Elsa's house after a pretty gruesome twelve-hour bus trip. Elsa now acts like she's my older sister. Everyone's happy to see me. I tell them what I've been planning. They all think I'm crazy. They say I'm their loony friend. We laugh for a while and then get ready to go out partying in the evening.

After about three hours in the shower and getting dressed, Elsa's finally ready and we head out. It's one o'clock in the morning. It's far too late for me, but apparently not for them, nor for the entire town. The bars are swarming with people. The night's very exciting. We get to a nice place and order some beers. After a little while, one of Elsa's friends shows up. Her name's Vienna.

Vienna's a bit on the chubby side. She reminds me of my middle sister. She's very nice and outgoing. By the time the night is over, I'm one very drunk sailor making out with Vienna.

I wake up the next day with a big headache and completely in love with Vienna. Loony-ass me. I forget all about my big adventure and cancel the rest of my trip. I've decided to stay here and get to know the girl better. And so, just like that, I have a new girlfriend. We hang out for the next couple of days until it's time for me to head home.

Two weeks later, I'm back to see Vienna. But things are not at all peachy. I feel submissive around her. Her strong personality overwhelms me. She doesn't value me. She rejects me. She's rude to me in front of her friends. And since we haven't had sex yet, I have no power over her whatsoever. And my pattern says that's absolutely unacceptable.

And so begins my new power quest. It's a matter of life and death. I need to win Vienna over and gain control of the relationship. I must have sex with her. I'm on automatic.

Soon it's June and I'm on vacation. This time I'll be able to stay with Vienna for about ten days. We have an exciting camping trip planned. We're going to spend some time on a deserted island with a few friends.

I get to her house after my long trip and in the evening we have sex. Finally. Maybe now I can turn the tables. But I'm wrong. Although sex was decent, she doesn't seem to value it very much and is still not under my control. Damn it.

I notice one thing during our camping trip. Vienna has been watching me as I do my usual athletic stuff around the island. I climb trees, swim to other islands, run around the beach, go into the woods. I love this sort of stuff. Sport's my nature. I see she appreciates me for it. And she's falling for me. Finally.

After our trip, I hang around for a few of days before going home. Vienna has definitely become infatuated with me. She's even into sex now. I get the power I've been longing for. And of course, I start losing interest in her. I feel bored. I feel revengeful. Like I always say, I just can't help it. I want to make her pay for all the times she rejected me and made me feel inferior.

Then comes the last straw. The evening before I leave we go to a party. Vienna's younger sister (whom I've had my eye on for some time) comes up to me and hands me an anonymous note. Some girl's letting me know how handsome she thinks I am and how she can't believe I go out with Vienna.

I feel good and bad at the same time. I feel good because this woman thinks I'm hot. And I feel bad because she's right. What am I doing with this girl. She's not exactly attractive. She's not at all my type. I feel embarrassed. I feel like a fool. I feel I've been selling myself cheap.

Back home, I've been thinking about my relationship with Vienna. I no longer feel like traveling twelve hours to see her. It's just not worth it. I decide to give her a present and buy her a plane ticket to Rio. She's thrilled.

A couple of weeks go by and I'm at the airport to pick up my girlfriend. But as soon as she arrives, I start feeling like shit. I'm not attracted to this girl any longer and I want to break up. There is nothing else in this for me. I know this is sort of cold-blooded, but I cannot pretend to feel something I no longer feel. Too bad for Vienna, because by now she's completely in love with me.

I get an uncontrollable urge to act. I waste no time and break up with Vienna the same day she arrives. She's devastated. I put her on the first plane back and go smoke a big joint to forget the entire thing. I guess I got my revenge after all, but I swear it was unintentional.

Not Again

Once again I dream I'm back in the States. I have no support, no money. What am I going to do. I'm desperate. Fortunately, I wake up. It takes me a while to convince myself it was just a dream. Damn. I think I need some therapy soon.

September 1990

After three years living in my father's office, I'm making my big move. I'm happy to be a bit more independent. I'm moving to a new apartment, which I'll be sharing with my brother, who has recently returned from college. Although we don't get along, I'm excited and think this will be a positive change.

I've also asked my dad to refer me to a good psychotherapist. I'm studying to become a psychologist and it makes sense to go and treat myself so that I don't screw up other people's minds. He refers me to one of his wife's colleagues, a Freudian therapist.

I go to my first session. I get to the therapist's office, which is also her house. The lady greets me as I walk into her office. She calls me "sir." I think that's weird. Too formal. She makes me lie down and I start talking. I can't see her at all. What the heck kind of conversation is this. And she doesn't say much either. After my first session, I leave and never come back. Hey, I want things to be a bit warmer. I must find another therapist.

One month later, I start therapy with one of my former college professors. His name is Sergio and he was my group therapy teacher. Sergio's sort of a quiet guy. He listens a lot during our first session. And I have a lot to say. I'm full of anger and fear and strong feelings. At least we sit and face each other. He makes few, but striking, comments. After my first session, I feel relieved. It feels good and I'm willing to continue. At first I'll be seeing him twice a week.

My brother and I have barely moved in together and already there is plenty of friction between us. I think he's a slob. He has a stupid nosey cat, and I have to keep the door to my bedroom closed to prevent the beast from raiding my fish tank. Wow. I've been angry with my brother for a long, long time.

I've been feeling down lately. Hey, I haven't had a girlfriend in a while. This relationship business really pisses me off. I just can't get it right. If I have a girlfriend, I want out. I'm jealous, I throw fits, I worry about rivals, and I feel as if I were in a prison. But when I'm alone, I crave having a girlfriend. Jesus. How long will my own contradictory feelings juggle me around.

But I'm not strong enough to stop the vicious cycle. At least not yet. I soon find a new object of desire. Her name's Mary and she's a Literature major. We get along very well and often talk for hours. I think I'm falling in love with her. She's shy, so I can't tell if she's attracted to me or not.

Eventually I start bugging Mary to go out with me, but she always has an excuse. This thing's starting to do me more harm than good.

I'm acting weird. I have now become a stalker. I hang around Mary's building on a couple of occasions. I'm looking for a rival, but haven't found one yet. Apparently Mary has no boyfriend.

So I finally decide to make my move on her and see what happens. One afternoon, I invite her to my house. She comes into my room, and after some sweet talk, I try to kiss her. She's in shock and doesn't move. A one-way kiss is no fun. The situation gets awkward and she leaves. Enough. I decide to cut Mary off my life. The usual way. I smoke a nice big joint to ease my rejection pain.

Lately I have been playing games with another of my classmates. Her name's Fay. Fay is very naughty—a real tease. I constantly try to grab her and she pushes me away. I'm enjoying another power game, which will surely end as soon as I have sex with her.

In December, I invite Fay to spend the holidays with me at my older sister's beach house. I'm okay with this relationship. It doesn't involve my projections. I just want to have sex with her, and the more she teases me, the more excited I get.

Unfortunately things don't turn out that well. Several times, I try to make out with Fay but she pushes me away. I'm quickly getting sick of these games. It's been a while and it's been fun, but now it's time for action. Still Fay keeps rejecting me. I give up. I don't need this shit. I decide I'll be cold as ice from now on.

Back home, I once again resort to my cousin Tammy and her Tarot cards for advice. I come over to her house and we talk for a long time. Her reading is great. She foresees another relationship coming. Big changes. I promise her I'll be back more often to chat.

My strategy with vampish Fay has worked. As soon as I let go and show no more interest, she wants me. No more tease. I'm really no longer interested, though. I feel I've given her up for good. But if she wants to have sex with me, I won't push her away.

Then one day it happens. She comes over to my place and we have sex. I make sure she has a great time. I make sure she knows what she's been missing. I feel very powerful. And of course, I don't want to see Fay ever again.

In the meantime, I get to know my next-door neighbors. I don't know why I hadn't noticed them before. Yes, two women, a blonde and a brunette. I'm immediately attracted to Cecilia, the curvy blonde bombshell, and we plan to meet up sometime.

Cecilia and I meet at her apartment. We talk for a while. She tells me she's a flight attendant. Whoa. I like that. But I'm just killing time, waiting for an opportunity to strike. Eventually we do make out and cuddle for a while. Hmm. Special. I think I might have a new girlfriend.

Therapy with Sergio has been helpful. We mainly speak about my relationship with my parents. He helps me see many things. It's amazing how one can carry a very heavy load for long periods of time and not even notice it. I feel lighter and more hopeful than ever. I'm keeping very busy working and studying and now I even have a girlfriend. What more could I ask for.

But not all is a bed of roses. Things between my brother and me aren't going well. We have a hard time dealing with each other. One day my father decides to give us a car. We're supposed to share it. I soon start giving my brother hell for not taking proper care of the vehicle. He then tells me to shove the car up my ass and that I do. Ha, ha. The car's now mine.

After this terrible argument, the situation at home becomes truly unbearable. I have to find a place of my own.

It was easy. One month later I'm all ready to move into my new apartment. It's quite small, but seems adequate for my needs. I also think I'm ready to live with a woman. It seems convenient and logical to ask my girlfriend if she wants to be my roommate. Cecilia is thrilled and we move in together.

But trouble soon sets in. Right. Tell me something I don't know. Sex with Cecilia is pretty good, but like Vienna, she's not really into the act. And as a flight attendant, she's away most of the time and also not into our relationship. The less she cares, the more I want to bang her. Once again, my power struggle is on. A fucking seesaw. And I absolutely need her to be submissive. It's either her or me.

April 20, 1991

Today we're going to Cecilia's parents' house in the country. We get there and I immediately feel uncomfortable. I'm unable to approach Cecilia. She's embarrassed in front of her parents. I think this is ridiculous. After all, she's one year older than me and has led an independent life for a while. I try to be alone with her, but she pushes me away. At night, we sleep in separate rooms.

It seems I'm not the only one having problems with family patterns. After watching her parents a bit, I can see why Cecilia has a hard time dealing with affection and sex. Her father's very rude and not a warm person at all. Her mother's obviously hysterical and has probably never had an orgasm. Their relationship seems to suck big-time. And as for Cecilia's siblings, her twenty-four-year-old sister has never had a boyfriend. Her older brother's married and has two beautiful kids, but treats his wife like shit. And she seems to be used to it. I think to myself, *is this the future I'm heading to.* Hell, no.

After a pretty uncomfortable night, we drive to her family's apartment at a nearby town. Her younger sister comes with us. What the heck. I want to be alone with Cecilia and I need her to want me. We get to the apartment and in the evening, we manage to ditch Sis and have sex twice. Good sign. I'm getting there.

Cecilia's unable to meet my sexual needs. She's away most of the time and I naturally start looking towards other women. I keep saying to myself whatever happens will be her fault. I'm a man. I must provide for my needs. And one day, she'll get what's coming to her. Yes, payback's a bitch. I'm full of anger and long more and more for revenge. I constantly warn Cecilia that she'll eventually lose me if she doesn't change. And I mean it.

But I won't give up my fight just yet. Before rejecting Cecilia, I must have her in the palm of my hand. She must be under my spell. I'm such a mean fuck. And the one thing that really bothers me is the fact that she has sexual inhibitions. No matter how I try, I can't make her have an orgasm upon penetration. She can only reach an orgasm if I masturbate her. What kind of sex life is this.

But by now I no longer think there's something wrong with me. Hey, after all I'm a sex god. She's the problematic one.

Damn. I can't even see I've turned this woman into an enemy. Just like my momma. Unfortunately, I don't realize how ruthless my attitude is—this thing runs on an unconscious level.

Dude Looks Like a Lady

Cecilia's not around. I feel incredibly naughty and horny. I crave for some action. It's pretty late. I think I'll drive around town.

I'm cruising by the beach. I'm checking out the prostitutes. This has never been my style, but hey, there's always a first time for everything. I think I'll check out what it's like to have sex with one of these whores. With a condom, of course.

I see a most beautiful blonde standing on a corner. I'm instantly attracted to her looks. She's petite, has nice, thick legs and is tight all over. Just my type.

I stop the car and she gets in. I drive off and we start making conversation. But I'm not in the mood for conversation. I'm drooling all over her. I stop at a red light and start feeling her up. Yes, red light is exactly right. As soon as I stick my hand under her tight skirt, I notice something that shouldn't be there. It feels like a penis. It is a penis. Holy crap.

I retreat in complete shock. I want to puke. The transvestite is laughing his ass off. He can't believe I thought he was a woman. But, man, he looks just like a woman.

I have nothing against homosexuals, but this is really not my cup of tea. I want him out of my car immediately. He agrees, but tells me I must pay him for his time. What time. We hung out for like five minutes. Ah, what the heck. I'm definitely not in the mood to argue. And I also don't care to find out what else he's got hidden under his skirt. I give him some money, drop him off, and get the hell out of there. And so ends my adventure. And all my horniness is gone. I mean, completely gone.

Jealousy Fit

Cecilia and I have been invited to a barbecue at her uncle's house. Everyone's outside enjoying the day, and all the men are enjoying the view of my girlfriend's body in a bikini. Time for another jealousy fit. I shut down and start being mean to Cecilia. I question her. I doubt her feelings for me. Who's she looking at. Where's she going. I've gone completely mad.

The girl is just trying to enjoy herself, but I'm making her life miserable. We end up fighting and she tells me off. Shit. She still has the power in this relationship. I feel submissive. I manage to control myself and pretend everything's okay, but when we leave I'm incredibly relieved.

Horny Granny

My constant thinking about sex has been attracting all kinds of strange energies. Take my elderly neighbor, for example. Every time I enter or leave my apartment, she's there on the hall waiting for me in her nightie. That would be no big deal except for the fact that she's like ninety years old. I hate to say it, but I think she's hitting on me. Seriously. Apparently she'd been a very good swimmer when she was young. She shows me pictures taken in the 1920s. Yep, she was hot. But now she's cold. It must be hard to accept old age and changes in the body, especially if you had a great body when you were young. Anyway, I start sneaking in and out of my own apartment in the hope that Granny will eventually forget that I even exist.

I'm thinking of moving once again. Our apartment is too small. There's also this Granny thing that has been freaking me out. It's just not right. I don't know what she wants, but I don't like it.

One of my professors at the university is a close friend who owns an apartment in a very nice part of town. I speak to her and she's willing to rent it out to me. Problem solved.

But another thing has been bothering me quite a bit. Cecilia has been pretty much living off me and does not contribute towards rent or any other expense. Her only contributions are the leftovers she brings from her trips. And it's not like she doesn't have any money. In addition to being an international flight attendant, she brings plenty of things from abroad and sells them here. Cosmetics, silk, and the like. Actually, she's got a pretty successful little business going. The entire issue gets on my nerves. After one year, she should be more involved in our relationship, which has basically been fueled by the awful me-trying-to-get-close-to-her-and-she-pushing-me-away thing.

I talk to her about my concerns. She agrees that she must contribute financially as a sign of her involvement. I mean, by now I earn quite a bit of cash and would most gladly support her if she needed it, but the fact is she earns money as well and must contribute. It's only fair.

Cecilia also asks me if I want to make more dough by taking some of her stuff to college and selling it to my friends. Hmm. I don't think I'm capable of selling cosmetics to women. She tells me not to worry because the stuff will sell itself.

So after a bit of hesitation, I decide to take some cosmetics to the university and see what happens. I'm shy about the entire thing, but Cecilia's right. As soon as I tell a few women about my new occupation, all I have to do is step back, let them fight over the stuff and receive the money. I kind of like that. In very little time, I run out of products and go home a happy man, with some extra bread in my pocket. Soon money starts to accumulate, and after only about a month, I've managed to save about $500. This seems to be taken care of.

March 1992

I've been in therapy for over a year and have managed to do away with many of my fears and much of my anger. I realize there's still much to do, but see myself as a changed man.

Well, I mean, I'm doing okay. I've settled into my own comfortable little life. I keep my pains under control and sweep the dust under the carpet. After so many years haunted by stressful thought patterns, my improvement seems like heaven.

One very big issue that takes up a lot of therapy time, though, is my dependency on my father's money. My finances are pretty stable and I no longer depend on him as I did in the days of the predated checks, but there is this lingering psychological aspect to the situation, which keeps me bonded. One way or another, I eventually find myself asking him for cash. And as usual, my father makes it hard on me. I always have to do something stupid in return, but mostly I have to embarrass myself, beg, and listen to all kinds of shit.

But then again things aren't always hard. Remember what I told you before. Whenever my father's in a good mood, he'll give me money before I even ask for it. This relationship has been confusing my mind for a long time. I really don't get it.

Guinea Pig

Cecilia's lack of interest in our relationship and the fact that she's constantly traveling has me craving for sex all the time. I can't say that enough.

One Sunday afternoon, I'm lonely and horny. Again. It's a gorgeous day out. And I absolutely need some action. Of course,

I haven't learned my lesson from the other night with the transvestite. I decide to do an experiment. Well, I've never been to a whorehouse. I wonder what it's like. I pick up a newspaper and check out some ads for escort services. I find one that looks nice, get in my car, and drive over.

The place is in an apartment facing the beach. I ring the doorbell. A good-looking brunette opens the door. I tell her I've come to see what a whorehouse is like. I'd like to try one of her ladies please. The woman looks puzzled, but nevertheless happily lets me in, and tells me to make myself comfortable. She says her girls are out at the beach and should be coming back soon. She turns on the TV and takes off to another room.

While watching a very hard-core porno flick, I wonder what these girls look like. What if they're all dogs. Can I just say I don't want them and leave. Maybe I should just leave. I'm scared. Come on. Quit it. I must think positive. And now that I'm here, let's see what's in store for me.

It doesn't take long before the first girl walks in. She's blonde and tall, but very ugly. She greets me and disappears through the door. My hostess walks in and asks me about the girl. I tell her I'd rather wait a bit more.

Soon another woman walks in. And another. And another. Damn. They are all pretty gross. My expectations are going down the drain.

After a while my hostess comes in and tells me this is pretty much all the girls she has. Only one left. I'm kind of bummed out. Well, she's not that bad looking herself. Maybe I can do her. I ask her if she's willing to be my girl for the afternoon. She laughs and tells me that's not her role. I guess I'll have to wait for the last girl and pray very hard she's good sex material.

A few minutes have gone by and I'm getting nervous. What have I gotten myself into. Again. I'm about to storm out the door when the last girl comes back from the beach. She's hot. Hot. Hot. Beautiful and young and hot. Her name's Ursula. She has black hair and a cute little face. Her tiny bikini barely covers her small, shapely body. I can't take my eyes off her. In the meantime, my hostess comes back and tells me she has decided to make herself available to me after all. She wants my sexy body. Oh, well. Too late. Now I want Ursula.

Ursula leads me into an adjacent room. There's nothing in it but an enormous bed. I make myself comfortable while she takes a shower.

Pretty soon she's back. She drops her towel, has me lie down and starts giving me a hot blowjob. Then she gets on top, cowgirl style, and rides me pretty hard. Weird. I'm supposed to be enjoying this, but the situation's completely phony. Never before in my life had I had sex without any real desire, any feeling. The woman doesn't want me. She's getting paid to play a role here, which is to please me. I feel terrible. I feel sorry for her.

Fifteen minutes later and it's all over. I get up, get dressed, and thank her. The woman looks at me as if I'm crazy. What am I thanking her for. I don't know what to say. I don't know what to do. I feel awkward as hell. I pay her and rush out of the place. Well, that didn't go so well. Again.

Lap Dance

I've been flirting with this girl at school, Caleigh. She's incredibly feminine and sexy. Naughty classmate Fay, the prick tease, has sensed something in the air and is on the lookout like a watchdog. What's up with this woman. Maybe she thinks she owns me or something. She tries to interfere in my games with Caleigh. She says nasty things about me. She tries to stand between us.

I get fed up and decide to talk to Caleigh. I tell her what Fay's trying to do. I tell her Fay's an asshole. She agrees. We both tell Fay to get lost and she finally backs off for good.

Then we set a date to have sex. Yes, you heard me right. We agree to meet on the following weekend. Cecilia won't be around. Although she's technically still my girlfriend, I feel no guilt whatsoever for cheating on her. I'm getting to the point of wanting to break up with her anyway.

The weekend has come and I'm ready for some action. In the evening, some friends are over at my place and I'm waiting for

Caleigh to show up. And boy, does she show up. The doorbell rings and I open the door. Caleigh is standing there. She's wearing a very short black dress. Full exposure on her gorgeous legs. No bra. What a sight for my sore eyes. She comes in. We all chat for a while and then my friends get the clue. Time to go.

I merrily entertain my very special guest. We have drinks. We talk. We laugh. We even make music. She sings pretty well and I record a duet with her. Then we start making out in the living room. I slide my hands along her legs, slowly caressing them. She gets up and takes off her dress. I remove her black panties and kiss her entire body. I turn her around. She slowly sits on my upright manhood and gives me the lap dance of my life. We then go to my bedroom and have some more great sex. She has multiple orgasms. Oh, yeah. Power, power, power trip. I'm the king of this whole wide world.

That's the good news. Now for the bad news. Right after sex, Caleigh tells me she's not on the Pill. And I wasn't wearing a condom either. We're both worried she might end up being pregnant. Shit. I guess we'll have to wait a month and see what happens.

Well, convenient or not, the pregnancy thing is a good excuse for me to avoid Caleigh. I got what I wanted and lost interest in her. But this time, I resent my feelings. We could have had a great relationship. Not going to happen. Even when I get the news that she has had her period a few weeks later. Close, but no cigar.

I've had it with Cecilia. I'm going to break up with her. The first thing I do is tell her that we should no longer live together. She's got to get an apartment of her own. She seems sad, but agrees to look for a place to live. She finds a small apartment pretty far from my house and moves out. We're still going out, but certainly not for long.

October 1992
I feel strong and confident. I feel I'm in control of my life. I tell Sergio I'm ready to quit therapy. He agrees. We can at least give it

a try. He tells me he'll be available in case I need him. I'm excited, but sad at the same time. Sergio has become a father figure to me, one much different than the one I had been carrying inside for so many years. I really wish he were my father. It's hard to let go. Hopefully, I've internalized that positive image enough to keep me away from further trouble. Yeah, sure.

I'm making one last attempt to revive my relationship. Cecilia and I try to reconcile things by spending the weekend at my friend's mountain cottage, which has become a very special place for me. I feel peaceful and relaxed when I'm there.

As soon as we arrive, we drop off our bags and head for the forest. I feel good. I feel strong. I feel naughty. My deteriorated feelings towards my girlfriend and my new attitudes have started to turn the tables in my favor. Cecilia is now much nicer to me. She also wants to have sex more. But the more she wants it, the more I reject her. Naturally.

We get to a waterfall. We're completely surrounded by nature. My girlfriend's perfectly shaped semi-nude body's really turning me on. I approach her, pull down her bikini, and give her steamy oral sex. I delight myself in power while she has multiple orgasms sitting on a rock by the river.

Graduation's only a few months away. Seems I'll finally have a college diploma. I'm currently working on my thesis and have an internship at a mental hospital. I'm getting ready to follow in my father's footsteps.

One day, I get a call from my dad. One of his colleagues is looking for someone to join his team. Great. A referral. Carlos is a psychiatrist who works with drug addicts and people with very serious personality disorders. Damned hard work. I don't mind. I can handle it. And I can most certainly handle some more money. I call the guy and set up an interview.

And sure enough, Carlos hires me. In all, there are four psychologists in his team. Our work basically involves following up on patients. We accompany them on walks, we take them to the movies, we care for them in their homes. Carlos sees his patients every once in a while. We're the ones present on a daily basis.

Although I'm still a private tutor, I find time to have many patients under my responsibility. I see very crazy people.

This one guy loves to play chess and listen to Black Sabbath. He's also into astral projection. When I come to see him, he just babbles incoherently for hours. We play chess and he kicks my ass. I take him for walks on the street and he's very loud. We attract a lot of attention.

There's another poor guy who spends hours in the bathroom washing his hands. I really pity him. He's very young, maybe fifteen. And then there's another guy, an older guy, who never takes a shower. He's terribly afraid of going out on the streets, so we mainly stay in his house and talk. He likes me.

December 14, 1992

I get an urgent call from Carlos. He wants me to go check on one of his patients, who has locked herself in her apartment and won't answer the phone. I get there and she's in the midst of a psychotic crisis. She's completely paranoid and won't let anybody in.

We call an ambulance to take the lady to a hospital. I stand outside her door and spill out my very convincing arguments. She opens the door. The woman looks like shit. And she's half-naked. Gross. The ambulance guys arrive and take her away.

December 18, 1992

One of my patients has tried to kill herself and is in the hospital. Carlos wants me to go and see her. I get there and the woman's lying in bed. Her mouth's all white. She has swallowed enough sleeping pills to kill a horse. Wow. But she'll be all right. They've pumped her stomach. I remain there and talk to her for a while to make her feel better.

I'm not surprised to see that these episodes don't shock me at all. After all, my dad is a psychiatrist. I was practically brought up in a mental institution and have seen all kinds of crazy people. One thing's for sure, though. I'm thrilled to see that patients' checks have started to come in by the bucketful.

The Final Act

Cecilia and I barely see each other anymore. She's fucking problematic and I don't need this shit. I have enough patients already. Time to make my final move.

She comes back from her latest trip and I tell her we need to talk. I think to myself, *if she's been paying any attention to what has been going on between us this should come as no surprise.* Boy, am I mistaken.

She gets to my apartment and I go straight to the point. I tell her the truth. We don't get along, we seldom have sex, we don't have a good life together. She just sits there for a while, and then suddenly throws a fit. She yells and yells and yells. I'm introduced to a new and mean version of my girlfriend. I'd never seen Cecilia do this before. She then storms out the door and refuses to give me her key to the house. Who cares. I'll have the lock changed.

Soon I get calls from our mutual friends. They're all startled. We seemed like the perfect couple.

I tell them our relationship had been bad for a while now and Cecilia should have known it was coming. I had warned her many times. Some of her friends understand. Others try to act like my parents and I tell them to fuck off.

SIX

The Devil in Disguise

By now the spiritual tools I picked up in 1988 have become effective means of feeding my neurotic personality. Hey, what can I say. I often seek guidance from the oracles, but am so emotionally involved in my stories that I misinterpret the fucking things and all I see is bad news. The bad news generates more bad feelings, which in turn make me seek more advice from the oracles. This cycle repeats itself again and again, *ad nauseum*, which means until I puke.

December 23, 1992

Carlos has asked me to take one of his patients to a Narcotics Anonymous meeting. The kid's only nineteen. He smokes plenty of pot and drinks, but his main thing is cocaine. He only weighs about sixty pounds. The little fuck's constantly giving his parents a hard time. He steals things from home to buy dope. He's away for days at a time. A very difficult case indeed.

After our meeting, I take him to his house. In a few days, I'm supposed to drop by and interview his parents. Chemical dependency is a family thing.

December 26, 1992

I ring the doorbell at my patient's home. His mom opens the door and greets me. I come in and interview her and then his brother. They are very crazy people. Then I interview his sister. Her name is Kate. She's skinny and short. She's a single mom. I'm attracted to her. I know. My damned needs are at it again. Kate also seems to be interested in me. But you know me and my Godforsaken moral values. There's no way on Earth I'll ever mix business with pleasure...

December 28, 1992
I'm back at my patient's house to treat his family. I go into Kate's room to speak with her. She hands me a letter. She wants me to read it. It's not addressed to anyone in particular, but I can tell it's obviously for me. It's a love letter. She has hit my soft spot. I can't stop myself and we make out. Dear Lord.

January 5, 1993
Kate and I are dating in secret. I feel bad because she's a patient's relative. Crap. I really shouldn't be doing this. It's very unprofessional. I decide to ask my boss Carlos for advice. Carlos has been married four times and has nine kids. Not exactly the best person to advise me, but all I want is approval. He tells me if I want to go out with a patient or a relative, fine. I should just make sure this doesn't turn into a habit. It must be a one-time thing. This is all I need to hear and I have a new girlfriend.

I invite Kate over to my house. We're just sitting around talking when the doorbell rings. It's Cecilia. Surprise, surprise. She looks like shit. She wants to raise some hell and argue. I don't even let her come in. I tell her I want my keys back. She's crying. She's hysterical. Kate's in the bedroom and doesn't say a word. After some more heavy metal talk, Cecilia throws the keys at me, tells me to go fuck myself, and storms off. Again. I think this one's gone for good. I'm sure glad she didn't see Kate.

Things are progressing very quickly. I'm now completely under Kate's spell. We've decided to get married soon. Lightning-fast decision. I tell all my relatives about her and everyone's in shock. They don't think this is a good idea. I'm dying to tell everyone off.

My siblings are afraid of me and don't really say anything. And that's good because I haven't asked them for their opinion. But my mother and father both want to talk to me.

First comes Mom. We go out for lunch. We have our conversation in the parking lot just outside the restaurant.

She babbles and babbles and babbles. After evaluating my situation, she has concluded I'm following the footsteps of my uncle, her brother, who married a poor woman and adopted kids. I'm thinking, what kind of weird Freudian distortion is this. She tells me Kate's taking advantage of my potential. What's that supposed to mean. I'm sick of these people trying to tell me what to do. *Look at your own screwed up life*, is what I say. Who the fuck are you to advise me about anything.

Last but not least comes my dad. We set up a meeting. From the tone of his voice I know he's going to give me a hard time. Our duel takes place at his clinic. He's being his old authoritarian self. Daddy has always been right. Daddy's putting me down once again and making me feel unworthy. Nothing I do is right. That woman's going to ruin my life. I'm making a wrong move. Wrong, wrong, wrong.

I tell him all I want is the freedom to do what I think is right. He doesn't have to approve of what I do. I just want him to support me as a person, as his son. He says no. That really kicks my ass. I'm devastated. I feel horrible. I feel powerless. This guy's a dick. That same evening, while trying to have sex with Kate, for the first time in my life, I cannot get my penis up.

I'm in the prime of my rebelliousness. I don't care what anyone says. Kate and her four-month-old daughter move in with me and her relatives are delighted. They see that she has found a young and promising psychologist who will take good care of her.

I try to play it cool but in reality I'm completely overwhelmed by the entire situation. I can't think straight. Things are happening too fast. I need time to stop and think, but I simply cannot get my act together.

Psycho

Kate and I are at my home and we're doing it in the bedroom. Her baby girl's in the living room, asleep. After sex, we're relaxing in bed when Kate suddenly starts complaining about her life. I can't really understand what she's saying, especially because it seems she's not really talking to me. She's lying down and has her eyes closed. She's saying, *you guys this...and you guys that.* How can that be. I'm the only one in the room. She's getting very upset. Disproportionately upset. God. I think I've seen this before. Yep. In the fucking mental hospital. My girlfriend seems to be having a psychotic episode of some sort.

When she calms down a bit and finally opens her eyes, Kate's nowhere to be found. I mean, she's here, but she's not here. She has channeled a spirit and now calls herself Annie.

I had plenty of experience with channeling in the old days at the religious temples, but this is a first. My own girl, in my own home. Shit. What have I gotten myself into. Anyway, I chat with Annie for some time. At least she's not psychotic.

I must be going nuts. I can't believe I got myself into this mess. And what's worse, I'm still willing to go through with this nonsense. Although I'm somewhat excited about my marriage, deep in my heart, I feel heavy. I have this very bad gut feeling. On the other hand, I want to inflict revenge upon my parents. After all, I am *the* true rebel. Tell me not to do it and I'll do it. But the truth is, I feel as if I'm in limbo. I can't see clearly at all.

Kate's mother has been taking us to a religious temple. During a divination session, I'm told former girlfriend Cecilia's still around and is trying to harm me through magic. And I believe it. That must be why I now have a weird rash on my penis that won't go away. So Kate and I do all kinds of purification rituals and food offerings. Damn it. It seems like my mother all over again. I am up to my neck in this mess.

Hostage Situation (and a Fun-Filled Weekend)

I've borrowed my friend's cottage and we're off for the weekend. Before leaving, we swing by Kate's mom's house to pick up her daughter, who'd been with Grandma for a couple of days.

As soon as we get there, Kate starts arguing with her mother. What's that all about. Apparently Kate has a debt on her mother's credit card and crazy Mom wants her to pay it back. Now. Great. Actually I'm pretty sure she wants me to pay it back, but she won't say it openly. I tell them we can solve this issue later. Mom refuses and says Kate must pay her now.

Then she does something that completely blows my mind. She holds the little girl hostage. She tells us that she'll not let her granddaughter leave the house until Kate has paid her debt. Shit. I can't believe it. I intervene. She can't do that. What's she thinking. This is her granddaughter we're talking about. She can't treat her as if she were a thing. But Grandma's completely insane and insists she won't let the little girl go.

I'm forced to resort to the persuasive abilities acquired after many years of practice with my own father. I manage to cut a deal with Kate's mom. She can keep my ID until her daughter's debt is paid and she'll let the baby girl go in return. The woman agrees and we leave for the mountains in shock. Unbelievable.

Once arriving at my friend's cottage, we leave Kate's daughter with the caretaker's wife and head for the forest to relax a bit. We're ready to have sex, but once again, I fail. I feel frustrated and powerless. Kate's visibly annoyed. I give up trying to get my penis up and we put our clothes back on. After smoking a joint, we light up cigarettes and just hang around for a while, gazing at the amazing jungle scenery around us.

Then suddenly two guys and a dog emerge from the woods. We're scared. They come closer and start talking. They tell us they're forest rangers. They tell us this is a restricted preservation area and we're not supposed to be here. Whew. We're relieved. We thought they were some crazy dudes ready to do us all kinds of harm. I'm also happy we weren't having sex. That would have been embarrassing.

And so my life goes from awesome to awful in the blink of an eye. Sadly, my old motto is fully functional. *Let's see what happens*, I say to myself. *There's no real reason to break this off. Not yet.* I feel I must withstand this situation until I can no longer take it. Super. Me and my wonderfully masochistic attitude.

Kate and I legally tie the knot on March 4, 1993. There's no ceremony, just a toast on the street in front of the notary's office. My family has given up trying to convince me not to get married, and everyone's present. Kate's family members are also here.

After dinner at a pizzeria, we're off to our honeymoon at a rented beach house. We're taking Kate's little girl along because I desperately want to minimize contact with crazy Grandma.

All's well during our honeymoon, except for sex. The stupid rash on my penis has gotten worse and now hurts like crazy. Kate complains all the time. She doesn't understand my problem. She doesn't care. This kills me because I feel I've lost all my power.

Psycho II

Kate's trying to find her pen. She looks and looks and looks, but the thing is nowhere to be found. She gets hysterical. I tell her to calm down. No big deal, it's just a pen. But she won't stop and tension builds up. I want this shit to be over with, so I stop what I'm doing to help her out. We still can't find the damned pen.

Now the girl's really ticked off. She's throwing stuff around. She's screaming. I'm just standing here in disbelief. How can such a small thing lead to this crazy whirlwind of activity.

Then she forgets about the pen and starts attacking me. She hits me and tells me how her life sucks. She tells me she'll make my life hell. I really have no reaction. I don't know what to do. I try to reason with her, but no dice. My system is too stressed out. I tell her I'm going for a walk. I've got to breathe. She doesn't let me. She tells me she's going to follow me. She tells me she's going to harm her little girl. I give up and stay in the room, listening to all kinds of insults.

After a long time, her episode finally wears out and she falls asleep. And I'm not even thinking there's still time to escape this horrible situation. I'm not even thinking I can still cancel my marriage. All I think about is how I can save this poor soul. I want to be her savior. I feel bad for her. I'll do my best to treat her. I can manage this situation. Crap, oh crap. I'm projecting Momma very strongly on this one.

I am annoyed because Kate's relatives bug us all the time. Her mother calls her every day. She's one hundred times crazier than Kate, if that's at all possible.

I find some relief at work, but not much. I no longer have private students. My work with Carlos has led me to a position at my father's psychiatric clinic. Yeah, some relief.

I do have a few good friends at the clinic who help me get my mind off the terrible stress, but overall it's craziness all day long, and more craziness once I get home from work.

Death Wish (Please Don't Try This at Home)

Kate has come up with a new and fun tactic. During one of her episodes, she tells me she's going to kill herself. I get very scared and don't know what to do. She locks herself up in the bathroom and tries to cut her wrists. Fuck.

I then remember my therapist, Sergio, telling me there was a time when his wife used to do the same thing. He solved the problem by telling her that if she wanted to kill herself, there was nothing he could do about it. And when she took many pills one day, he didn't do a thing. I don't know if I have the guts to do that, though. I guess I'll have to wait and see.

And it doesn't take long for Kate to try to kill herself again. This time she tells me she's going to swallow all her stomach cramp pills. I gather up courage and tell her that if she wants to kill herself, it's her wish and I can't do anything about it. She then takes the pills and laughs in my face. I'm terrified but manage not to show my feelings. Fortunately, nothing happens. After a while, she complains that her stomach hurts. I really don't give a rat's ass. That's the last time Kate does anything of the sort. Blessed be my therapist.

May 5, 1993
And now for some great news: Kate's pregnant. My stomach's churning. Even though I think I'm ready for fatherhood, I'm horrified to see I'm now stuck with this woman forever. And then there is also Kate's girl, whom I have really adopted as a father. My moral values tell me that Hell will freeze over before I even try to escape this situation.

Things are going from bad to worse. I lose touch with most of my friends. Kate and her daughter take up all of my energy and time. And now the fact that she's pregnant makes me worry even more when she has her episodes.

The Spaghetti Affair

We're over at Kate's folks' house for lunch. All her immediate relatives are here and we're having an okay time. Then Kate starts arguing with her mom. Naturally. The argument becomes heated. Uh-oh. She starts freaking out. I try to calm her down. Then Kate suddenly grabs my plate of spaghetti and dumps it on my shirt. Her relatives kind of reprimand her, but it's no surprise to them. They've probably seen this many times before. But not me. I've only seen this on TV. I mean, I've had many arguments with women and even with my mom, but never to the point of physical abuse. Man, this is bad soap opera material. And I am the co-star.

After pondering my situation for a while, I conclude that bad influence is mostly to blame for our troubles at home. And by that, I mean Kate's family. Maybe we should move to another town. I might be able to handle things better then.

The one place that comes to mind is my friend's mountain cottage. The nearby town is close to Rio, but at the same time, far enough to minimize daily contact with any nosey family member.

Wild-West-Style Finale

One evening, Kate and I go out with my good college friend Tina. After dinner at a nearby restaurant, we walk Tina to the bus stop. We're about to cross the street when we see two guys running in our direction. They zoom past us. Then two cops come right behind them, shooting all over the place. I only have enough time to shove the girls against a building wall and protect them with my body. We're very lucky we don't get shot.

That's it. Now I definitely want to leave this place. It's way too dangerous. I contact my friend and he lets us borrow his cottage until we find a decent place to live in our new town. And soon we're on the move. I quit my work with Carlos but keep the job at my father's clinic. I've made arrangements to come and work three times a week.

But things don't turn out well from the start. I can't stand getting up so early for work. I leave home at four in the morning and return late in the evening. As usual, my father helps out with some money and especially food. And I've become a true beast of burden, carrying heavy bags of food from the clinic to my home. Hey, at least I'm in good shape.

I use the rest of my time to find a new job closer to home. I go everywhere handing out résumés. I find a clinic nearby and hope they hire me soon. I also drop my résumé off at a renowned English as a Second Language, or ESL, school and they seem to be interested in me.

As the days go by, my daze begins to fade and I can clearly see what an asshole Kate is. I can't trust her alone with the child. Sex is also pretty rare, due both to our bad relationship and to my physical issues.

I'm in constant touch with my urologist, who writes me prescriptions and the rash on my penis goes away for a while, but soon returns. I believe someone's really trying to fuck up my life and that someone is Cecilia. I feel pretty screwed up energetically.

To make things worse (or better, I really can't tell), there's a gorgeous woman at my father's clinic who's very attracted to me. Joanna's one of my interns. We instantly become very close. I'd love to have sex with her, but I'm afraid of Annie, the spirit, who would certainly find out and tell her lunatic host. I can only imagine what that would be like.

Joanna's not the only woman I have my eyes on. I flirt with many other women at the clinic but dare not touch them. These games are driving me up the wall, because my libido's very high and I have nowhere to discharge it.

The hard work of peddling my services doesn't take long to pay off and I'm soon hired as an ESL teacher. Forget psychology for a while. I'll initially be working part-time. Nice. This will allow me to make a smooth transition from my activities at the clinic.

And perfect timing, because my current job really sucks. My patterns have turned work into a weird game with my father. The same old song and dance.

Mostly I only pretend to be working and hardly ever see any patients. On Saturdays, for example, I get to the clinic at around seven and sleep in my office until noon. Then I hang around and wait until it's time for me to go home. All I want is my allowance (my paycheck) at the end of the month.

Kate and I argue all the time. She's very aggressive on every level—including physically. I abhor this kind of behavior. I wasn't brought up that way. But Kate was. She once told me that when her father was angry, he used to throw her brothers against the wall headfirst. Jesus.

Our baby is almost due. It's been a rough ride. Many times, I've had to beg Kate not to harm our unborn child by hitting herself and doing other senseless things. And now she wants to have the baby in Rio. I think it's both unnecessary and dangerous, because after all, we're a two-hour drive away from her physician and if anything happens, I'll have to rush like a maniac to get her to a hospital. But I let her have her way. The fewer things that make her unhappy, the better.

Luckily, we quickly find a pretty decent apartment downtown and plan to move before the baby arrives. Our new home is pretty small, but perfectly adequate for our needs. It's located over a bar and a bus stop on a very busy street. There goes my peace and quiet. I was used to sleeping to the sound of frogs and crickets. I guess I'll have to settle for the sound of car engines and loud people laughing all night long. But we're okay. I know this is only temporary. I'll immediately start looking for a better place to live. There's no hurry now. All I really wanted was to leave my friend's cottage as soon as possible. I didn't want to abuse his generosity.

False Alarm

Kate is hysterical. Again. She's having contractions and we think she's going into labor. We call her doctor, who tells us to drive to the hospital immediately. I also call my relatives and everyone's very excited.

Two hours later, we get to the hospital. My sister Veronica's already here. We're rushed to a room. The doctor soon arrives. She examines Kate and tells us it was a false alarm. I'm bummed out. This is precisely why I didn't want her to have the baby here.

And so, in order to avoid other unnecessary trips, we decide to stay at my mother's house until the baby is born. It won't be much longer now. The doctor says we should spend the night at the hospital just to make sure everything is okay.

My sister leaves and Kate and I are in the room alone. Kate is furious. I ask her to calm down. It's not yet time for the baby to come and there's nothing we can do about it. I tell her everything's going to be all right. But she's going into another episode. It's about one o'clock in the morning.

Kate starts complaining. She's being very loud. I beg her to lower her voice. We're in a hospital, for Christ's sake. She blames me, her parents and everyone else for what's happening with her.

Then she grabs the lever on the bed and starts banging it. She says she's going to wake everybody up in the damned hospital. I'm very embarrassed and extremely annoyed. I'm also very scared for the baby. This can't be a good thing. But I don't know what to do and so I just do nothing. Anything I say will only make things worse. After a while, she winds down and falls asleep.

The following day, we're at my mother's home. Kate has quieted down. Mom's dishing out her usual bullshit instead of being there for me. She tells me that she's been working like a dog. She tells me she's been working on some great project but no one cares about it. She tells me how poor she is. She spills out her entire victim repertoire and makes me feel even worse than I already feel. She's hinting that I pay some of her bills. I think this is all crap. She has had—and even has—plenty of opportunities to sell her work, but has rejected them all. She wants to take me down the gutter with her. So I tell her to go take a hike. Too much for her patterns. She gets very mad and kicks us out of the house. Unreal. I don't even argue. We just grab our things and leave. Fuck her and her selfishness.

We have no alternative but to drive to Kate's mother's house and ask her if we can stay there. She welcomes us with open arms. I finally feel a bit more relaxed and hope things will go well in the next few days.

February 3, 1994

Once again, I'm thinking about my situation and what led me to it. I think about how my family life was kind of make-believe. I think about how my parents were "so happy together" for seventeen years and wouldn't divorce because of the kids. I think about how that led to their mutual hatred, which affected us all. I think about how I'm doing the exact same thing.

My musings are suddenly interrupted. We're at the hospital and my beautiful baby boy has just been born. He looks just like me. I'm delighted beyond belief, but I'm also worried. What's our life going to be like now.

It's not long before we leave the hospital and go back to my mother-in-law's house. We'll have to stay here for ten days before the baby is allowed to travel. I tell them I'm going back home because I have things to do in the apartment and also have to work, but will be coming to see them every two or three days. Good for me. I get a decent and well-deserved rest.

Everything works out fine and we're all home after a couple of weeks. I'm finally hired full-time at the ESL school. No more getting up at four in the morning and taking a two-hour bus ride to work. I couldn't be happier.

But now we have two children to care for. And I also have to take care of Kate and her episodes. Fortunately, I have found a way to minimize her crises. This is what I do: after enduring her episode for a while, I convince her to let Annie come. She resists a bit but channels. And then I can relate to Annie. Yes, my friend, this is very weird. I don't know who or what this Annie character is—a spirit or an alter ego of some sort, but I really don't care, as long as I don't have to deal with "bad Kate."

While things are shitty at home, my new work is great. The place is owned and managed by four people: Wendy, Jade, Myrna, and Fred. I like Wendy the most. Jade is nice as well. She's a very sophisticated lady. She's what my mother probably would have been like if my father hadn't divorced her. Myrna's also very nice. She's the youngest of the bunch. She's blonde and short and chubby. Oops. I think she's attracted to me. She's very friendly, perhaps a little too friendly. But I definitely want no piece of that. Fred's the most distant of the bunch, but I also get along with him. In fact, he was the person I spoke with when I applied for the job. My colleagues, the secretary, the cleaning lady...all seem to be very nice. I think I'll be here for a while.

Some more good news. I've found another apartment in a very quiet neighborhood. It's only about two blocks from where we live now. The two-bedroom apartment is larger and our rooms face the forest.

Reflection

It's funny how I'm now living a divided life. Again. On the one hand, there's my new professional life, which has been improving on a daily basis. Relationships are great and I feel terrific all day long. I find that I very much enjoy teaching.

But life at home is a nightmare, the complete opposite, and it gets worse and worse every day. While I strive to find a way and make things work out between us, Kate doesn't seem to care at all about our marriage.

Three's a Crowd

Kate and I have been talking some naughty stuff lately. I casually mentioned to her that it would be nice to have a threesome some time and she agrees. It also turns her on. So we decide to invite one of her friends to our home for the weekend so that we can do the heck out of her.

Kate's friend Alicia arrives on a Friday afternoon. In the evening, we put the kids to sleep and the three of us are chatting and having fun. I'm very aroused, but nervous. We really don't have a plan, but I think things will be easier if we all start drinking and smoking. Alicia refuses the weed, but drinks with us.

We're having whisky and our libidos are getting mighty active. I can smell sex in the air. At one point, Kate tells Alicia she has some aerobics clothes a friend has given her to sell. The idea is that they try them on and show them to me and I express my opinion. Yeah, right. But before they do that, they tell me they're going to take a shower. Prick teasers.

I can hear the women giggling. I want to storm in the shower and join them, but I have a big problem—the rash on my penis, which has gotten worse and hurts very much. I really don't think I'm able to have sex without feeling a lot of pain. I'm also embarrassed Alicia will see the rash. So I stay in my room and beat myself on the head.

After their shower comes my very own fashion show. Enter Kate with very tight leggings and a tank top. She looks amazing. Then in comes Alicia and her delicious curves. Nice. Very nice.

While Alicia's changing, Kate and I work out an improvised plan. She'll go to the kitchen to make us something to eat while I come on to Alicia. Then she'll return and join in. Genius plan. Dumb asses. And we don't even have a plan B.

Alicia's still in the bathroom. The door's open. I go in and totally grab her. I go straight for her private parts. She's in shock. I tell her I really want her. What about Kate. I tell her Kate won't mind. I try to kiss her, but the woman is paralyzed.

Alicia eventually gives in. She tells me to leave so that she can go to the bathroom and then we'll have sex. She closes the door, but when she opens it a minute later, the woman's completely dressed. And so our plan goes down the drain. We're all sort of embarrassed and just pretend nothing has happened.

The next day, I take Alicia home. During the two-hour drive, she pretends she's asleep and we don't say a word to each other. When I drop her off, I apologize and she says everything is fine. Well, I know I'll never see this woman again.

I'm relieved because the kids are now enrolled in nursery school. I can finally go to work and forget about Kate. I no longer have to worry if Kate's feeding the children properly or taking good care of them. They do it all at school.

The kids leave for school at seven and are not back until five. I'm thinking this will be great for them as they will interact with other children, as well as with some healthy adults.

Kate's also happy. Looking after two babies is hard work. She tells me she's going to look for a job. Hey, maybe there's some hope for our marriage after all. Maybe Kate will get better if she's busy. Maybe she'll relax and stop having the episodes. Dream on.

My boss Myrna has referred me to one of her friends, who owns a private tutoring center in town. I thank her but maintain my customary healthy distance. I can see that Myrna's starting to get annoyed because I want nothing to do with her.

So I'm now a full-time teacher once again. Psychology's on hold. Except for the daily sessions at home, of course.

Contact with my family has become a thing of the past. Kate still speaks with her mom almost every day, but now she has finally found a job at a clothing store and has been keeping busy. Let's see how long this will last.

Clueless

I come home from work one day and see there's new furniture in da house. Kate has bought a huge and fancy new shelf. I'm pretty sure it cost a lot of money. I'm sort of angry. She didn't talk to me about it. I'm the sort of person who likes to share things in a relationship. That's how we grow and control our finances.

But Kate doesn't care. She tells me she's now working and will purchase whatever she wants. And since she doesn't have the money to pay cash, she has arranged to pay for the shelf in twelve monthly installments. I tell her this isn't in our budget and that she shouldn't have done that. What if she loses her job. She tells me to fuck off.

Sure enough, one week later, Kate loses her job. She tells me she was fired for no reason whatsoever, but I don't believe her. Awesome. Now she's back home getting high all day long, and I have an extra burden to carry for the next twelve months.

Thank goodness things are looking good in my professional life. I've just been offered another job, this time as a chemistry teacher in a private school. I'm supposed to teach basic chemistry to tenth, eleventh, and twelfth grades. My week's pretty crowded with work—the ESL school, private tutoring, and now this. And the money's really starting to pour in.

Soon after I start working at the private tutoring center, I meet a girl. Her name is Cassandra. Cassie's the center secretary. She's in her early twenties and is very pretty. She's tall, blonde, has a great body, and what's best, she's into me. We get along great and I immediately start to have feelings for her.

I spend my free afternoons at the private tutoring center with Cassie. I think I'm falling in love with her. She's also in a crappy relationship. She tells me her boyfriend doesn't treat her well.

She knows about my ordeal. We start playing flirting games on a daily basis. The situation at home is intolerable, and it sure feels great being with Cassandra.

At the ESL school, Myrna now treats me like shit. She tolerates me, but that's about it. I comment on her behavior to my other boss, Wendy, who says Myrna has problems with men. Figures.

November 27, 1994

One evening, Kate and I are in our bedroom when she decides to look for a sweater. Oh, dear. Here we go again. By now I'm fully aware of her process and try to stop it before it even begins, but am unsuccessful. She looks and looks and then starts to freak out. I tell her I'm going to the living room to play the guitar. The kids are asleep in their room.

After about a minute, she storms into the living room. She looks very mad. I tell her to leave me alone. I can't stand this any longer. I really can't. I get up and lock myself in the bathroom. I need some peace and quiet.

In the bathroom, I notice my system has completely closed down. My jaws are locked. I have a terrible frown. My sphincter is very tight. For the first time, I really feel I must do something about this situation or else the stress is going to kill me.

Kate soon starts banging on the door and says she'll make my life hell. No surprise there. It's already been hell for quite some time. She's very noisy, and I end up opening the door because I'm afraid she'll wake the kids up. I'm also embarrassed because the neighbors will certainly hear us. I'm becoming a respectable figure in town and I don't want to ruin my image. And also, I'm a bit more polite than that.

I go back to the bedroom. Now Kate's really provoking me. She wants me to hit her. I tell her I won't do it. She insists. *Hit me, hit me, hit me.* I tell her to stop and calm down. She continues. And then I completely lose control and give her a swift kick in the ass. I don't kick her hard at all, but it's enough for me to immediately retreat in absolute guilt.

Kate's having a field day. I've done exactly what she wanted. Now she's telling me what a coward I am because I hit her. She's screaming and I'm speechless, motionless. We hear a neighbor banging on the wall. She's telling us to stop fighting. Kate yells back and tells her to fuck off.

After a while she starts to wind down. She ends up falling asleep and channels Annie. I tell her I can't stand the situation any longer. Annie tells me I'm the only one who can save Kate. If I give up, there is no hope for her. But the thing is, I feel like I'm about to have a heart attack. Who is going to save me.

December 12, 1994

I am now completely in love with Cassie. This is very weird. I feel great and I feel shitty at the same time. In the afternoon, we see each other and finally kiss. Wow. I don't think I've ever felt anything like that before. One single sweet, true, soft, amazing kiss. I'm in heaven. But I'm also in hell. I have no way out. I have to do something about my situation.

In a moment of clarity, I decide the best thing I can possibly do is leave that hellhole I call home. I think of the children, but my desperation is much stronger than my moral values. They'll probably be better off anyway. My feelings for Cassie have given me the strength I need to see this through to the end.

December 15, 1994

Early evening. Kate and I are in the midst of another argument. I tell her I'm leaving. She freaks out. She says she won't let me do it. I tell her I can no longer live like this.

She goes into another episode, but this time, I really don't care. I'm surprisingly calm inside. She does her usual thing and then Annie comes. She begs me to stay and help Kate. I tell her I can't. I've reached my breaking point. And then another spirit comes. I don't know her name, but she's trying to convince me to stay as well. Fuck that. Then Kate's back and we decide to call her folks.

Her parents arrive at eleven. They're not surprised I've decided to leave. They know their daughter only too well. The huge commotion has awakened the kids. I'm trying to think of a way to save them from the stress and suffering. I beg Kate's father to take them somewhere else, but Kate won't let him. I beg and beg and beg her parents to take the kids away.

Finally, the children are led to their room while I'm left with the two crazy-ass women. But I don't want to deal with this any longer. I simply can't. Kate's mom manages to calm her daughter down. I see a window of opportunity and quickly make my move. I grab my clothes, tapes, and guitar and take them to the car.

Things seem to be under control. I can finally leave. I have Kate's parents promise they'll stay with the children for a while. I tell Kate I'll be back the next day to pick up my books.

I drive straight to my friend's empty cottage. Lucky me, just a few days ago I had purchased large quantities of marijuana and can smoke myself into oblivion.

December 16, 1994

Back at the apartment. I see Kate has stacked my books outside. Good. I won't have to deal with her. I start gathering the books and notice she has spent the night ripping every single page of every single book in half. I don't care. I just want to get rid of her.

Just as I'm about to leave, she opens the door. She begs me to stay. I don't say a word and leave the building. She goes out on the street and threatens to throw a tantrum. She knows how I hate that. But I don't care anymore. I get into my car and drive away and don't look back for a second.

SEVEN

Variety

I'm sitting alone in my friend's cottage looking out at the dense forest in front of me. I can't believe I had enough courage to break free. An enormous burden has been removed from my system. I'm light as a feather. I must now rest. The past few weeks have been just awful.

I sleep like a log for twelve hours, then purify myself under a waterfall and head to town for my last day at the private tutoring center before the holidays. I'm dying to see Cassandra.

I've gotten her a gift. I bought her a small gold cross with an emerald in the middle. I carefully opened a box of chocolates, placed the jewel inside and resealed the box so that it looks like it hasn't been opened.

At the center, I give Cassie her present. She smiles and thanks me for the chocolate. I tell her to open the box. When she sees the cross, her face turns pale. I can tell she's delighted. My hopes are high. Even though she has not broken up with her boyfriend yet, I'm very confident it will happen anytime now.

Cassie tells me she's going to the beach for a couple of weeks. What a coincidence. So am I. We plan to meet. It'll be great to see her and maybe we can get it on then. I feel better than I have felt in a long, long time.

Breakdown

I am spending Christmas at my mother's. My entire family's here. There are tons of kids running around all over the place. People are happy. But I feel like shit. It's 1988 all over again. I try to hold back my feelings, but my tactic isn't working very well. My relatives know what has just happened, but no one speaks about it. I guess they're waiting for my reaction.

At some point, I feel I'm having a breakdown. I lose control and start crying. I absolutely need to let it all out. I tell everyone I feel horrible. I tell everyone I feel guilty. I can't stand seeing my nine-month-old son suffer. And there's also the little girl. What a horrific situation. My relatives listen to what I have to say, then get together and envelop me in a beautiful group hug. I cry even more. And I feel supported and loved. For once.

Soon after Christmas, I head for my older sister's vacation home at the beach. I'm looking forward to seeing Cassie.

One sunny afternoon, I drive to the restaurant where we had agreed to meet. I get there and Cassandra has not yet arrived. No problem. I'll wait. And I wait. And wait. And wait. After a couple of hours, I realize she's not coming. I'm very sad. But deep down inside, maybe I knew this was going to happen.

Back home a few days later, I see her. I ask her why she didn't show up at the restaurant. Cassandra tells me she was there and didn't see me. I guess I just missed her. Or she's lying. Whatever. I'm beginning to see that our potential relationship isn't going to happen. I'm completely heartbroken.

And things get worse when Kate somehow finds out about us and seeks revenge by having an affair with Cassie's boyfriend. Now Cassandra's really freaking out on me. I tell her he's a prick anyway and that we should be together. She's mad at me. I realize she thinks I'm causing her too much trouble. She tells me off and I finally give her up.

I've also had it with this rash on my private parts. I call up my urologist and this time he prescribes this weird orange spray. I start using the medication and it seems to be working. It takes some time, but I'm finally free from the stupid rash. The orange medication worked wonders, or maybe it was my separation.

It's been one month since I last saw the kids. Things have cooled down between Kate and me, and I decide to get in touch with her. She's happy to hear from me and gladly agrees to let me see the children. I realize something must be done about the dissolution of our marriage and call a lawyer to resolve the situation legally.

Things improve little by little. I've been allowed to crash in my friend's cottage—at least for now. One weekend, my middle sister's over for a visit. She has come with her boyfriend, a long-time acquaintance of ours. They're fun and like to drink and get high. In the evening, we decide to go and visit our cousin Tammy, who coincidentally has also moved into town. She rents a farmhouse surrounded by beautiful mountains in a remote neighborhood.

Tammy's brother, Chuck, a wacky psychologist, has set up a therapeutic resort in the area, where he holds workshops pretty much every weekend. He also rents an old theater nearby and has turned it into an avant-garde bar for his clients.

After searching for a while, we finally find the frigging place and spend the night in a small and friendly family gathering.

The following weekend, I get a visit from the owners of the cottage. My friend's parents are very fond of me and regard me as a son. They want to talk to me about my separation. They're very religious people. They give me a sermon about the institution of marriage and how important it is for the kids and blah, blah, blah.

After they leave, I'm furious. I feel as if my own parents have been invading my personal life once again. Who are they to tell me what to do. I decide to write these people a very strong and rude letter reminding them that they're not my parents. I need to get this off my chest pronto.

It only takes a couple of days for me to feel the consequences of my tactless letter. My friend's here to see me about it. He's telling me how ungrateful I am. He's telling me how his parents are outraged. He also tells me he heard I've been taking advantage of their hospitality and have been inviting all kinds of people to his cottage. Shit, the only people who came over were my sister and her boyfriend. I don't say a word, but realize I'll soon have to leave the place.

D-Day

My kids are over at the cottage for the weekend. On Saturday, my friend's parents suddenly arrive at the house. I know. They're here to kick me out. Bummer. Few words are spoken. I just pack my stuff into the car, take the children and drive off. Fuck them.

That caught me by surprise. Kate's away for the weekend, so I can't take the kids back to her. I have no choice but to go to a nearby hotel. It's pretty nice. Ten cottages surround a small lake. Eucalyptus trees and pines all over. Fresh mountain air. We're the only guests here.

By evening, I'm feeling horrible. My victim pattern has really kicked in. I put the kids to sleep and cry like a baby all night long. I'm feeling terribly sorry for myself.

As the morning comes, I get my act together and assess my situation. I must think clearly. Things aren't so bad, after all. All I have to do is find a new place to stay. Tamara immediately comes to mind. Maybe she'll be able to help me. I think I still have her phone number. I stop by a public phone and give her a call. Cousin Chuck answers. He's very happy to hear from me and tells me to come over right away.

What a relief. I drive for about half an hour and arrive at his resort. There are many people around. Things look exciting and busy. And I'm most welcome. My mood changes instantly. The kids are free to run around and I'm able to relax a bit. My cousin Tammy and my aunt are also here, along with many other people who seem to be very cool.

Chuck's neighbor, Beatrice, has also turned her property into a therapeutic resort. On weekends, people come and stay at both properties, which are pretty much connected. I really like the vibes of this place. In the evening, after having dropped the kids off at Kate's, we're sitting around a bonfire. I tell everyone about my most recent nightmare. Cousin Chuck says I can unpack my stuff and stay here. The people seem to be one happy family, and I'm now part of it.

I'm told I can stay in a small apartment in the main house, which is comprised of a storage room and a small kitchenette, with a fridge and a sink and a bathroom. I'm grateful and happy to have a new home.

Things between Kate and me have improved quite a bit since our separation, and we're now able to talk about the technical and practical aspects of our situation. We soon get together with my lawyer to discuss legal matters. Kate's very friendly, especially because the lawyer's bill's on me. She sees no need to find her own lawyer and my lawyer will act on our behalf.

Our conversation's very quick and straight to the point. I'm doing things like my dad. I'll pay for the children's needs—rent, school, food, clothes, and health insurance (including Kate's).

But I don't want to have the legal obligation of paying for everything. No way. So Kate ends up signing a paper that says I'm only obliged to pay the kids minimum wage child support. As for her, we all agree that she can find a job and needs no alimony.

She knows she has the kids to bargain with if anything goes wrong. And I'll keep my word, even if only out of fear. I agree to pick up the kids on Fridays every other weekend and return them on Sundays. And so we happily part after my lawyer tells us our separation will probably be legal by the end of the year.

In the evening, I'm at my new home. Things are pretty quiet during the week. There's no one here except for the caretaker, his wife and kid and myself. They live in a house a few yards from where I'm staying.

My new home's pretty shabby, but will do for now. At night, I have a hard time falling asleep because of the mice crawling all over the place. I solve the issue by getting very high and banging on the walls until they are quiet.

Soon Tammy takes pity on my situation and invites me to come live with her in the farmhouse. She lets me stay in a small room just outside the house. I'm happy as can be. Tammy's cool. She gets high and drinks. And we get along well. We have a great time in the evenings after I get back from work. We chat quite a bit and I also play my guitar.

We both look forward to weekends. That's when everyone comes up from Rio to party. The therapeutic groups are mostly women and that's great. We spend our evenings at Chuck's bar, now named *Cine Theatro*, drinking and eating pizza.

I regain some self-confidence as my life becomes somewhat more stable. I'm doing well at work and see the kids often. Most of my money is spent on them and on Kate, but at least she leaves me alone. I'm starting to feel weird, though. The shyness and introversion have returned. Maybe I'm smoking too much weed.

June 1995

I help Kate rent another apartment. It's nice, about the same size as her previous place. We've also started seeing each other again. I go to the apartment and wait for the kids to sleep and we drink and have sex all night.

I soon start feeling very, very naughty again and want to do every woman in town. You see, my horniness is one thing that completely eclipses the shyness and introversion I was telling you about. I see a sexy girl and feel this intense heat, which seems to spring from my genitals and moves on up to my belly and then to my heart. I'm then totally taken by this fire and feel compelled to discharge it, even if only through masturbation.

Let me tell you, this happens a lot. My mind's filled with fantasies involving every interesting woman I know and I anxiously wait for an opportunity to turn them into real sexual episodes.

And one of these opportunities comes up a couple of days before I'm supposed to return the keys to Kate's old apartment.

Kate tells me that one of her friends, the one who sells gym clothes and who supplied the outfits for my quasi threesome, has boasted to her that she's had sex with me. I tell her this is bullshit, but I reckon it's a sure sign the woman wants me to bonk her.

I call her up and ask her to meet me at the empty apartment because I'm supposedly interested in some gym clothes. We both know I'm full of shit, but who cares. I'm really horny and proud of myself because I had the courage to call her.

I go to the apartment and wait for her, but she never shows up. I called her bluff but she backed down. What can I do. After a while I take my pants off, masturbate for about an hour and go home. I'm such a crazy bastard.

Old-Fashioned Fun

My relationship with women has become one emotional roller coaster. And I can't see that it's a complete reflection of my relationship with my mother. Always some kind of power struggle. Although I have little contact with her, the pattern remains fully active with other females. Amazing.

Take Myrna, my boss, for example. Our relationship has been deteriorating for no apparent reason. What have I done to this woman. She wants to control me at all costs. She puts me down whenever she can. She tries to correct my work all the time. She finds ways to punish me.

One day, one of my ESL students is making trouble in class. I resort to one of my effective teenage control tactics and ridicule him in front of his friends. I make him write *I'll behave in class* one hundred times on his notebook. The other students are cracking up. Silly, yes. Old-fashioned, yes. I'm trying to make a point here.

After he's done, he hands me the sentences. I rip up the pages and throw them away. He can't believe I just did that. I tell him this is how it feels not to value someone's work. I tell him this is what he's doing to me in class. Then I tell my students I like them and understand they want to have a good time, but I have a job to do and will do it no matter what. Everyone seems to understand my message and things seem to have turned out fine.

Later, Myrna calls me into her office. She has heard about my actions and harshly questions my methods. She asks me if I've gone crazy. She tells me the nuns in her school used to do that kind of thing when she was a child in the old days. I try to make her understand my point. I wanted to teach the children an unforgettable lesson by making use of exaggeration and ridicule. It was a nice prank and no one was harmed. And it's not like I made the kid kneel on corn or something.

Of course she doesn't understand me. Of course she doesn't want to understand me. I see all she really wants is to give me a hard time. She makes me apologize and promise her I won't do that again. What a dumb ass. Just like my mother…

In the romantic arena, my life is still haunted by Cassandra, the chick who recently gave me the boot. Although I haven't seen her in a while, I still have feelings for her. I need to free myself from this prison. The entire thing has become a nuisance.

Luckily, I meet a woman during one of Chuck's workshops. Her name is Ellen. Although we don't have sex, we make out and cuddle all weekend long. Perhaps I've found a new girlfriend.

After the workshop, Ellen and I plan to be in touch and get together again in the near future. Cassie is gone from my head. In a flash.

The days go by and I don't hear from Ellen. I try to get in touch with her but she doesn't answer my calls. Apparently what we had was a lie. She's rejecting and ignoring me. Anger builds up and very quickly turns into rage. How dare she play around with me. How dare she disrespect me this way. I feel like speaking my mind and write her a very nasty letter. Damn. This nasty letter business is becoming a habit.

I soon get news from Ellen. The woman was surprised to have received such an emotional letter. She thinks I'm exaggerating because we barely know each other. Whoops. I suddenly have a moment of clarity and realize she's right. I feel embarrassed. I feel stupid. Once again, I see my patterns have completely taken over. When will I learn to let my emotions settle before I take action. Oh, well. There goes Ellen. She's an asshole anyway for not keeping in touch. At least I was able to vent out some bad feelings.

Backdoor Man

As for my sexual needs, I have Kate to quench my thirst. I'm over at the apartment to see the kids and have it off with her. Only my timing's not too good. There's someone else here. To my surprise, she's apparently seeing another guy and I meet the dork face to face. The good thing is that I'm not jealous at all. There's no way I'm going back to Kate. I only want her for sex and she knows it. I know she'd rather have me than her boyfriend, so I pretend to leave and wait at the bus stop down the road until the fella takes off. After a while, I see him walking down the street. As soon as he turns the corner, I head back to the apartment and bang his girlfriend for hours.

Reflection

This whole situation makes me feel like I have a double personality thing going on. Part of me is naughty, dirty, detached, and extremely sexual. The other part is gentle, submissive, vengeful, and hopelessly romantic. Which part plays out depends on the woman I'm with.

I'm confused. I really don't know what I want. My mind's in turmoil and I'm attracting all kinds of trouble. My chemistry classes at the private school are filled with sexy teenaged girls, and they all want a piece of the mature teacher. Shit.

This one student, Lucy, is very attracted to me. I'm attracted to her as well, but won't dare touch her mainly because this is my work and after all she's only sixteen years old. But I must admit it's very hard to resist.

One day, Lucy stays behind after chemistry lab. She says she wants to help me clean up. Hmm. Naughty Lucy's up to no good. She's wearing tight jeans shorts. Why do they even allow these things at school. She leans over to clean a test tube and I can see her perfect ass. I desperately want to lock the door and do her on the lab bench. I can feel the energy rising between us, but I manage to gently push her out of the lab before I lose control.

To make things worse, there is also another student, Felicia. She's very attracted to me and is always inviting me to go over to her house. For the sake of friendship, eventually I agree.

I get to her place and of course she's alone. We talk about the Tarot and crystals. Felicia is very mature for her age. And she's also hitting on me.

At some point, she tries to sit on my lap. My first impulse is to rip off her clothes right here and now and teach her a very dirty lesson, but some higher authority prevents me from doing so. I gracefully change the subject and slip away from her sharp little claws. Damn, this teaching job can be hard sometimes.

At my ESL job, things are no different. There's this one girl who's always around after I finish my evening classes. I wonder why. She's cute, but she's also kind of young.

One evening, I'm the last employee to leave. I go into the teachers' room to drop off my stuff and, lo and behold, the girl's here, waiting for me. She has somehow managed to sneak in and is cornering me. Her body gets very close to mine. I can feel her warmth. I can feel her desire. She's all smiles. And libido. I think this time I won't be able to resist. I want to take her to the bathroom in the back and do unnamed things to her. But the higher power once again intervenes and I send her away. She insists, but finally leaves. I'm shaking all over. I get to my car, light up a big joint, and suffer from intense priapism, which means a chronic hard-on, until I get home and masturbate for hours.

Crisis of Conscience

Lord, what should I do. On the one hand, the angel in my head is desperately trying to save me from big trouble. I don't want to have anything to do with minors. And there's no way in heaven I'm mixing business with pleasure. I remember well the one and only time that happened. It fucked up my entire life. But on the other hand, the devil in my lower head is screaming for a good time. I'm between a rock and a hard place. I mean, literally.

Fortunately, my angel's getting its way. By force. The fear of future traumas has prevented me from acting out these forbidden situations and has kept them in my mind as fantasies.

Unfortunately, though, these unlived experiences have filled me with regret. I'm constantly thinking of the good times I could have had and didn't. What a load of crap. Another goddamned emotional seesaw.

Reflection

While I fight and fight and fight these sexual feelings, more and more and more situations appear before me. I really need to get my mind straight. I really need to find some women I can relate to without feeling fearful or guilty.

Cool. No sooner did I wish for available women than they started pouring in. Maybe they had always been around. Maybe I hadn't seen them before. Or didn't want to. I don't know. The fact is that one day I notice this very attractive girl who lives near the farmhouse. Her name's Adele and she's completely infatuated with me. How could I not have seen her before. Well, who cares. I certainly see her now. And what do you know, I overcome my stupid fear, this weird inner laziness, and ask her out.

I pick Adele up from work one evening and take her home. Before I drop her off, we make out for a long time in the car. We barely speak to each other. No need.

But I don't feel she's girlfriend material. You know how it is. She's too attracted to me and will do whatever I ask her to. So there's no struggle, no one to win over. My pattern will simply not activate. Still, she's by far the most beautiful woman I've ever dated. She looks like an exotic Indian princess. So it's beyond my powers to really reject her and we plan to meet again in the future.

The Cavalry Is Coming

My aloofness towards Adele is getting on my nerves. She's a great gal. I could be going out with her. I must do something to free myself from this pattern. So I start looking for a new therapist.

A friend refers me to a woman. Her name's Angela. I call her up and set an appointment. We have our first session. I like her very much. I think I can start seeing Angela once or twice a week.

September 13, 1995

In the evening, I'm hanging out at *Cine Theatro* as usual when a couple comes in. To my utmost surprise, I see it is Joanna, my old crush from the clinic in Rio, and her boyfriend. Oh boy, am I thrilled. Joanna's looking good. Too bad she has a boyfriend now that I'm single. But wait. They seem to have been arguing.

Joanna's extremely pleased to see me. She says her boyfriend owns a house in the area and they're here for the weekend. She also says he's an asshole and she's happy that I'm around.

She dumps him and sits at my table. We talk for a long time. The vibes are very sexual. We both want to go somewhere and have intercourse, but it would obviously not be appropriate. She secretly writes down her phone number and urges me to call her. And I will. That is, if I manage to overcome this darned shyness.

It takes a couple of weeks for me to finally gather enough courage to call Joanna but I simply can't get hold of her. She might have given me the wrong number or I'm just too afraid to speak with her. Maybe it's too late. I kick myself in the head for not having called her before and give up. Fuck. One more regret for my long list. And one more kick in the head.

Tamara and I are no longer alone. My aunt, Tammy's mother, has moved in with us. Tammy's twenty year-old daughter, Ashlee, has also been spending longer periods at the house. We suspect that she'll be moving in sometime soon, especially because she has started to date a local guy, Larry. I get along very well with sweet cousin Ashlee and love her dearly. (I suppose I should call her my first cousin, once removed, but that's too technical. So from now on Ashlee's officially my *sweet cousin.*)

So my saga continues, and this time, fate has a cute joke in store for me. It so happens that my car has broken down from driving on the rough country roads and I'm forced to take the bus for a while. However, since I live in the boondocks, the bus only takes me as far as *Cine Theatro*. I'd have to walk the remaining two miles home. But I'm lucky to have such a caring sweet cousin. Ashlee has offered to pick me up at the bus stop whenever she's around.

The second time I take the bus, I notice a beautiful woman, who happens to get off at the same stop. I'm desperate to know who she is. And of course Ashlee, who is a true social butterfly and knows everyone around, tells me her name's Julia. Julia lives just around the corner from *Cine Theatro*. She's cute. She has an awesome body. I want her. Boy, am I glad my car broke down.

The perfect opportunity comes along a week later, when the local neighborhood hosts a beer fest. *Cine Theatro* is open and I've been asked to help at the bar. Well, sort of. I'm free to come and go as I please.

After a few beers, I feel good. I feel confident. I'm ready to rock and roll. I introduce myself to Julia and we chat for a while. Then we make out. And make out. And make out. And make out. Then she tells me she has to get up early for work the following day and needs to get some sleep. Too bad. But we have started a nice thing and I'm in love once again. Just like that. I'm totally psyched. I want to marry the girl.

However, the night's young and I soon forget her when I see Adele, my exotic Indian princess. Wow. This must really be my lucky day. She's completely wasted. She's all over me. Again. But I feel sort of guilty. My pattern thinks I'm already married to Julia and urges me to be faithful. Unbelievable. Fortunately, I'm very drunk and have no trouble taking Adele to the back of the bar. We make out for a while. And then she's gone. No problem. I'll surely meet up with her later and we'll have dirty relations under the counter or something.

As the party wears on, I start feeling lonely. Julia's gone. And Adele's nowhere to be found. I get depressed and finally go home, feeling like shit.

The following day, I look all over for Julia but can't find her. I start thinking she's trying to avoid me. Of course. I'm moving too fast. Pretty soon I'll be writing this woman a nasty letter, just as I did with Ellen a while ago. My pattern's repeating itself and I can't help but freak out on the situation, albeit this time I'm able to clearly see what I'm doing while doing it.

I finally find her, give her hell, and she gently tells me to fuck off. But this time I manage to stand up for myself. So I just say to myself, screw her. And it works. I decide I'm no longer going to want to marry every woman I fall in love with. And it works. I decide I'm going to stick to loose affairs for a while. And it works. I decide I want to have a good time, relax and not have any serious commitments. And it works. Somehow this pattern is releasing its grip on me. I must be doing something right.

One week later, I test my newly acquired freedom. I meet a woman during a workshop. She's okay. She likes me. We make out and talk. We have sex in my car. Then she leaves and I really don't care. I don't even know her name. I don't want to call her or see her again. I just wanted a good time. This is surely news to me.

Alas, more problems rear their ugly heads. A couple of students I'm tutoring tell me the private school biology teacher has been bad-mouthing me. What the heck, I barely know the bitch. She's suspicious because most of my students do well in class. She says I must be manipulating grades or something. I get very irritated. What have I done to this woman. I'll most certainly clear things up at our upcoming teachers' meeting.

During the meeting, I quickly see what the fuss is all about. Teachers here pride themselves that their students get bad grades. It makes them feel smart and important. Ooh. My class is hard. Ooh. I'm on a power trip.

I think they're all full of shit. I try to make my classes fun and easy so that my students learn and get good grades. I also test them a lot so that they're able to make up grades they have lost. But the teachers don't understand what I'm doing.

It's a good thing I get along with the school coordinator. She seems to understand what I'm all about. After the meeting, I talk to her and she tells me not to worry.

The Last Dance

One Saturday, Kate and I have sex at her apartment. My condom breaks while we're engaged in some advanced acrobatics. No big deal. We wash up and I don't think much of it.

A few weeks later, she calls me and tells me she's pregnant. I completely freak out. This is my worst nightmare come true. The last thing I want is to have another child with fucking Kate. I ask her if she's sure. I want to see the positive results. She won't let me. Strange. She wants money for an abortion. Hmm. Fishy. I tell her she's full of shit. She says I don't really need to give her the cash. She'll just have the baby. Whoa. I immediately fork over the money. I guess she wins.

Another week goes by. I'm worried sick. Then Kate calls me and tells me she's had the damned abortion. Whew. I make sure I visit her and see how she's doing. I get to the apartment and see she's just fine. In fact, she's doing so well I can't even see her scar. I'm such a dumb ass. Just as I thought, she's been playing me all along. But this time, I don't want to argue. I feel I've really had it with this woman. I decide it's about time I cut all sexual ties with Kate. She's simply not worth the trouble. I kiss her goodbye and whistle on out of the house.

I haven't heard from my mother in a long time. Oddly enough, a few days after the abortion episode, she calls me up. And guess what. She wants money. She tells me life is hard. She tells me she has no money to pay her bills. She tells me she has no money to eat. Poor Mom. I wish she didn't have to beg for money. I wish she didn't have to lower herself like that. I can feel the defeat, the shame, and humiliation in her voice. I feel very guilty. I feel very bad for her and lend her some cash.

Later on that same day, I'm speaking to one of my sisters on the phone and casually mention my mother and her dreadful situation. To my surprise, she tells me Mom wanted the money so that she could go fix her hair. I'm appalled. Whatever happened to her poverty talk. Once again, I've been conned. Man, that was a low blow. My own mother emotionally blackmails me for cash.

Just as I'm going into a very heavy downward spiral, I'm able to see how this pattern is projected onto my relationship with Kate. Wow. Awareness slaps me in the face. This is therapy material for sure.

I bring the entire thing up during my session with Angela. Forget about Kate. I want to work on the source of it all, which is my mother. I whine and whine and whine. Angela makes me see that, in order for her pattern to survive, my mother has become a vampire. By persuading people she's a big victim, she sucks on their energy to avoid facing her own feelings of inadequacy. No wonder I feel depressed and guilty when I'm around her.

Then I see that my mom really can't help but act out her own pattern. However, her poverty and dependency thing is actually none of my business and she must get rid of it by herself. She's a great artist and must learn how to sell herself and make money. I can see that by lending her money I'm doing her more harm than good. So I decide the best thing to do is to stop "helping" her.

I'm in awe. I feel I've come to a major turning point in my life. The recent troubles with my mother and Kate and the way I dealt with them have made me realize I've had it with this vampire bullshit. Sorry, they'll have to find someone else to suck the living crap out of. And now that I'm no longer willing to feed this pattern, all I have to do is clean up the mess.

I call up my mother and tell her she can expect no more help from me. She then attempts her victim thing. I try to make her understand what she's doing, but she won't listen to me. I can also see I'm not strong enough to resist her pleas. You know, the little boy in me is still very much influenced by his mommy. Well, once our conversation is over and I'm feeling like shit, I see that the only thing I can do to preserve my sanity is to stay away from her until she changes her ways.

One down, one to go. Now I have to deal with Kate. The situation here's a bit more delicate because it involves the children. However, I feel strong and I have Angela's support.

I tell Angela I'm sick of working like a dog and not having enough money for myself. She tells me I'm overwhelmed because all my money goes to Kate and the kids. I agree that I must go on paying for my kids' needs but as for Kate, she must find her own means of support. Although I'm afraid she might retaliate on the children when I break her the news, this is a risk I'll have to take if I'm ever going to be free from this attachment. Boy, am I glad I made her sign that financial waiver.

So Kate and I go out to lunch and I tell her I can't afford to give her money anymore. I tell her I'll still pay for the kids' school and meals and clothes and health insurance. But her easy days are over. She'd better get a job. I'm surprised she really doesn't have much to say. She doesn't complain at all. And I feel free.

Before we part, Kate has another issue she wants to discuss. Her asshole parents have been threatening to take the children away from her. They say we don't take proper care of the kids. I'm extremely annoyed. Kate might be lazy and careless sometimes, but she's doing her best and I'm around to ensure the kids are all right. So I decide to write the fuckers a very nasty letter. Yep, me and my nasty letters.

Sometime later, Kate calls to let me know her parents have received my letter. My words were very effective. The fuckheads have backed off. They have apologized and will probably leave us alone. Nevertheless, I instruct the school not to let anyone pick the children up except for Kate and me.

A few more days go by and my father unexpectedly comes to town. He gives me a call and says he tried to see the kids at school, but they wouldn't let him. I apologize and tell him what has been going on. I feel bad because the children don't get to see Grandpa very often, but better safe than sorry.

November 20, 1995

I have decided to add some fun to my chemistry class at the private school. I've written little jokes for each one of my students and am reading them aloud. It's Lucy's turn. I tell her the gods in Olympus have invited her to a party ('cause she's such a goddess). Everyone laughs. Then she says she would be happy to go if only I give her my address. Wow. My students are cracking up, mainly because I'm blushing. Fuck. This is meant to be a joke. I pretend not to hear her and quickly move on to the next student.

Quasi Orgasm, Part Two

I'm spending Christmas at cousin Tammy's. Ashlee's also here and has brought two slutty friends along. One of them is voluptuous and I want to do her. I follow her around the house. I give her naughty looks.

One day, she's all alone in the kitchen washing dishes after lunch when I walk in. My heart's pounding like mad. I want to say something naughty to her. I'm completely out of control. I have an incredible hard-on. I want to have this girl right here.

Not really knowing what to do, I pretend to grab something on the far side of the sink and slip behind her. Just as with Daisy years ago in the movie theater, my hard penis finds her buttocks and for a moment, slides in between her ass cheeks. I almost have an orgasm. I excuse myself and leave.

Finger-lickin' good. Another one of those unforgettable moments. I'll most probably be making use of this as a masturbation fantasy for years to come.

Sweet cousin Ashlee's pregnant. Cool. The entire family's giving her shit. What a bunch of assholes. They think she's too young and immature to have a child. They think Larry's not right for her. But she couldn't care less about the entire situation. Cool. I really like Ashlee.

A Vision

Although I now have enough money to rent a place in town, I still feel I'm not ready to leave my comfortable womb in the country. However, my movement towards civilization has already started. I've left the farmhouse and now rent a small cottage nearby.

I'm happily settled into my new home. I smoke a nice big joint to celebrate. I get high, sit back and close my eyes. Suddenly I have a vision. I see myself inside an egg. Although it's nice and cozy inside, I want out. I poke a hole in the shell and take a peek at the outside world. I can see a shiny presence. It's my new me. I'm strong and glowing. I'm surrounded by wonderful people and things. I feel great. I'm independent and complete. What a sight.

I breathe deeply and open my eyes. I leave the house and look around. All I can see are mountains. This is indeed my womb. I feel warm. I feel protected. I know I must soon leave this place. The night sky is clear. I remember there's supposed to be a lunar eclipse tonight. I lie down on a big rock in front of my house and gaze at the beautiful spectacle until I fall asleep.

Tammy has a new boyfriend. The guy's name is Tom. He's okay. Tom's an addict. His thing was booze. But he's been sober for a while. He's over for the weekend and has brought a lady friend and her young son. She's married to one of Tom's friends, a cocaine addict. The woman's life is hell. Her husband doesn't care about her. Well, I do.

In the evening, after everyone goes to sleep, she comes to my house. We have sex. I can tell this woman's needy. I mean, very needy. I can tell she hasn't gotten any in a long, long time. She's incredibly horny. She's insatiable. She grabs me and bites me and scratches me. Damn.

The next morning, Tamara's pissed at me. She says the woman's little boy woke up in the middle of the night and wanted his mommy, who was nowhere to be found. Tammy says I'm slutty, just like her brother Chuck, who fools around with every woman he meets. I smile and take it as a compliment.

A few more weeks go by before I get some more action. This time there's a huge party involving both Chuck's and Beatrice's resorts. There are loads of people here, including many locals. I meet up with bus stop lady Julia. I know she gently told me to fuck off. But, hey. Let bygones be bygones. She's looking good. Her bulgy breasts are almost bursting out of her tight blouse. Her jeans hug her perfect round ass like a second skin. She's coming onto me. I'm relaxed. No attachments or obligations.

I take her to an empty cottage and we get it on big time. After a while, we go back to the party. Julia's gone. I see my gorgeous Indian princess Adele. She's looking good. She looks very, very tempting in her tight T-shirt and denim miniskirt. She's coming onto me. I'm relaxed. No attachments or obligations. I take her to the same empty cottage and we get it on big time.

When the party is over, I'm exhausted, but feel great. Two women in one night. Almost as good as a threesome. I'm finally making up for all the lost opportunities in the past. I'm becoming a regular Don Juan. And I carry around a bunch of condoms in my pocket. You never know.

I'm through with my country life. It's no longer financially viable and I'm ready to rent an apartment in town. And the way I see it, my social life won't suffer because I plan to spend the weekends with my cousins anyway, at least for now.

I find a two-bedroom apartment in a quiet neighborhood in town. Nice. I'm close to everything. I'm closer to the children. I can get to work easily. I don't have to carry tons of grocery bags for long distances. I can fix my car. I welcome myself to civilization by smoking a nice doobie and relaxing in my new place.

The new apartment's great, except for a few wacky neighbors. There's an old lady who lives downstairs and knows everything about everyone in the building. Typical.

There's also a crazy woman who lives right next door. She thinks she's a beauty diva. But she's gross. She's very loud and throws her garbage bags out the window instead of placing them on the curb. Ah, city life.

Tough Love

It's September 8, 1996, and I get a call from my father. He tells me he has a spare car and has decided to give it to me. He knows I already have a car, but I'm not surprised. It's my good old dad expressing his love. My old car's fixed, so now I'll have two cars. What the fuck for, I don't know, but I take the bus to Rio to pick my gift up anyway.

When I get to his place, he hands me the keys and starts giving me shit about how I should take good care of the car and yak, yak, yak. Hold on, buster. I tell him to leave me alone. I'm too old to be hearing this kind of crap.

I tell him I'll accept the car under one condition: The documents must be in my name. I know better than to allow him to blackmail me later and take the car away or something. He agrees and I drive back home in my new station wagon.

I'm indeed in high demand. The mother of one of my private students is having a hard time dealing with her two daughters and needs a psychologist. She has heard of me and wants me to help. Man. I haven't had a patient in a while, but this could be fun. A good friend lends me her office and I agree to see the woman.

A week later, I'm in my friend's office waiting for my patient when I hear a knock at the door. My, oh my. I'm startled to see a mighty good-looking momma. Here I go again. But I've been through this far too many times. I immediately suppress my thoughts and focus on my patient's needs. I soon realize what her visit's all about. Her husband's rejecting her. She probably hasn't had sex in a while, and she's desperate. We barely talk about the girls, and I can see she wants me. I can see she's here to have sex and pay for it. Fuck that. I'm no gigolo.

Although I really do want to get laid right here in the office, I behave myself and do my best to help the woman. I make her see what she's trying to do. She eventually notices her advances and is embarrassed. At the end of our session, she thanks me for everything and takes off. I have a feeling she isn't ever coming back. Oh, well. At least my conscience is clear.

At the private school, things are getting increasingly out of hand. I'm really fed up with the damned biology teacher, who keeps on projecting her failures onto me. She goes so far as to tell people that if I'm not manipulating grades, she'll eat her diploma. Of course, my students spill the beans to me. What an asshole that teacher is. She'd better get a very big glass of water to help her swallow all that paper.

I'm tutoring math to a few students. I see their teacher has made a mistake and I correct it. No big deal. The following day, my students tell me the fucking lady has tried to make me look bad by twisting things and telling her entire class that I'm the one making the stupid mistake.

So, as the old proverb goes, the last straw breaks the camel's back. To hell with the damned job. To hell with all these fuckers. I really don't need this shit. I tell my coordinator I've had it with this harassment and won't be returning next semester. She's kind of sad, but seems to understand my point of view. And after all, there's really nothing she can do about my situation. No problem. I've finally realized the regular school system's not for me.

Fatal Attraction

Sharon, one of my co-workers at the ESL school, has asked me to help her niece, Robyn. Robyn is as skinny as can be. She's very depressed due to problems in her relationship. Her husband has left her and she's desperate. She has a young son but has been unable to take care of him. Robyn has no money, so I agree to see the woman for free at Sharon's apartment, which is in the school building itself.

My first session with Robyn goes pretty well. She basically needs some guidance. She tells me her story. I then give her some initial advice and am happy to see that she's feeling better already. At the end of our session, I teach her a couple of techniques to keep her spirits up until we meet again and off she goes.

Everything's just fine and dandy until I notice she's projecting her husband onto me. Initially I think nothing of it. It's part of the therapeutic process. I'll keep her projection under control and use it to resolve her patterns within the therapeutic context.

But Robyn does not seem to understand this and thinks she's in love with me. She thinks I'm her savior. She's coming on to me during our sessions. I try to make her see that I'm only her psychologist, not her lover. No use. She doesn't listen. The situation gets worse. Then one day, I end up telling her that if things go on like this I'll have to stop treating her. But still she doesn't listen.

Poor woman. She's so lost she can't help but to be infatuated with me. I decide the best thing to do is to stop seeing her. At our last session, I try once again to explain what's going on. No use. I give up. I advise her to keep working on the techniques I taught her and vamoose on out of her life.

But things wouldn't be that easy. A few weeks go by and I notice Robyn's around every time I leave work. She's been stalking me and I'm getting ticked off. I talk to her aunt Sharon and tell her what's going on. I ask her to talk some sense into her niece. This is beyond therapy now. But nothing seems to work. I figure the only way to get rid of the bitch is to tell her off directly every time I see her, and that's what I start doing. It does take almost a month, but she eventually gives up.

Opportunity's still knocking, whether I want it or not. It seems that everywhere I go, I meet a woman and get into some kind of trouble. Sometimes it's good trouble, sometimes it's bad news.

One weekend sweet cousin Ashlee and I are at her boyfriend Larry's house. There are many people around and we're getting high. I'm sitting on a corner and can't utter a sound. I'm feeling very shy again. I'm thinking these people have the wrong idea of who I am. By now I'm pretty sure all the marijuana I smoke is to blame for my shyness, but I'm hopelessly addicted.

Anyway, Larry lives here with his divorced mom and his two brothers. His older brother's girl, Sasha, also lives in the house. She's mighty juicy and likes to show off her great bod. She enjoys parading around the living room in her hot and sexy gym shorts, making us guys drool. Hmm, this spells trouble.

In the evening, we all go to *Cine Theatro*, which is just a couple of blocks away from Larry's house. I'm talking to Ashlee and mention Sasha. I tell her how I'd give an arm and a leg to roll in the hay with the lusty wench. Ashlee tells me Sasha wants me, too. Goddamn. I ask her to set up a secret date this same night. She giggles and takes off. After a little while she returns and tells me Sasha will be waiting for me outside the bar at eleven o'clock. I can hardly believe it.

At eleven I drive by and sure enough Sasha's standing there. I pick her up and we drive to my apartment in town. I feel pretty shy, but I know I'll show her otherwise very soon.

As soon as we get to my apartment, I grab her and pull her towards me. I give her a long, passionate kiss. She melts in my arms. Hmm. This is going to be good. I then proceed to pull down her dress and expose her wonderful knockers. I kiss them for a while and then move further down. She stops me. She says she doesn't feel right about cheating on her boyfriend. Yeah, right. She's just playing hard to get. I dish out the old you-only-live-once routine, and indeed, it doesn't take much to convince her to get naked. Nice. I take Sasha to my bedroom and get to know her really well. In the biblical sense.

When it's all over, Sasha tells me she's pleasantly surprised to see a very seductive and mature man has replaced that shy little boy. Oh, well. I just smile and smooch her some more.

I take her back home. When we get there, I see that her boyfriend's sleeping in the van right in front of his house. Shit. What if he wakes up. I drop her off and luckily he doesn't even move. The fucker is passed out from all the booze he'd been drinking. Now that's what I call good trouble.

Suddenly, I realize it's been a couple of years since my last steady relationship. I've used women and women have used me. I've had quite a bit of sex. This affair business is great, but I'm starting to feel lonely. I think I'm ready for a new girlfriend. I long for love. I long for companionship. I long for a woman who I can share my experiences with. Yes, my pattern's about to reverse polarities. Let's see what comes out of this.

The Last Temptation

My chemistry class is holding an end-of-year party at a club, and they want me to come. Sure, why not. I get there and it seems like a lot of fun.

The party is by the pool. There's alcohol and food. All my students are here. Including lab helper Lucy. She looks awesome in her teeny-weeny bikini. She's coming onto me. Again. And I'm drinking a bit. Just a bit, because I have a therapy session in the afternoon and I don't want to be too wasted.

After lunch, I tell them I have to go. Lucy urges me to return after my session. Hey, maybe I will. I don't know how much longer I'll be able to reject this girl. I'm leaving this school anyway, so who knows.

After my session, though, I'm sober and decide it's best not to return to the party. Not a good idea. Hot minor. Shit.

EIGHT

Crazy Cara

It's early 1997 and I have the need to do an extreme cleanup. I desperately want to release all the crap I've been internalizing all these years. I feel compelled to take a pen and paper and write out my entire life.

I figure the astrology I've been studying lately might come in handy. I start making notes on planetary aspects, transits, and progressions. I set up an astrological matrix of my puny existence and then relate my findings to events in my life. I end up writing about five hundred pages. Wow. I'm really exposing myself here. And to make my self-exposure official, I mail the entire thing to a friend and ask him to read it. I also make a couple of copies and give one to my therapist Angela. I take the other copy and burn it along with all the old photos and documents I can find.

But that's not enough. Of course not. I need more. You know me. I need something physical. So I take the most strenuous and exhausting active meditation I can find and work on it for twenty days. I jump around, scream, break things and rip all my books apart. I'm finally clean. I have even managed to quit smoking pot and cigarettes.

A few days after I finish my ordeal, I'm leaving the apartment when I encounter a very attractive blonde. We exchange quick glances and I can't help but notice her fantastic curves and luscious long legs as she walks out the building. Now who could that be. I'm most certainly going to find out.

One morning I'm leaving for work when I see the hot blonde at the local bus stop and offer her a ride. She gladly accepts and we get to know each other on the way downtown.

Her name's Cara and her aunt lives in my building. She's an only child who lives with her parents in a nearby neighborhood. I also find out she has a way with children—she works at a local nursery—and is into fashion. Cool. Nice. The woman has a very captivating smile. Gorgeous green eyes. I can't take my eyes off her. And the more she talks, the hornier I get.

Before I drop Cara off, she tells me Auntie's throwing a party on Saturday and I'm invited. Great. This woman excites me and I can't wait to see her again.

It takes me a while to overcome my stupid shyness, but eventually I manage to show up at Cara's party. She seems thrilled to see me, but constantly forgets my name—a minor inconvenience when I consider the possibility of having sex with her.

We chat for a while and then head on up to the building terrace to check out the night sky. At some point, we stop talking and start kissing and I have a new girlfriend. As quick as a wink.

I'm on cloud nine. Again. I fall for the same old story and think Cara's the girl of my dreams. Again. I want to marry her. I want to have kids with her. Shit. I haven't felt those uncontrollable urges in a while.

But I do notice things are a bit different this time around. In the midst of my bewilderment, I can somehow perceive Cara as a real person. And I don't like many of the things I see.

I immediately notice that her values are completely different from mine. She's also ten years younger than me. Although I'm totally involved (already) and will most certainly dive into this relationship headfirst, I can see from the start that it's not going to work out. I think to myself I must be very stupid to embark on another crazy ride.

But then again, maybe this is just a dumb voice in my head trying to prevent me from having endless intercourse with this babe. There I go again. Thinking with the wrong head.

After one or two dates, Cara wants me to meet her parents, a very humble couple with local country customs. Her mom's an extreme neuropathic character who works from home baking and selling sweets and pastries. I can tell by her overweight figure that she eats half of her production. Her father sleeps all day and drinks all night.

Even though she's twenty-two, Cara's not allowed to come to my house alone. You know, local country customs. Respectable young ladies cannot engage in such dubious activities, not unless they're married anyway. So we have to sneak into the apartment whenever we want to be alone because nosey Auntie's constantly spying on us. As a thirty-one-year-old man who has lived alone for over ten years, I find this ridiculous, but play along because sex is my neurotic priority.

May 1, 1997

Tonight, I pick Cara up at home and we go out for dinner. Then we go to my apartment and manage to sneak in without her aunt seeing us. As much as I try, Cara won't sleep with me. She's very naïve. I talk to her about it and she tells me she has only had sex once before with her former boyfriend, who obviously didn't do the job right. She's still a virgin.

May 15, 1997

I've spent the past two weeks employing my persuasion skills on Cara and today we finally do it. It's a bit awkward. She really was a virgin. She bleeds all over the place. She has no experience whatsoever. She has a lot to learn. She's full of taboos.

As for me, I feel somewhat fulfilled, because I know I have the power from the very beginning. I'll teach her to enjoy sex and she'll be under my spell in no time.

May 25, 1997

Cara is the talk of the family. Although we've been trying very hard to hide our pornographic situation as best we can, everyone knows what's going on. Her relatives find it absurd that a decent girl is going alone to a man's house at an ungodly hour. They're asking themselves how it is possible for a single girl to have sex and not be a slut.

May 27, 1997
I want to take Cara to my apartment and bonk her brains out but am forced to stay at her house and watch TV with her watchdog mother. After a while, we manage to go downstairs to make out a little, but she soon has to go back home. I'm pissed. The woman doesn't stand up for herself. I try to make her react in some way, but no dice. Things are quickly getting weird between us.

May 31, 1997
Today Cara kindly lets me know she's been talking to her mom about our relationship. She's happy to inform me they have found a way out of our indecent situation. They have decided we must get married. I'm shocked. My head is spinning. Shit. The pressure is all on me. I tell her I need a little time to think and go home.

Reflection

It's the same old song and dance, my friend. I meet a woman and two months later we get married. I have no time to really get to know her and when I do it's too late.

You might ask why I might want to persist on this obviously harmful path. The thing is, I see it and I don't see it. I can see that Cara is not right for me. I can see we are completely out of sync. I can see our relationship is never going to work out. But I'm extremely needy. I'm possessive. I'm afraid of being alone. It's a sad thing, but my sick emotions still have the last say when it comes to relationships and sex. You know what that means…

June 4, 1997
I reluctantly agree to have Cara move in. Hey, at least this time, I'm adamant on not signing any legal papers. So in the afternoon, while still in shock, I help her bring all her stuff over to my house.

June 9, 1997
I'm once again a married man. Just as I expected, Cara and I don't get along at all. We don't understand each other. Conversations

come and go and it's like we're speaking different languages. But that old conviction of mine insists I must live through the experience. I say to myself *I've got to be strong and face the test life is providing me.* I'm such a masochist.

June 15, 1997

I'm on vacation and have made plans to go on a honeymoon trip with Cara. Nothing fancy. We travel to a nearby historic town and stay at a nice hotel. Cara spends the day shopping for clothes. I'm lonely. I'm bored. I also start feeling very anxious. It's as if something is terribly wrong. I cannot identify the problem, but this makes me start smoking cigarettes once again, which does not seem to bother Cara. Well, her father smokes.

June 20, 1997

Back from our short honeymoon, we have our first argument. No big deal. Couples argue. It happens. But to my immense surprise, Cara suddenly tells me she's leaving. Say what. I can't believe this is happening. We have only been living together for a couple of weeks and the crazy-ass woman wants out. Just like that.

While the fucking drama queen's packing her things, I try to explain to her the commitment involved in a serious relationship. I tell her that leaving is pretty much the last thing we do before the entire marriage falls apart.

I feel I'm talking to a little kid—a little kid with a very dirty mouth. She starts cussing. She doesn't seem to understand the meaning of commitment. She's a little girl completely involved in her victim drama. She tells me I'm a bad person. She calls me names. She tells me I'm ruining her life. The chick's out of her mind. No use trying to convince her. Cara grabs her stuff and takes off to her mom's.

I'm completely desolated, to say the least. But fortunately I can see things clearly. I'm not legally bound to her. And what's more, there are no children involved. So I can just forget about Cara and look for a caring, understanding, loving, and respectful woman. Yeah, sure. I can, but I don't. My crystal clear clarity goes just as quick as it came.

As I sit around the house thinking, I get more and more and more entrenched in my patterns. I've been rejected. Cara doesn't like me. I no longer have power over her. How could she do this to me. And what about sex. I simply can't stand the thought of Cara doing it with another guy. I'm sure this has been a terrible misunderstanding. I'm sure I can make her see my point of view. After all, we love each other.

And so yours fucking truly decides he'll head to Cara's house and ask her to come back. How dumb is that.

When I get to her apartment, Cara's hiding behind her fat-ass mom. I'm forced to explain the entire situation to them. Again. Mom helps me convince Cara she has overreacted and she agrees to come back to my place. I'm relieved and determined to make things work between us. Little do I know this is only a sample of what's to come.

June 27, 1997

After over seven years, I've decided to retrace my footsteps and return to the forest for a new adventure. I tell Cara of my intentions and she thinks I'm going crazy, but has no major objections. So she spends the night at her mom's house while I head for the mountains.

June 28, 1997

I'm back from my adventure. Once again it was pretty scary and intense. I feel I've closed the cycle, which began in 1990. Cara welcomes me home. She still thinks I'm crazy, but takes good care of me while I sleep pretty much all day.

July 2, 1997

Cara grabs all her stuff and takes off after another silly argument. Once again, I struggle with myself but end up at her mom's house asking her to come back.

July 14, 1997

Guess what. Cara has left me again. And I'm at her mom's house begging her to come back. This is becoming a routine.

July 29, 1997
Cara and I have just returned from her mother's house. Yes, she had just left me.

September 5, 1997
Unbelievable. I'm off again to Cara's house to pick her up after another argument. When am I going to learn. Unbelievable.

September 16, 1997
I wish I had something new to say. But I don't. Cara has stormed out of my apartment with all her stuff. And I'm on my knees yet once again.

September 25, 1997
No, I'm not kidding. For the seventh time in a couple of months, Cara has taken off. Funny how I promise myself this is the last time I'll forgive her—for the seventh time.

Sex in the Bunker

I decide it's about time Cara and my mother met. What a bright idea. We pick up my son and drive to Mom's house for the weekend. Of course the two women don't get along well at all. Mom despises Cara because of her humble origins. Mom thinks she's such a big shot because she comes from an aristocratic German family. She thinks I deserve better than that. Boy, have I heard all this bull before.

But who cares. We're only spending the night anyway.

My mother sets up our bed in her living room floor. It's late at night and we are lying down, watching TV and making out. We are both very aroused. Foreplay time. A lot is going on under the sheets. Shhh. My son's sleeping right next to us. Cara quietly crawls on top of me and puts me into her. The feeling is intense. I have surely taught her well. She slowly wiggles and wiggles her warm body until we're both exhausted and utterly satisfied. Now you know why I insist on this relationship.

Soapy Delight

Cara and I are taking a long shower. We slide our wet and soapy bodies against each other while the steaming water runs down our naked skin. I lift her by the buttocks and she wraps her legs around my thighs for some reverse piggy-back action. Wet and wild. I've become a regular sexual position encyclopedia. She has multiple orgasms. We have to sit on the bathroom floor after it's all over. My legs and arms are shaking from holding her. What a way to keep fit. Tonight I sleep very, very well.

October 8, 1997

Despite our great sex last night, we have another argument in the afternoon and Cara takes off to her mom's once again. By now I've lost count of the times she has left me. I've also lost count of the times I've begged her to return. I'm getting fed up with the situation. Really fed up. There's only so much even a sick pattern can take, you know.

Even though cigarettes help me control my neediness, I sure wish I had a nice fat joint to smoke. Maybe then I would be able to get rid of Cara for good. I could just bury myself in smoke and pretend this is all a bad dream. While I ponder whether I should buy a pound of weed or go pick up my girlfriend, time goes by unnoticeably, and pretty soon it's too late to take any action. I end up sleeping alone and decide to postpone my decision until tomorrow. For once.

Murderous Intention

It's October 9 and I've realized that I've transferred my marijuana needs to a woman. I hadn't thought that possible, but I'm hopelessly addicted to Cara. So my decision is obvious. I drive over to her mom's after work.

When I get there, I notice both Cara and her mom are scared. They don't let me come up to the apartment and we talk on the street, next to her building. I'm told her father's awake and really annoyed. So what. We talk and argue for a while, and then suddenly I see a man walking out of the building. It's Cara's dad. He's drunk and has a big kitchen knife in his right hand. He's coming in my direction. I think he wants to stab me to death. But I feel completely calm. The situation is far too ridiculous for me to be nervous. Or maybe I'm in shock.

I try to reason with the guy and tell him he's exaggerating. Cara's mom is completely terrorized and urges me to leave. Cara walks down the street with me. There are many people looking. Her mom finally convinces the drunken fuck to back off. I talk to Cara some more and, guess what. I convince her to come home with me. Apparently all that crazy shit was not enough to make me give up the relationship. My neediness is stronger.

December 31, 1997

I'm totally overwhelmed by the mess I have gotten myself into. My relationship with Cara sucks big time.

We take the bus to her mother's. We're going to celebrate the New Year eating homemade pastries like pigs in front of the TV. I've had it with Cara. I can't even stand looking at Cara. I want to be somewhere else. I want to be at my cousin's resort, where they're throwing a New Year's bash with exotic belly dancers and plenty of cool people.

I'm bored to death sitting in the living room. I feel like shit. Cara's father is sleeping off his drunkenness, as usual. I tell Cara I'm not feeling very well and go to her old bedroom to take a nap. Bullshit. It's just an excuse to get away from those fuckers.

While lying in the dark bedroom, I'm thinking of a way to get out of this hellhole. And out of Cara's life. The thought of tying some sheets together and sneaking out the window crosses my mind. I'm really desperate.

After a while, Cara comes in and we start arguing. Her nosey mother soon joins us and starts defending her daughter, as usual. I feel lonely and mistreated. I have to get out of this place. Cara's dishing out her usual crap. She's a victim. I'm a crook. Her mom's constantly warning us that her father will hear us, get up, and wreak havoc.

Then the drama gets worse. The plot thickens. Suddenly, on the spur of the moment, I tell them I can't stand the situation any longer and get up to leave. My girlfriend starts crying and gets in my way. I get by her and rush out the door. She follows me. Her mom's almost having a heart attack.

I'm in the hall. Cara tackles me, trying to prevent me from leaving. I'm appalled. What kind of behavior is this. I manage to get her off my back and head for the stairs. In a truly spectacular move, the stupid bitch runs ahead of me and throws herself down the stairs. This is her big drama opportunity. She truly deserves an Oscar. She stumbles down and falls right in front of me. She's now agonizing. What a load of crap. I walk towards her and just as she thinks I'm going to help her get up, I jump over her sorry ass and run out. She still tries to grab my legs, but I'm too quick.

Once outside, I waste no time. I take a back street and run like there's no tomorrow. I'm afraid her weirdo father will come after me with a knife or a gun. I arrive at the bus stop just in time to take the last bus to my cousin's party. Boy, am I relieved to be here. I tell everyone what has just happened. I guzzle down a few beers and start playing the guitar and singing like never before. Then someone hands me a joint. I think I'll stick to Mary Jane. Sure beats crazy Cara.

January 25, 1998

It's been almost a month since I've last seen Cara. Although I've been getting high pretty much every day, I still feel very lonely and needy.

I come across Cara on the street. My heart's beating faster. I can't think straight at all. I want her badly. Jeez. Apparently this dumb ass hasn't had enough. We start chatting, but Cara's afraid someone will see us. She's not allowed to talk to me.

I'm soon trying to convince her we should get back together. For once, she's the voice of reason. She tells me we're no good together. She says things between us will never work out.

But all I can think about is sex, sex, and more sex. And of course I end up convincing her we should give our relationship one more try. No comment.

January 27, 1998
Cara has moved in with me once again. I now live in a different apartment, away from her stupid family members. Maybe now we will have some peace of mind. Oops. I think I've heard this one before.

February 5, 1998
Uh-oh. This morning I notice a strange liquid coming out of my penis. Weird. There's no way I have an STD. After all, Cara's the only person I've had sex with lately. Unless...

I question her. We argue and she finally confesses that after drinking a few beers one night a couple weeks ago, she slept with some guy. We weren't together then, but to me, that's completely beside the point. I feel intense waves of jealousy running through my system. I'm furious. She could at least have told me. I'd have worn a condom. We argue and argue. I'm outraged. I'm grossed out. This is our final act. No, really. My insane pattern tells me I've been betrayed, and that's more than enough to justify a permanent breakup.

Sensing the gravity of the situation, she throws herself at me with her usual soap opera drama. She tells me she's not worthy of my love. She tells me she deserves to be punished. She begs me to beat her. Oh, man. Not again. This is absurd. I give her hell. I tell her she's crazy. What's up with this beat-me-up crap. I tell her our relationship's over for good.

I make her call her mother, who immediately comes over. I explain to the bitch what has happened, but she still backs her daughter. Yes, she knows Cara's wrong, but she tells me she has to defend her own daughter. Enough. Anything's better than this torture. This time I'm the one telling Cara to pack her things and leave. For good.

NINE

The Destroyer of Demons

There have been big changes around the countryside. Sweet cousin Ashlee is pregnant once again. She's now living with Larry and their daughter in their own home. My aunt has moved to Chuck's resort, where she keeps busy taking care of the place. *Cine Theatro* has closed down.

As for Ashlee's mother Tammy, I think she's going nuts. Her new home is on the same lot as Ashlee's. She no longer has her friends over. Her boyfriend Tom is gone. She just hangs around and drinks all day long. She's constantly talking to her dogs and her cats, and to herself. Country life has made her mad. I'm sad because I like Tammy. She has helped me a lot. I want to help her, but she wants no help. She's too much into her vodka therapy.

Back in the Fast Lane

My awful experience with Cara has made me give up serious relationships for a while. I'm once again on the lookout for carefree sex. I have my eye on this girl who lives next door to Ashlee. I'm completely besotted by her simple charm and beauty. Short dark hair, blue eyes, a real gem. Oh, and let's not forget her awesome bod. An undiscovered top model hanging out in the countryside. She's always standing outside her house whenever I visit my cousin, and I can see her smile at me as my bus comes by. (I no longer trust any of my cars to the rough country roads.)

Of course, Ashlee knows who she is. The woman's name is Adrianna. She is Tammy's new housekeeper. It doesn't take long for me to ask Adrianna out. We meet on the road near her house one day and are soon kissing. Boy, is she appetizing.

From then on, we start playing a fun cat-and-mouse game whenever I'm at my cousin's. No matter where Adrianna is in the house, I'm right there grabbing her all over. She giggles, pushes me away, and tells me to stop being a naughty boy. I stay away for about two seconds and grab her again. We kiss, she pushes me away, and we start all over. Fun, fun, fun.

But this cat eventually catches up with the mouse. One day, Tammy's out shopping and won't be back for a while. Adrianna and I are alone in the house. Let the games begin. I pinch her butt and grab her. She pushes me away. We talk some trash to each other. She's such a prick tease. We kiss. She pushes me away. I come back for more. I'm incredibly horny. Finally, neither of us can stand it any longer.

I throw her against the pillar in the middle of the living room. I pull down her shorts. She starts wiggling her beautiful behind, teasing me some more. Whore. Then I stand behind her and hold her waist tight. Time to rock and roll. Hmm. Dirty stand-up sex. Priceless.

Strangely enough, after we're done, Adrianna starts getting sentimental on me. I push her away. No way, Jose. I don't want to get emotionally involved, especially with this girl. She's a slut. I just want to keep her as my fuck buddy, although I do fantasize taking her away from this place, marrying her, and giving her a good life. In a weird way, I feel we are very much alike. Dang it. History repeating itself. Again. Did I mention she has a daughter.

I've been in therapy with Angela for over two years now and my life has changed quite a bit. It's been about a year since I had one of those U.S. nightmares. After ten years, they're gone for good.

There's still one important issue I have to resolve. Although I haven't supported Kate directly in a while, I feel she has been living off the money I give her for the kids. She still hasn't found a job. Well, she doesn't have to. I pay for their rent, their groceries, their utility bills, as well as for the children's school and medical insurance. I guess she only has to scavenge money for her smokes and booze. The fucker's openly taking advantage of the situation.

And things will tend to become even more worrisome. The children are growing up and will attend regular school, which means more time around Momma and her "good" habits. Well, if caring for the children means dropping them off and picking them up at school and then feeding them, I'm starting to see that maybe I can do a better job at parenting than her. At least I'm a better role model.

I bring this up during therapy one day and tell Angela I'm thinking of taking the kids away from Kate. I don't want to force her into anything, though, because I know she'll retaliate on the children. Well, I don't think I'll have to. I'm pretty sure she will give them up once I tell her I can no longer pay for their expenses.

Angela and I finally agree that I'm ready to take on the extra responsibility. And if I'm ever going to free myself from Kate's manipulations, that's pretty much the only way out.

Of course my strategy involves a certain amount of risk. I'm scared shitless of what she might do to the kids. She really doesn't care. But I feel that this time I must swallow my fear and follow through with the plan.

A few days later I meet the ex-wife on the street and tell her about my decision. Kate freaks out. She does not mention giving the children up, though. Instead, she says they are the ones who will suffer because she'll be forced to move to her mom's and they will go crazy there with all the bad influences.

I can see the skank is blackmailing me. But just as with her pseudo-suicide episode a few years back, I decide to call her bluff. I tell her she's gotta do what she's gotta do, and I take off trembling inside. I'm gambling high stakes here.

It doesn't take long before my gamble pays off. Kate contacts me and tells me she's leaving for her mom's. She also tells me she can't support the kids and wants to give me full custody. This is exactly what I wanted, but I'm nevertheless astonished. Wow. She doesn't even want to take care of her little girl. Oh, well. I accept her offer and get ready for yet another change in my life.

Let's see. How am I going to do this. I'm a pretty busy guy. I need to figure out a way to take the kids to school in the morning, pick them up at lunchtime, and find them a place to stay until I get off work in the evening.

Luckily Matilda, a very dear old friend, has moved to town. Matilda worked as a housekeeper at another good friend's house for many years and wants a new life. I recently helped her find a new job and I'm sure she'll give me a hand with the children.

Matilda and I talk the situation over and decide the kids will go to a new school close to her house. After school, she'll pick them up and take them to her place, where they'll stay until I'm off work. Although this sucks, it will have to do for now. But I'm glad the children will at least enjoy some positive adult influence for a change.

Bummer. Our arrangement hasn't worked out that well. Kate's daughter hasn't adapted to her new life. She wants to go live with her grandma and her mom. I feel rejected but agree. I speak with her grandma, who immediately comes and picks her up. My son remains with me, and this makes things much easier. I know he misses his sister, but there's really nothing I can do about it.

This situation has brought up a new and delicate issue that needs to be dealt with. Kate's mother has taken full possession of her granddaughter and is filling the little girl's head with all kinds of crap against me. I'm really disgusted. These people are assholes and have no respect whatsoever for the kids. Whenever my son comes over to visit his mother's relatives, Mom takes off to party and the poor kid stays with his mean sister. She has learned from mean Grandma that her brother's as bad as his dad. She's given privileges while my poor son gets the leftovers.

I bring this up at therapy and Angela makes me see that these people are involved in some kind of counter-prejudice pattern.

They're trying to make up for the fact that I'm not the girl's biological father by overprotecting her and mistreating my son. Shit. Fucking cuckoos.

I tell Angela I don't know what to do. I see that my influence, although otherwise beneficial, causes the child more harm than good. She hints that I might be repeating my father's repertoire. My dad wasn't really there for me, but then again he wasn't really absent either. And it was exactly that indecisiveness that did me the most harm.

So I'm left with an important decision to make. I must either accept full responsibility for the girl's fatherhood or give it up for good. Either way, the child will suffer.

After much pondering I decide that the best thing for the kid at this point is for me to back off and no longer act as her father image. And I'm not buying into the girl-needs-a-father hypocrisy. I want to do what's best. No matter what it is. And who knows, we might be given a chance to reconnect in the future when she's grown up and away from her grandma's influence.

I communicate my decision to Kate, who is saddened, but seems to understand my point of view. After all, she knows her own kind. She agrees to come see her son whenever she can, and we turn the page on another ugly chapter of our lives.

One-Day Stand

In the meantime, my sexual adventures are on the rise. I've been flirting with my next-door neighbor for some time. She is kind of ugly and skanky, but certainly doable (you can label me a chauvinist boor anytime now). The recent affair with Tammy's housekeeper Adrianna has really boosted my self-esteem and I think I can handle a swift approach without being bothered by stupid feelings of shyness.

I'm coming home after work and neighbor girl's in her apartment, looking out the window. We greet each other, chat a little and I invite her to my place for some coffee. Oh, well. I don't drink coffee. We both know what this is all about. We get into my apartment and she immediately plunges her hungry tongue into my mouth. Then she chucks me on the bed, rips my clothes off, and rides me like crazy until she's satisfied. She scratches me. She bites me. She moans. She screams. Damn. I can tell this bitch hasn't had sex in a long, long time.

It's the weekend and my son and I head for the country. He'll enjoy the open spaces and family company while I'm looking for some more action. Unfortunately, Adrianna isn't around. But the good news is, there's a therapy group over at the resorts, so I decide to check it out.

It's not long before I meet a woman. Her name is Fiona. She's not exactly a great looker, but her laid-back attitude, messed-up hair, and crooked teeth kind of attract me. We chat all afternoon and by nightfall, we're kissing and cuddling. We spend the weekend together, and before she leaves, Fiona invites me over to her house in Rio.

Another Bad Trip

My son's spending the weekend with relatives and I'm at Fiona's. Fiona's kind of freaky. She's into Santo Daime, a spiritual practice based on the collective singing of hymns while under the influence of *ayahuasca*, some heavy psychedelic shit. She has invited me to attend a ceremony at her church. Hey, why not.

The place is filled with strange people dressed in white. It's now noon. We're supposed to take a dose of *ayahuasca* every two hours until ten in the evening. Dense rainforest surrounds the church. It's kind of cold.

I take the first dose and soon realize I'm having one hell of a bad trip. I'm deprived of my social masks. I feel people can see through me. I'm radiating my flaws, my failures, my negativity. I feel I'm defenseless. I feel naked and scared. I curl up in despair. I also curl up because I'm terribly cold. I can't stop shivering.

A couple of hours later, I take another dose. I look around. The people are dancing, chanting and going crazy. I want to find a hole where I can hide but there's nowhere to go.

I refuse a third dose. I decide to wait for my bad trip to wear off. I can see Fiona on the other side of the room and wish she were closer, but men and women aren't allowed to be together.

At some point I see a few people sitting around, singing and working. Great. Some exercise to keep me warm. I join them and peel *ayahuasca* roots for the rest of the evening. I feel like shit, but manage not to puke.

At ten o'clock, the ceremony is finally over and we drive to Fiona's house, where I get to warm up a little. I need a hot shower. It would certainly be nice if Fiona were to join me, but for some unknown reason she's treating me like crap. And yet once again, the more she rejects me, the more I want her.

We end up sleeping on the same bed, but don't have sex or even kiss. I don't know what to make of the situation, and I really don't know what to do. I feel rejected, but I'm also annoyed. Well, fuck her. I'm far too tired to lose sleep over this anyway.

After a terrible night's sleep, I dash out of Fiona's apartment. What an asshole. I don't ever want to see this woman again. Fuck rejection. Fuck submissiveness.

Back home I get a call from Fiona. What does this woman want. I don't want to talk to her and basically tell her to fuck off. She suddenly changes her attitude. She's all nice and sweet. I tell her she has treated me like shit and I don't want to see her again. She begs me for another chance. Fuck that. I hang up the phone and never speak to Fiona again. Wow. Way to go.

A Blast from the Past

I'm extremely happy with my newly acquired inner strength—the "fuck off" factor. Cool. Just in time for another test.

I'm in Rio visiting my sister Veronica. She tells me she and her husband have met up with my former girlfriend Monica. She tells me Monica asked about me and wants to see me. I don't have a problem with that. We went through some rough times in the past, but I'm in a pretty good place in my life, so it must surely be safe to get in touch with her.

And so I call Monica and we decide to meet at her apartment. We're both excited to see each other. After all, we have a lot of catching up to do.

We find that we still have many things in common. Our marriages didn't work out. She has a daughter, who's around the same age as my son. While we're chatting away, I can't help but think that things could have been different between us. A sweetly painful sense of nostalgia crawls into my system and I soften up. Is it possible that after ten years I still have feelings for this woman.

Over dinner, she tells me she's involved with a married man, a much older man. As usual, I start analyzing her. You see, I'm acting on personal interest here. She tells me she's not happy. She has been stuck in this relationship for a while. Hmm, maybe I can save her. I can be her knight in shining armor, who has come to rescue both her and her daughter from a loveless life of suffering.

Oops, hold on. I excuse myself and head for the bathroom. I look at my face in the mirror and start laughing. I can't believe how full of shit I am. It takes a few minutes for me to get my act together, but I manage to see Monica's not my mom. My mother is the one the damned pattern's trying to save.

I sit on her sofa to watch some TV. She lies down next to me and places her head on my lap. I feel somewhat awkward. I tell her maybe we should give ourselves another chance. I don't know if I really mean it, but I tell her anyway. Things might be different after such a long time. We have both been through a lot. We have both matured. But she resists. She tells me I live in another town and things will be complicated. I sense she's scared. I insist a little more and she backs off a little more.

After a while, the whole thing's really getting on my nerves. It's the new me kicking in. I'm tired of begging. I no longer need this shit. Why am I doing this. What am I thinking.

Then in one of those moments of clarity, I simply change the subject and decide in my mind that it is about time to cut ties with Monica for good. Well, maybe I'm just making up an excuse to avoid feeling rejected once again. Really, who cares. My feelings for her are not as strong as they used to be. I think she also senses this is our last chance, our last opportunity. But she does nothing about it. Going, going, gone. I'm out of the apartment and hopefully out of her life.

August 1998

My life has stabilized quite a bit. I've enrolled my son at a Waldorf methodology school. Now I get to drop him off and pick him up. He also has swimming and English lessons and has his own therapy sessions with Angela. He's getting some needed psychological support. Although we no longer need Matilda's help, we often drop by for dinner.

As for Kate, she has vanished. No calls, no contact. I kind of knew this would happen. To come see her son, she has to take a bus and travel for two hours and she's too lazy for that. I feel bad for him, but then again, he's not exposed to her bad influence and now has the support of a special school and therapy.

But even though my female friends and family members help fill the gap left by his scatterbrained mother, I start thinking he'll eventually need a real mommy—someone who's there for him; someone who cares for him and helps me raise him. And you know what that means. I'll have to get married again. Brrrrr. Just the thought of it makes me shiver.

Well, I think for now I'll settle for a nice girlfriend. I'm confident that my new attitude towards women will lead me to the right person. Oh, and of course I start passing the word around.

And so it happens that a co-worker at the ESL school tells me she'll hook me up with one of her friends, Vanessa. She's supposedly gorgeous, gentle, loving, and overall a great gal. We'll see.

Vanessa and I meet at the local mall. Although not exactly a beauty queen, she has attractive curves. And she seems to be very nice and gentle indeed. A *Sound of Music* kind of girl. We get to know each other for a while and set up another date.

The following weekend, I leave my son at Matilda's for the night and go out with Vanessa. I barely recognize her. She looks very sexy in her black mini skirt and high heels. Her make-up is perfect. Her very provocative white blouse reveals her cleavage in a big way. Whatever happened to the innocent-looking valley girl. Oh, well. I'm not the one who's going to complain.

We go out for drinks, then come back to my apartment and get down and dirty. I mean, real down and dirty. What can I say. I think I have a new girlfriend.

My new mindset has affected my relationship with money—and for the better. One day, one of my sisters calls me and tells me my father has decided to be unexpectedly generous. He has given us a very expensive watch from his fancy collection. He has handed the watch to my brother, who's supposed to sell it at an auction and then divide the cash among the five of us. The watch ends up selling for around twenty thousand dollars, which means I get an extra four thousand in my bank account. Nice. For the first time in my life, I have extra money in the bank. I'm rich. It feels good. I feel safe and powerful. I can't believe all these good things are happening to me.

Hiccup

My new relationship's great. Vanessa is very nice to me and to my son. She's gentle and sweet, but also sexy and independent. She's like a much-improved version of Cara. Much improved.

And speaking of Cara, I'm at home one afternoon when my doorbell rings. I open the door and nearly faint. Cara's standing in front of me. She wants to come in. I hesitate for a moment, but what the hell. She can do me no harm. Although I have no more feelings whatsoever for her, she's looking mighty good. Uh-oh.

We go into my room. She tells me she loves me and asks me if I still love her. Say what. I look at her and very calmly and coldly say no. Then she takes off her blouse and shows me her perfect breasts. Ouch. I just can't resist and start feeling her up. But then I come to my senses and tell her I really don't have feelings for her anymore. She begs me to have sex with her. I try to be honest and tell her I'll most definitely bang her brains out, but it won't mean a thing. I tell her to go home and think about it, and if she still wants to have sex only for sex's sake, fine. She can come back tomorrow and we'll do it. Cara's very sad. As she walks out the door, she kisses me. I don't feel like kissing her back. I stand as still as a statue.

I later meet up with Vanessa and tell her what happened. She is very mad and wants to have a word or two with Cara. No need. She can clearly see I'm not interested in the least bit. I assure her Cara won't be coming back. And indeed she doesn't.

TEN

Liberation

I'm doing pretty well, thank you very much. I have money. I have plenty of free time. My son's being properly cared for. I have a great girlfriend who gives me love and sex. Just about time to fuck things up again.

I've been on an inner quest now for a few years. There's this uneasiness, this awkward feeling, compelling me towards something. It might be peace of mind. It might be a better life. It might be truth. I haven't got the slightest clue. But I am nevertheless searching.

After unsuccessfully scrutinizing pretty much every religion and spiritual teaching I could find, I remember J. Krishnamurti and his very awkward ideas. I re-read his stuff and become utterly fascinated with the idea of freedom from my own mind. I also read a few books by a guy named Osho, who says the exact same thing: the problem with my life isn't what happens within it; the problem is who I think myself to be. Wow. How radical. I love it. I'm somehow fully convinced that this is what I have been looking for all these years.

Thus I have suddenly decided I'll devote the rest of my life to freeing myself...from myself. But I have a problem. Reading has taken me only so far. I need to meet people who share the same convictions. I need to ask questions. I need to see these ideas in practice if I'm ever going to progress in my spiritual life.

Amazingly, a few days later I'm at my therapist's office when I run across a promotional leaflet. An Osho facilitator will soon be in town for a rebirthing workshop. I'm thrilled. I have no idea what to expect, but I sign up anyway.

Rebirthing kicks ass. My ass. I'm at the workshop. Before our first session, Roberta, our therapist, explains that rebirthing employs certain breathing techniques to release old patterns and tensions from the body and mind. All right.

The other participants and I lie down and start breathing. Some Indian music's playing on the background. I enter a kind of trance state. It's not very nice. I feel tense. My body feels tense. In fact, soon I feel like I'm wearing heavy shoulder pads. My hands are clenched into claws. I'm sweating profusely. My mind's filled with all kinds of painful memories. I'm crying. Someone gently touches my chest and tells me to keep on breathing.

I realize the music has changed. Now it's wild. Now it's ripping me apart. Now I want to scream. Now I want to die. I'm in hell. My whole body hurts. My head hurts. My soul hurts. But I just keep on breathing. And breathing, and breathing.

After what seems to have been an eternity, the music changes once again. We're told to breathe normally and simply relax into the moment. And relax I do. I can hear celestial vibrations and angelic choirs. (Actually, I think it was just a Vangelis CD, but what the heck. Let's not spoil the fun.) I'm immersed in a deep, almost catatonic state. The burden is gone. The bad vibes are gone. I'm in paradise.

Ding, dong. The first session is over. Break time. Everyone goes out for lunch but I stay behind. I'm too weak to even move from my mattress. But I feel very, very light.

By the time the workshop's over, I feel completely renewed. Roberta lets us know this is only the beginning. We're all invited to take part in a real, hard-core rebirthing training, which is due to happen in a couple of days. We will be spending sixteen days in a nearby resort without any outside contact. This is the first stage of a two-part program, by the end of which we'll be certified rebirthing therapists.

I tell her I would love to go but I really can't make it. I have many responsibilities. Many things to take care of. What about work. What about my girlfriend. What about my son. Especially my son. I can't just leave him like that. Then Roberta warns me not to use my son as an excuse because in the future I might end up blaming him for not having allowed me the freedom to attend the training. Shit. The perfect sales pitch. That hits me like a bucket of cold water. I already feel so guilty for having my son go through so much that I immediately see she's right and sign up for the damned training. Good for me.

September 3, 1998
I feel really crazy and irresponsible. I feel good. I feel free. I unexpectedly take off from work. I tell my employers I absolutely need this time off. I've never even called in sick in six years. They're in shock, but agree to let me go. I tell the girlfriend I'll be away for a while with no contact. She finds it hard to understand, but accepts it. I leave my son with my good friend and fairy godmother Matilda. I know he'll be in good hands. I am ready to go to my rebirthing training.

On the way to the resort, I'm scared. No, I'm terrified. What have I gotten myself into. I don't want to expose myself. I look around at all the other people in the chartered bus. Who are all these weirdoes. Well, they look scared too. I don't think anyone here knows what to expect. I feel better already.

The training starts in the evening with an introduction and initial instructions. Roberta's the head therapist and tells us that from this moment on we can't be in touch with anyone outside the group. In case anybody has special needs, we should contact one of her three assistants. Also, no gum or candy or chocolate or any kind of sweets are allowed in the training. No alcohol or cigarettes or drugs. Shit. Don't know why, but I'm shaking all over.

September 4, 1998
We begin the day with a very hard-core, very physical, dynamic meditation. Just what I need to get all the pattern crap out of my system. Then we move on to several rebirthing sessions, along with other therapeutic exercises. I kind of like this. Our first day comes to an end and I think to myself, *that wasn't so bad.* And to make things even better I meet a woman, Sophie.

September 5, 1998

I'm holding up all right. I haven't had to expose myself very much. I'm in control here. Oops. Not so fast.

The early afternoon brings a very nasty exercise that ends up changing my whole life and shattering my hopes of leaving this place in one piece.

We're standing around the room and must address our feelings out loud, as if they were standing right in front of us. We're encouraged to express ourselves freely and earnestly. Everyone's talking at the same time. I can handle this. No big deal. We talk to our anger, our regret, and our pity.

Everything's just peachy until I address my jealousy. I'm nice. I'm gentle. I'm suave. After all, I'm speaking to an old friend. I kindly ask Jealousy to go away. I don't want any more trouble. I'm so involved trying to persuade Jealousy to leave my life peacefully that I don't notice that one of the assistants, Samantha, has been standing behind me listening all along. She shocks the hell out of me when she suddenly yells, "Fuck, is that the way you are going to talk to your Jealousy? What kind of pansy-ass talk is that? Is that shitty feeling going to control you forever?"

At that moment, something inside me breaks open and I start crying. And I cry. And cry and cry and cry. I'm fully exposing myself, but I just can't help it.

We have now formed a circle. One by one, each participant walks to the center and introduces their shadow. I'm still crying. It's my turn. In the center of the circle, I introduce my shadow: Anger. I feel intense heat. I'm grinding my teeth. I can't stop crying. I can barely speak. Roberta thanks me and asks me to return to my place in the circle.

After about three hours, I finally manage to calm down. I feel great relief. I'm light. I'm a little boy. I want to go outside and run around, jump and sing and scream. And I do just that.

September 8, 1998

I'm fully into my process. Today, during the morning meditation session, I rip the heck out of a shirt my father has given me. It's time to break free. I'm very angry with Daddy. I'm angry with the fucker for having abandoned me. I'm angry with the fucker for having given me a hard time all these years. I'm angry with the fucker for having screwed up my relationship with money. And so I completely and utterly destroy him. After the meditation, I'm exhausted and take a long, freezing cold shower. Wow. I feel great clarity of mind and inner peace.

September 10, 1998

I've noticed that this training has had the effect of regressing us all to childhood. I feel more and more as if I were in lower school or something. Very weird.

Today we get to work on the mother image. I'm scared to death. This is very, very hard for me. My mother has also been an object of hatred for years. Damn, I realize I have become one big hatred machine.

During one exercise, we are asked to draw Momma. I draw a very ugly monster. I'm scared of it. But I must face it. Then there's a rebirthing session where I gather my little boy courage and tell the image to fuck off for good. It seems to work. I feel stronger.

In my free time, I get together with my woman-friend Sophie and her skinny-girly body. We play around. We giggle. We cuddle. We hide from the mean grown-ups and do naughty things. Just like good old times with my cousin Pam.

September 13, 1998

Today's a big day. We have finally been regressed to the moment of birth, and two rebirthing sessions will recreate its stages. We'll first be in the workroom and then in the pool. I'm shaking badly. I'm fucking scared. Fucking terrified. My birth process was not easy at all, and I don't expect it to be easy now.

My turn has come. Twelve people sit around the room at the edge of mattresses, legs spread out. They represent the mothers who are ready to give birth. The remaining twelve, including me, lie down between their legs and are covered with sheets.

We start breathing. I feel I'm in my mother's womb. It's dark and gloomy. After a while, I feel really uncomfortable. Things get tighter. And tighter. And tighter. I start moving around.

Someone places heavy things on top of me. Maybe some mattresses. I think one or two people even sit on them. I feel very claustrophobic. The situation's unbearable. I want out.

I hear voices telling me to get out. I'm about to be born. I try to force my way out. I push with all my strength, but there are about ten people sitting on me, and I can't see shit. I'm suffocating. I force and force. No dice. I'm in despair.

Then a voice tells me to simply slide down. I realize I had been trying to burst my mommy's belly when all I really had to do was slide down and out of her vagina. I easily squeeze through the opening feet first and am finally born. That was awful. I'm sure glad it's over.

My relief doesn't last long, though. After birth, I'm left alone. I'm cold. I'm lonely. I'm a helpless baby. I'm sobbing. I'm crying. I want my mommy, but she's nowhere to be found. I cry for about an hour until the session is over. Holy crap. What an experience. So that's what my birth process felt like. Pretty dang shitty. No wonder I'm all fucked up in the head.

In the afternoon, we gather for the second rebirthing session. We'll do the birth thing once again, but the objective this time is to replace our traumatic experience with a nice, warm, and supported process.

Again I'm shaking like hell. Fuck, enough already. I go into the pool. The water's warm. My partner's holding me in her arms. I start breathing. Surprisingly, the entire session is smooth. Great. Fantastic. I finish my birth process and some people carry me out of the pool. Samantha, the assistant, is there for me. She wraps a few towels around me and embraces me. I feel protected. I feel cared for. I feel loved.

By the time the whole thing is over, we have become a bunch of silly kids partying in the pool, spitting water on each other's faces, blowing whistles and laughing. It's amazing.

September 15, 1998

I'm fed up with Sophie. I don't want to cuddle anymore. She's too easy. She's under my spell. Same old, same old. She wants me. Therefore, I don't want her.

September 18, 1998
Today is our last rebirthing session. It involves death. We've been preparing for it for a few days now. We've written goodbye letters to our loved ones. We've walked around and said goodbye to the Earth. I feel somewhat melancholic.

The session is incredible. In the end, we're all reborn to a new and exciting world. I can't wait to get back home and make some changes.

After our last process, we have a party. Since I ditched Sophie, she decides to get friendly with some guy, one of our fellow participants. Crap. A rival. I didn't see this coming. Sophie employs the same tactic as my old high school girlfriend Jill many years ago. It worked then and it's working now. I'm incredibly jealous. I feel rejected. I clearly see my pattern, but am defenseless against it. Sophie and her new friend are having a good time, while I sit around defeated. And I thought I was done with this for good. Stupid neurosis.

My feelings for Sophie change completely. Once again, my logic's very straightforward: she doesn't want me. Therefore, I want her. But now it's too late. We're soon going home. Before I leave, I express my newly emerged feelings by writing her a love letter. What a lunatic.

Back home after the rebirthing training. I feel I've gone through five years of therapy in two weeks. I'm enlightened. I'm a changed man. I must make dramatic changes in my life. My old life's got to go. Right now. I quit therapy. I break up with Vanessa. She's nice and all, but I've tasted freedom and know I don't have to compromise any longer. I can get exactly what I want. And she's not exactly what I want. I also decide to quit my jobs and skip town. I don't know where to go, but that's a minor detail. I'm free to move anywhere I want. I see I've been living in a prison all my life and I want out.

Sophie writes back and clearly lets me know she has strong feelings for me as well. We speak on the phone a couple of times.

I'm bummed out she lives about two thousand miles away. But I've lost all interest anyway. Fuck it. All I can think about now is rebirthing. There'll be a workshop in October and of course I'll be there. I'm too excited to even think I might be going too fast for my own good. Silly me.

I let my bosses at the ESL school know I'll only be staying until the end of the semester. They think I've gone crazy. They're appalled because I'm leaving work again to attend another group, but they have no choice but to let me go.

My second rebirthing group is lots of fun. I'm much more relaxed. Our head therapist, Shima, is Roberta's boss and has been with Osho himself. She's German (figures) and seems very knowledgeable. This workshop focuses on chakras, our energy centers.

I soon get friendly with Samantha, the same assistant who helped facilitate the rebirthing training. I had been checking her out ever since we met a few months ago and was dying to get my hands on her nice, firm, yoga body.

We get to practice plenty of dirty yoga every evening after group activities. I just love the way Samantha makes cute, little, weird facial expressions when she's having an orgasm. And here I go again, getting involved with another broad.

But Samantha's not the only flower in my garden. I also meet another woman, Nicole. She's pretty and all, and we even flirt a bit, but Samantha totally wants me for herself and keeps the new girl away. It's okay. She keeps me very, very busy.

Bad Vibes

One evening, we're doing some chakra energy transmission work. My partner's a strange, skinny woman with bulging eyes. I don't like her vibes at all. After the exercise, I feel strangely tired. I feel drained. My emotions start shifting very quickly. Soon I'm completely exhausted. I can also see a shadow from the corner of my left eye. It's constantly moving like a wheel. I'm scared as hell. I mean, I've been to all kinds of religious ceremonies and séances, courtesy of Mommy Dearest, but nothing like this has ever happened to me. There seems to be some sort of entity draining my energy and making me feel like shit.

I'm weeping. I ask Shima for help, who, along with Samantha, spends hours getting the entity out of my force field. Wow. Please get that skinny woman as far away from me as possible.

Group activities are over. Samantha and I are madly in love. I've decided to travel south to her hometown for Thanksgiving. It'll be nice to spend a few days together outside the group environment. Kate has also called and finally wants to pick my son up for the holiday, so things have worked out just perfectly.

Thanksgiving is a blast. Samantha and I spend six marvelous days enjoying ourselves and having sex all the time. Her mom's very liberal and allows us to do whatever we want in the house. I even sleep in Samantha's room.

Roberta, the head therapist of my rebirthing training, is also around. Oops, did I mention Roberta and Samantha are sisters. The three of us chat and laugh and share memories from our recent groups. I'm having so much fun that I secretly decide this is the place I want to move to. A little voice in my mind tells me this might be about the lady, but I completely ignore it.

I tell the two women of my decision and they seem thrilled. Roberta will even allow me to stay in her place when I return for house and job hunting. Samantha will be going to India for a couple of weeks. Well, we can get together when she gets back.

On the bus back home, I'm dreaming about my new life. The Southern part of Brazil, especially this city, seems very cool. It seems like the place for me. With my knowledge of English, I can easily find a job. I can leave my son with his mother for a little while and later send for him. Perfect. And then there's Samantha. Ah, Samantha. Fucking neurosis.

ELEVEN

The Leap that Never Was

Great news. My daddy's finally coming to visit. This is his first time in my home since my move five years ago. I'm really excited. Bullshit. I know what this is all about. He has heard about my new and crazy intentions and has come to see what his irresponsible son is up to this time. Whatever. I'm ready for the dude.

He drops by my apartment with his wife and starts giving me hell. He wants to know what my plans are. He's mainly worried about his grandson. Is the child going to be safe. Will I be providing him with stability and support. Shit, what an asshole. How about supporting me for a change.

As usual, I give him hell back. I basically tell Dad to mind his own business. What's the matter with these people. After much fruitless arguing, he gives up trying to convince me of whatever it is he wants to convince me of, and they leave.

I'm pretty satisfied with my attitude. The way I see it, my dad has once again tried to castrate me, but this time I managed to hold on to my *cojones*.

The transfer of the scepter from father to son is part of becoming a man. Too bad my father's simply not handing it to me. I'll have to take it from him by force. Fuck it. I'll do whatever it takes to find my own power.

My last day at the ESL school is no bed of roses either. Myrna wants to eat me alive for having literally abandoned work. On the other hand, I know she's thrilled to see me go. Although I leave on good terms with everyone else, no one quite seems to understand what's happening to me. And neither do I.

Soon it's time to leave my apartment. I pack all my stuff and take it to sweet cousin Ashlee's. I also sell my two cars cheap, one to my sister and one to Matilda. I feel Matilda deserves a good break after all the times she has taken care of my kid. As for my son, I decide he can stay here as well. Ashlee will take good care of him, better than his mom, anyway. The problem is that Kate has already agreed to stay with him for a while. Oh, well. I give her a call and tell her I have changed my mind. I lie and tell her he's coming with me. Kate gets really pissed, but that's her own fucking problem.

I'll also be staying in Ashlee's house for a few weeks until I'm ready to travel. One thing I feel I need to do is gather energy and strength to carry on with this very important change in my life, so I start a sixty-day active meditation workout. Every day, I lock myself up in the children's room for one hour of pure catharsis. The people in her house think I've gone crazy. Hey, maybe I have.

Meanwhile, Samantha and I exchange emails on a daily basis. She seems to be having a good time in India. And I'm already making plans for our future life together.

But things go sour when she suddenly stops returning my messages. Hey, she must be busy or unable to access a computer or something. Hmm, I have a bad feeling about this.

A few days later, Samantha tells me she has met up with an old boyfriend and it seems they are back together. She's basically breaking up with me. Cold turkey. Man, not again. I'm heartbroken. I'm devastated. I'm powerless.

The rival/rejection thing has really taken me by surprise this time. For a moment, I'm paralyzed. What about my move. I can now clearly see Samantha's a major factor in my motivation.

I desperately try to manipulate the situation. I call Roberta. Maybe she can shove some sense into her sister's thick skull. She seems genuinely displeased, but there's nothing she can do. She calms me down and we make arrangements for my trip anyway. Although part of me wants to call off the entire thing, I know I'm on the edge of a cliff and have no alternative but to jump.

Boogeyman II

I've decided to spend New Year's Eve in meditation. It's close to midnight and I'm alone in Ashlee's house getting ready for a rebirthing session while everyone else is at Chuck's resort partying. I turn on some music, lie down, and start breathing.

I soon realize this session's going to be heavy. Many layers of fear come up to haunt my conscious mind. They're like monsters around me. Dark. Sticky. Hairy. I can almost feel them physically. I begin to get really scared. Here I am, in this house on top of a mountain all by myself, and these creepy creatures are out to get me. There's no one to call for help. I'm a helpless little child. I continue breathing. Now the monsters have merged into one big beast. It's the Boogeyman. Now I'm really scared. I start crying. I can see it coming closer and closer. I'm terrified, but I know I must somehow face it.

Then something funny happens. I have a sudden change in perception and the entire thing loses its grip on me. The Boogeyman is now an idea and completely detaches from the fear, which reveals itself as a meaningless frequency passing through my system. I feel at ease. I feel relaxed and optimistic. I can see my fears are unfounded. As my session comes to an end, I clearly see it's time to stand up for myself. It's time to face the world. It's time to be brave, courageous. It's time to rise and shine. But for now, I'm going to get up and have a few beers at my cousin's party.

January 1999

I travel to Roberta's house and plan to stay until I have found a job and a place to live. I've put together a résumé and have made a list of places to visit. I feel very hopeful.

Surprisingly enough, I've gotten over Samantha. And I didn't even need to find another girl to transfer my feelings to. I guess I have too many things on my mind to even care.

Overall, I'm having a good time. I spend my days cruising

around town looking for work and in the evenings, I hang out with Roberta or write some music or read.

My efforts soon pay off. Within a couple of weeks, I manage to obtain four job offers. I'm having a hard time finding a place to live, though. The thing is, local laws state I need a co-signer in order to rent an apartment. Roberta's the only person I know in town, and I really don't think she's up for it. Yep, she's nice, but not that nice. No big deal. I'll deal with that later. First I must go back to Ashlee's for a while to see my son.

After spending a week with my son, I'm off to another workshop. Although Roberta is once again the facilitator, this group doesn't involve rebirthing. Instead, we'll learn about mental techniques aimed at deliberately shaping our own destinies.

The workshop is awesome. I feel very optimistic. I feel very confident. I feel powerful. I'm now under the illusion that I can create whatever I want for my life. All I have to do is make use of the techniques I've just learned and snap my fingers. I'm on top of the world.

Another week goes by and I'm back at Roberta's. I've rented a car and brought all my boxes over to her place. Everything's great except for one thing. Try as I might, I can't find someone to co-sign my rental. I'm beginning to get worried.

Finally, after two more weeks, Roberta has had enough of me and wants me to leave her place. And I want to leave. But I have nowhere to go. Besides, my job offers won't be available forever. I must act quickly, also because I'm running out of money. I leave Roberta alone for a while and travel back to Ashlee's to think and make my decision.

A lot has been going on at sweet cousin Ashlee's house as well.

An unexpected burst of creative energy has led me to write many songs over a short period. And I'm once again hitting on cousin Tammy's slutty helper, Adrianna. But this time I've been making some extra trouble for myself and also have my eye on her older sister, Shirley. Shirley's married but lives a pretty miserable life. Her husband doesn't care for her or treat her well. And of course, I must take advantage of the situation. And of course, Shirley has a young daughter. I guess in my mind I'm still trying to fix my relationship with Kate.

Needless to say, Adrianna's not willing to help me out with her sister. She's not too amused by my attitude, especially when I ask her to bring Shirley over so that we can have a threesome. Oh, well. I have other means at hand.

Coincidently, I've found my son's caretaker Matilda another job. She's now in charge of both resorts' kitchens and, guess what, that's exactly where Shirley works. I speak to Matilda about my not-so-noble intentions and she's happy to help me out. She talks to the girl and manages to get a date going.

Shirley and I meet at Matilda's house. We head straight to the bedroom and I show her a real good time. She's certainly not as seasoned as her promiscuous sister, but I don't mind. She has all the ingredients needed to feed my hungry pattern. She's poor and unhappy and needs a savior. She has a child. And she's somewhat unattainable.

Thus, months of effort and planning go straight down the drain as I suddenly decide to give up my big move to pursue another crappy relationship. No second thoughts.

April 25, 1999

I'm attending the second stage of my rebirthing training. Since I no longer have money to spare, I make arrangements with Shima to exchange the training fee for my translation work. You see, all participants are Brazilian. And that's a problem for Shima, who speaks fluent German and English, but can barely utter a word in Portuguese. Lucky me, she needs someone to interpret while she teaches her thing in English.

The group of participants is very small. Mostly women. I'm

definitely not in the mood for trouble. I've only come here to heal myself from these patterns and to finish my rebirthing training and become a certified therapist.

There's this one woman, though, who immediately takes a liking to me. From day one, she starts leaving notes on my bed. She stares at me non-stop during Shima's lectures. I think it's cute and flattering at first, but very quickly things get out of hand.

April 27, 1999
I come back to my room and find flowers along with a love note. I'm being stalked. Goddamned crazy chick. She says she's in love with me. She says she's crazy about me. How the fuck can she be crazy about me if we don't even know each other properly. This woman reminds me of my patient Robyn.

April 28, 1999
We're in the middle of a pendulum exercise. All of a sudden, I'm exhausted. I've been sucked dry. I think I have a fever. I need to lie down. Shima measures me with her pendulum. The pendulum barely moves. All my energy has been drained. Yep. Guess who. Shima lectures the group and indirectly tells the hungry woman to back off. It takes me a while, but eventually I feel better. Now where is that ten-foot pole.

The first thing I do after I get back home is rent a car and drive to Roberta's to pick up my stuff. No more moving. All I can think of is my passionate and forbidden relationship with Shirley. What a lame joke. I visit my potential employers and turn down all job offers. I then rush back to see Shirley. Stupid, stupid, stupid.

I have no job, but still have some money left. So I decide to rent an apartment in town. Although Shirley and I have had sex a few times in Ashlee's house, it's not safe for us to meet there. I hear her husband's getting suspicious and might want to kill me if he finds out about us.

Reflection

I'm quickly falling in love with Shirley. I'm submissive and needy. I'll do pretty much anything to impress her and have sex with her. Big-ass relapse. I'm even having those very, very funny ideas. The old I-can-save-her and I-can-take-care-of-both-her-and-her-child crapola. I can see history repeating itself once again, but there's nothing I can do to prevent it. I want to be her savior very badly.

I'm also trying to make it as a rebirthing therapist. I've teamed up with Virginia, a friend I met at one of my groups. An older woman, Virginia has been living in town all her life and knows many people. So while I run the rebirthing sessions, she's in charge of finding clients. At least that's the plan.

I'm happy because we have managed to put together a group of about ten people. Maybe there was a reason for having stayed in this town after all. I'm also psyched because Shirley's spending the night at the apartment and has agreed to be my assistant. She has no idea of what's going on. Who cares. I just want her around.

I spend the entire workshop dividing my attention between my group and Shirley. We make out and do naughty things while people meditate and breathe. Fortunately, all goes well and the folks seem satisfied. I even get compliments for having done a good job. I'm also excited I get to take some cash home. Virginia tells me she wants to set a date for a new group. Awesome. I have a large grin on my face and a hint of hope in my mind.

Love Between the Seats

In the meantime, my relationship with my mom has improved a bit. I take my new girlfriend Shirley over to her house to meet her. We get there and my mom's not at all impressed. As usual, she thinks I can do better. But she doesn't mistreat Shirley, and we have a decent time.

In the evening, Shirley and I take the bus home. During the trip, we start making out and things are getting exciting. The bus is pretty empty. It's dark and cozy in our improvised love nest. I kiss her forehead, her lush lips, her rosy cheeks. I unbutton her blouse to enjoy her deliciously perky breasts. My hands travel to her smooth thighs and she spreads her legs in response. I open her jeans and start stroking her until she has an orgasm right here, in the bus. Nice. Dirty. Naughty. I think another passenger might have seen us. I don't care. I feel powerful and in control.

But all my power and sense of control are gone as soon as we return. I'm completely insecure. I want Shirley to leave her husband and come live with me. She says she'll do it, but then doesn't. The woman's pretty smart. She has been screwing both guys. I simply can't understand. I can give her a much better life and yet she remains with that shithead. I really have nowhere or no one to turn to. Well, there's always marijuana. I haven't smoked pot in a while. I've been substituting the urge with my feelings for Shirley. Bah. Old story…

So suddenly life sucks. I live downtown in a nice apartment, but barely have any furniture. My relationship with Shirley's on hold. My money's gone. I'm depressed. My rebirthing therapist career is going nowhere. Virginia keeps telling me she's not able to find people for our groups. What a shitty producer.

I've been trying to find a job but haven't had any luck. And I can't return to my old job either. Myrna will only rehire me when Hell freezes over. All my private tutoring contacts are gone.

The only thing not stressing me out is my son. I somehow manage to pay for his school and Matilda helps me out quite a bit, especially with his meals. To me it's extremely important that he doesn't feel or see the hardships I'm going through. I made my poor choices alone and he has nothing to do with them.

I find some relief by managing to borrow some money from a bank. Actually, that's another bad move. How am I going to pay back the damned bank when I'm not making any money. I'll see. For now, I've decided to live one day at a time.

By now I'm certain Shirley doesn't like me. She has been toying around with me for some time and I have the feeling she'll never leave her idiot husband. I'm trying to stay away from her, but just can't. I'm not strong enough. All she has to do is snap her fingers and doggy boy comes running. Shit. Have I been through this before. I know there's only one way out.

Then I get a call from Virginia, and what do you know. She has managed to put a rebirthing group together. It has only four participants, but I'm happy. The group goes well and things get even better when Virginia's daughter shows up with the multiple-ounce bag of pot I had ordered. I go home and smoke myself to oblivion, and that's the end of Shirley.

TWELVE

The Final Cut

I'm off to yet another group. Shima's holding a month-long silent retreat. It'll be split into two fifteen-day sessions. I've once again been invited to exchange my fee for translation work. I ask myself, *what translation work*. Isn't this supposed to be silent. Whatever. I happily agree. To tell you the truth, I feel relieved I'll have a place to eat in the next thirty days. My son can stay over at Matilda's. She has helped me a lot lately. Oh, and great news. I'm also looking forward to a possible job opportunity. It involves translating sports articles online. It pays well and I'll be able to work from home. I'm extremely excited. If I get it, my financial worries are over.

July 15, 1999

First day of silent retreat. Shhh. It's fucking hard. I can't speak to anyone except when I have to interpret Shima's lectures. I'm all alone with my very crazy thoughts.

Our schedule's tight. We get up very early in the morning to meditate. We meditate all day long. In the evening, we meditate some more and go to bed, only to repeat the entire thing the following day.

My mind's in turmoil. I just can't get that job opportunity off my head. I'm worried sick I might miss out on it. What if someone calls me and I'm here, completely out of reach. I'm so stupid. Why have I come here in the first place. Why do I do these things to myself. Why. I want to run away, but the damned hotel's high up on a mountain and there's no way I can get out of here on foot. I guess I'll just have to tough it out.

July 23, 1999
My mind is calmer. Thoughts that were running wild have begun to settle. I feel present. I feel I'm in my body. I can see things I couldn't see before. I feel this retreat's going to help me a lot, as long as I don't freak out and leave first.

One thing I haven't been able to rid myself of, though, is the idiotic job-opportunity issue, which by now has become a full-blown paranoia. I simply can't see that my mind is making use of this story to stir up my feelings and feed its own patterns. I end up writing a note to one of the assistants and manage to make a phone call to Matilda in the evening. No news, of course. But at least I get to speak to someone. Hee, hee, hee.

July 30, 1999
Things have gone from bad to worse. I've been eating vegetarian food and haven't smoked in fifteen days. I can't get that job thing off my mind. I'm going insane. I can't stay here any longer.

The first fifteen-day session is over. Some people are leaving. And that surely includes me. I apologize to Shima and hand my translation job to one of her assistants. I'm out of here.

August 1-15, 1999
I'm back at the apartment but haven't told anyone. The first thing I do is light up a joint and then smoke two cigarettes. I then find a huge bag of Cheetos in my cupboard and eat the whole thing. It's my ego getting back at me for having deprived it of its dirty habits for so long. And, of course, I spend the next couple of days with a fever and diarrhea.

Although I'm back home, I'm still following through with the thirty-day retreat. Except for the cigarettes and dope. Funny. I spend my days meditating and reading spiritual texts as if I were with the group. This goes on for exactly fifteen days.

I'm still desperately trying to find a job. After a lot of expectation and stress, the translation position I was hoping to get does not come through. Now I'm in really deep trouble. My only solution is to try and find a job in Rio before things get worse. I have no choice. I prepare my résumé and mail it to about fifty companies. Something has to come out of this.

A month goes by and I don't receive a single reply. I'm depressed. But I'm not about to give up. I've also been searching for job opportunities in newspapers and one day I come across an ad that might be for me. A brand new business English school is about to open in Rio and is looking for an academic manager. I decide to apply.

I haven't worn a suit in ages. I feel kind of awkward as I walk into a fancy building in Rio for my job interview. The company's owned by a woman. She's young and attractive and full of energy. She's psyched about her new project. She's excited about me and my skills. She hires me on the spot. She is throwing a party this very evening and wants to introduce me as her new manager.

I'm fired up. My financial troubles might be over. But I start having weird feelings inside. I don't know if I want this job. I'll have to wear a suit to work. And I hate suits. I'll also have to face a long-ass commute every day unless I move back to Rio. I definitely don't want to deal with either possibility. I curse myself and my crappy life. Why does everything always have to be hard.

In the midst of my crazy questioning, I misread the invitation and get to the party very late. It's almost over. The woman's really pissed and disappointed. But the job is still mine.

A few days later, I'm back to the fancy building for my initial training. I don't feel well. Something's not right here. You know me. I follow my gut instinct. At lunch, I go out to eat. And I don't come back. I thank my employer for the opportunity and slink away with my tail between my legs.

Subtle Invasion

But my troubles in Rio are far from over. When I applied for the academic manager position, I also set aside a résumé to be sent to a renowned ESL school in case my interview didn't work out.

That was my backup plan. I left the résumé with my mother and told her that if necessary, she could drop it off at the school.

As soon as I decide there's no way I'm commuting or moving back to Rio, I call my mother and tell her to destroy the résumé. Yeah, dream on. The goddamned woman tells me she has taken the liberty of sending it to the school. After all, she'd be delighted if her son was back in Rio, close to Mommy. Never mind respecting any of his wishes or plans.

I'm mad as hell. I'm not going to take the job and don't want to portray a negative image to potential employers. My hopes are that they don't call me.

Of course, the school calls me. But instead of simply solving the situation with some white lie, genius here ends up setting an appointment for an interview.

The school's ready to offer me a decent amount of money for my time. The lady interviewing me says I should be honored I have the opportunity to work for such a distinguished company. I know she's right but tell her I need to think. I have one day to make up my mind.

By the time I leave the interview, I'm completely confused. I don't know what to do. I need the job badly, but I have my mind made up about not moving. I'm even considering the commute, but that might not even be financially worthwhile.

That evening, I speak with one of my sisters and her husband about the situation. They make me see that this is indeed a good opportunity, but I shouldn't take it if it's not going to make me happy. Now that was sobering.

The next day, I head over to the ESL school and tell the lady I've decided not to take the position. She's annoyed. Why did I send her my résumé in the first place. I feel embarrassed and angry with my mother for having invaded my life once again. The woman tells me that if I don't take the job I'll never again have an opportunity with that school. I thank her for her time and leave.

I feel divided. One part of me thinks I'm a complete idiot for having thrown away such good opportunities. But another part of me, the stronger part, is unwilling to compromise and wants to remain where I am. Dumb shit.

My financial condition has worsened. Now, in addition to a few bank loan installments, I owe a couple of months' rent. What am I going to do. I can barely support my son and his needs. I must find some money soon.

I am unknowingly being forced into an introversion period. No job, no women, no nothing. I hang around the house all day getting high and trying to figure out my situation. I soon reason I might be going about this issue the wrong way. It's no use having golden opportunities knocking if I'm not ready to take advantage of them. Maybe I should focus on doing something about my patterns and forget the outside world for a while.

October 1999

One of my fellow rebirthing therapists calls me and tells me she has referred my name to someone who might need simultaneous translation services. A few days later, I get a call from a woman named Joyce. She tells me an American shaman's coming to Brazil for a workshop and asks me if I'm willing to be his interpreter. Hell, yeah.

Soon Joyce and I are at her place overseeing the details of the upcoming event. Joyce is in her fifties and looks like a red-haired gypsy. She's a big momma figure. She has huge breasts. She also gets high. I wonder for a moment what things would be like if my momma got high. Joyce gives me a couple of the shaman's books so I can familiarize myself with the material. Hey. I'm beginning to like this translation business. I get to travel, learn new and useful techniques, get to work on myself, and get paid for it.

I'm steamed up about my new job—sure beats teaching English to teenaged kids by a mile. Joyce isn't paying me very much at all. But hey, better than nothing. I'm also sort of nervous. This work seems completely different from anything I've done in the past. Hmm. A translation is a translation. How hard can it be.

The shaman's group is very large. About fifty people form a circle around a mattress, which looks more like an operating table. One by one, participants lie on the mattress and get to have a spiritual session. The shaman says weird things and makes weird movements. He takes energetic spiders and ghosts out of people's bodies. I'm freaked. What exactly am I supposed to do here. Well, there's nothing I can do but play along. I say weird things, make weird movements, take spiders and ghosts out of people's bodies, only in Portuguese.

After the day's work, I'm completely overwhelmed and need to release a bunch of crap from my body. I go outside, lie on the grass, and just cry for about a half hour.

One more day of spiritual sessions and the workshop's finally over. We worked on all fifty people and I'm completely exhausted. But it was a great experience. And I have made some friends, too. Joyce tells me everyone loved my work. She says I was precise and completely present at the sessions. And she'll most certainly hire me again in the future.

Surprise

I'm in Rio hanging out with one of my new friends. We spend the day outdoors by the lake. It's my thirty-fourth birthday. Later, we are supposed to visit another friend I met at the shaman's group. Great. The more, the merrier.

We get to his apartment and there's a surprise birthday party for me. I'm completely amazed. Nobody has ever thrown me a surprise party. All my new friends are here, including Joyce, who organized the entire thing. We eat and drink and I sing and play the guitar. I feel loved. I'm very grateful and happy.

Another week goes by and Joyce asks me to be the shaman's interpreter at a one-evening workshop. This time, we walk around in a room full of people while the shaman does his thing to each person. We work for hours and in the end I'm totally burnt out. Once again, people like my work very much. I get many compliments and even a few presents.

As for my meager fee, trouble. Joyce now wants to pay for my services with post-dated checks, which I'll only be able to cash in a month. I'm taken by surprise. Damn. I thought she valued my work. I'm sort of pissed, but what the hell. The woman has just thrown me a birthday party. I'll just make sure next time things are different.

The pay I received for the shamanic gigs was a good start, but not nearly enough to significantly improve my critical financial situation. In January, I manage to supplement my almost nonexistent income by working as a psychologist. My only client is a very nice woman who's unhappy in her married life. I see her once a week in my apartment. I use this money to support my son and try as much as I can to provide him with a normal life. Whenever possible, I take him to Matilda's for a good meal. He also eats well at school. I'm the only one fasting here.

I've also been hanging out with Virginia, the woman who's doing her best to put rebirthing groups together for me. I like going to Virginia's. It's pretty much a no-worry zone. She also likes my son very much and helps me take care of him when we are over there. Virginia's divorced and has two kids of her own, but they are teenagers.

Although she lives in a pretty nice house and makes a decent amount of money running her aesthetics business, the woman's constantly complaining about her finances. She also complains a lot about having to take care of her grumpy elderly father. She feels he holds her back. She really hates him and openly wishes he were dead.

I soon notice that Virginia and I have developed this weird mother-son relationship. I hate this. I want to get rid of the stupid mother image. I feel she treats me like one of her kids. And fuck, I surely act like it.

One day, I decide to ask Virginia for a loan. She has recently received a shitload of cash from the sale of an apartment and has plenty to spare. The way I see it, she definitely won't mind loaning her friend a mere three thousand dollars.

Well, apparently she does mind and refuses to lend me the money. What kind of friend is that. I grossly overlook our sickly relationship and get ticked off, especially when I hear a couple of days later that she gave most of her cash to her teenaged son, who blew it all investing in online stocks.

I'm very hurt but don't say a word. Virginia's really not to blame. All I can think about is how I should have skipped town long ago, when the moment was ripe. I now realize I'm no longer supposed to be here, and the situation reflects the fact that life's kicking me out by force.

There's also this other woman, Wanda, whom I met at one of my rebirthing groups. Wanda lives in Rio but is always around. She's nice, but a little out of whack. Wanda often goes on and on about how she sees angels and how enlightened she is.

My relationship with Wanda is very unique. She constantly calls me to complain about her shitty love life. Our conversations start out nicely, but after about a half hour, the only thought that comes to my mind is how to end the conversation, how to say no.

After about three hours, she finally gets tired and hangs up. I feel drained. And even though I know the same thing is bound to happen again in a few days, I still pick up the phone when she calls. I'm lonely and pay for her company by putting up with her whining.

I spend the next couple of weeks trying to figure this pattern out. Why am I afraid of just saying no. Guilt; check. Pity; check. Sense of obligation; check. It's official. I'm once again struggling with my mother's image.

Wanda's a vampire. She calls me and sucks up all my energy. I can't hang up because I feel I've got to help her. I feel bad for her. And of course, I'm afraid she'll reject me and no longer call me. But this can't go on. I promise myself the next time she calls, things will be different.

Three days after that momentous decision, I'm sitting around the apartment getting high. It's late and my son's already asleep. The phone rings. It's Wanda. I hesitate a bit, but answer.

We start talking. I try to make good conversation but it soon turns into another feeding session for her. This time, though, I'm timing the conversation. Forty-five minutes go by. I decide it's enough. I gather courage. This is hard for me. I feel like I'm rejecting her, but I must put an end to this shit. I interrupt her in the midst of what she's saying and make up some lie and tell her I have to hang up. She's surprised. She insists, but I interrupt her again and tell her I really have to go. I finally hang up. I feel good. I feel powerful. But I'm anxious. I need another joint. I've won this battle, but I know I still have a long way to go before I win the war.

Three more days and another call. I time the conversation. I try to talk to Wanda about myself and about the weather. I ask her what she has been eating. I ask her about our rebirthing friends. But the moment I run out of questions, she starts babbling about her stupid romantic frustrations. Forty-five minutes go by and I tell her I have to go. She insists a bit and I almost hang up on her. This is becoming really annoying.

I start resenting Wanda and her calls. Sometimes I don't even bother to answer the phone. Better lonely than angry sounds good to me. Soon she doesn't call me as often. I guess my energy is no longer available; she'll have to feed somewhere else. Eventually she stops calling and, although we still see each other, our relationship has changed completely because I don't allow her to drain me of my energy.

I notice that whenever I break through some new threshold in my relationship pattern, things also change in the financial realm.

And it so happens that soon after having solved the Wanda dilemma, I get an email from an old high school friend who works as a freelancer, translating books and articles for a few publishing companies, including *Reader's Digest.* She says her employers are in need of good translators and offers to send them my name. I'm very, very worked up and can't thank her enough.

That same week, I get a few articles and a book to translate. I can now say I have a decent schedule. I wake up in the morning, take my son to school, come back, get high and translate all day long. I'm also still seeing my client. Hopefully things will get rolling for me.

Good Deal

Since I'm a responsible little fella, the first thing I do when I get my paycheck is set up an appointment with my building manager, who has wanted to see me for a while. Now that I have some money, I can pay past-due rent and building maintenance fees. I walk over to her apartment, which is just downstairs from mine, and ring the doorbell.

Holy crap. A goddess. We talk business for a while, make our deal, and before we know it, we're flirting like mad. She finds out about my Tarot skills and asks me for a reading—at my place, of course.

She comes over to my apartment after lunch. I see she's appropriately dressed for the occasion: she's wearing a very loose blouse and sexy running shorts. My, oh my. We completely forget about the Tarot and I bang her silly all afternoon. She gets to know my apartment really well. I show her the entry hall wall, the kitchen countertop, the living room sofa, the bathroom sink, and even my son's bed. A complete pleasure tour. Now that's what I call sealing a good deal.

I can't figure out why, but *Reader's Digest* has stopped sending me articles. It has also been a while since I translated my last book. Crap. Back on desolation row.

Fortunately, Shima has asked me to interpret at her advanced rebirthing training. This time, though, I feel it makes no sense to exchange the fee for my translation services because I've already done the training. I tell her I want to be paid. She hesitates, but at last agrees. The amount of money she wants to pay me isn't nearly as much as I should get as a certified translator, but what can I do. I need the money. And so there goes my son to Matilda's while I attend one more group.

Although my body is at the training, my mind's busy trying to find ways to scrounge up enough cash to survive another month. And the only thing I can think of is to beg. I ask Shima if I can borrow some cash. She says no. I'm outraged. I don't understand why she cannot lend me money. She has plenty. I then approach another good friend. I know he's rich and successful and will be able to help me. He's glad to lend me about one thousand dollars.

A Chapter Within a Chapter: Sneaky Bastard

It's hard for me to accept the fact that I'm now a freelancer. I was taught that to make a living I should have a good, steady job. The transition hasn't been easy in my mind, and for now, I can only feel safe and relieved if I have a nine-to-five position.

I've set up an interview at an ESL school owned by a guy named Joshua. Joshua's a sneaky bastard who, in addition to owning the school, makes his money selling and transporting metal.

During the interview, Joshua tells me he's unhappy with his current manager, one of my former English students, and sees me as the perfect solution to his problem. He wants to hire me as a teacher, promote me to manager, and kick the girl out. And he doesn't want any of his employees to know about our little secret until the changes are made. Fine. All I care about is that I finally have a decent job. I'll be paid well. And I'm not the one kicking the girl out.

June 3, 2000. My boss is about to promote me to manager. The situation has become somewhat awkward. His employees know he's up to something, but no one knows what. I feel really bad for the current manager. She's a nice girl. When she first saw me, she was very happy. She said she didn't believe I had come to work here since I was so overqualified. The poor girl hasn't got a clue of what's about to happen.

In the afternoon, Joshua calls her into one of the classrooms. After a while, she comes out and she's crying. He then calls me in and tells me the position is mine. He hasn't fired the girl, though. He has offered her a teaching position but she has told him to stick it up his ass. She's very mad at him. Unfortunately, she's also pissed at me.

Joshua and I immediately get down to business. The course needs new students. It has two branches in town. In addition to my salary, he agrees to give me a percentage of the tuition fee for every new student enrolled in the smaller branch as an incentive. Joshua knows I have a lot of experience with ESL schools and trusts me. I feel I'm in a very powerful position. I have great plans for the school.

That evening, we have a general staff meeting and my boss introduces me as his new manager. I'm not so sure everybody is fond of the idea, but I really don't care.

June 5, 2000. I now wear a shirt and tie to work. And I don't hate it. I feel it's good for my self-esteem. I transfer my son to a very nice private school. I hire a person to take care of him until I'm home from work. I don't want to overburden Matilda.

I start changing things at the school. I create a new course structure. I expand our services to include other languages and computer science. Joshua sees our quick progress and is very excited. He has been working on marketing his new school and has had good results. The word's getting around town and more people are enrolling.

I tell Joshua we're in need of good, efficient helpers. Gladys, his present secretary, is great but is unable to deal with the huge amount of work. We need another person like her. I immediately think of Thelma, a former co-worker of mine who happens to be unemployed. I think she's very competent and I want her to take care of our smaller branch. I speak to Joshua and he interviews her. Thelma's hired.

June 15, 2000. While working out finances with Gladys, I notice that in addition to dipping into school money as if it were his own personal piggy bank, Joshua has also made many sour deals. He has been using the school to return personal favors. He has been handing out scholarships and has been charging less to some of his acquaintances and friends.

I have a meeting with Joshua and basically tell him that his sloppy attitude is hindering his own business. Maybe not the wisest thing to say to your employer after less than a month in the job, but I'm just trying to be honest here. He sees my point and is willing to let me do my thing.

I immediately tell Gladys she can only give Joshua money at the end of the month, after the release of our financial statement. We also establish fixed prices for every course the school has to offer. That's it. No more Mr. Nice Guy.

June 23, 2000. I've lost respect for Joshua. Although a successful businessman, he shows up at the school dressed as a bum. Always in his sleeveless T-shirt, jeans, and baseball cap. His ideas make no sense. What a stupid fuck.

I treat him as if he were a very bad employee. No diplomacy whatsoever. I'm aggressive and tell him off. I make fun of Joshua behind his back. I feel like I'm dealing with some sort of bizarre shadow image of my father. Bad news.

June 27, 2000. Despite our not-so-peachy relationship, my boss is happy to see his school growing and making him a lot more money. After setting things straight financially, I'm now ready to take some product-quality measures. Most of my teachers are crappy and barely speak English. I think to myself, *how can they even be teaching.* I want to train them and send them to ESL school events.

My new actions start creating turmoil among the employees. One teacher in particular doesn't like me at all. He's very submissive and nice when addressing me directly, but I know he talks plenty of trash behind my back. Also, Joshua's former manager is back working as a teacher. A perfect recipe for conspiracy.

June 30, 2000. It's payday. Joshua's around and we are checking figures, closing statements, and paying employees. When he sees the amount of money he has to pay me, Joshua complains and says it's quite a bit of cash. Fuck. Just like my father. I work like a dog all month long to make the asshole a crapload of money, and all he wants to do is take advantage of me. Well, I tell him that's the price he has to pay for my services.

When it comes to calculating the percentage due to me for new enrollments, Joshua breaks his promise and awards me for my personal referrals only and not for all students newly enrolled at the smaller branch. I blow up and tell him that I'm leaving if he won't honor our verbal agreement. He begs me to calm down and ends up paying me for every single enrollment. Jerk. I let him know I won't work another day unless I have a signed document detailing my earnings. Joshua agrees and tells me he'll give me a document later. Anything to shut me up, I guess.

July 12, 2000. Things are starting to look better. Most of my bills are up-to-date. I've paid back the guy from the rebirthing group. I've gone to the bank and made arrangements for monthly payments on my debt. It might take a while, but now I have a steady job and hope things will eventually get back to normal.

My son likes his new school very much. His new nanny takes good care of him. Matilda's also happy for my success. She says I'm a great person and deserve all the good things coming to me.

As for steady relationships, I haven't been going out with anyone for a while now. I don't have the time. I'm doing okay with my fuck buddies and a lot of pot.

July 15, 2000. Frigging Joshua still hasn't given me the frigging signed document detailing my earnings. I confront his ass again, but this time he convinces me there's no need for written agreements between us. He assures me I have nothing to worry about. I normally wouldn't buy into this, but by now I'm fully entangled in a kooky father-son mess and accept his word. Lord, why am I such a blockhead.

I also get a call from Shima. She wants me to interpret at her upcoming silent retreat. Well, things are stable at Joshua's school. Gladys and Thelma can take care of everything while I'm away. I speak to Joshua and he agrees to let me go for a couple of weeks. I leave my son with his new nanny. He's getting used to my groups. Off I go.

July 17, 2000. Silent retreat. Shhh. The second time around has been much more pleasant, at least so far. My mind's much calmer and willing to let go.

July 23, 2000. I've been making extra efforts during this retreat. I meditate all day long. My main objective is to silence my mind completely, even if for a moment.

July 25, 2000. My intense patterns prevent me from emptying my mind. I've given up trying and have decided to turn the retreat into one long and arduous therapy session. I'll spend the rest of my time here healing unconscious behaviors by observing my thoughts and emotions.

July 30, 2000. An immense shift has occurred within my system. I've somehow detached myself from my thoughts and emotions and no longer believe in them. I'm now able to witness the contents of my mind without fully identifying with them. I feel my life has changed on a very deep level.

August 5, 2000. Sure enough, things have also changed around me. Upon my return, I find Joshua's different. He seldom shows up at the school. He's acting weird. I collect my monthly paycheck but feel very insecure. I sure do wish I had made him sign those documents.

August 12, 2000. It's Saturday and I decide to drop by the school to check on a few things. I get there and to my utmost surprise, my boss is holding an employee meeting. Sneaky bastard. Everyone has been invited except for me, of course. Uh-oh. I think I might be in for bad news. I greet everybody and take off. I think I'm in shock. I try to kid myself into believing that nothing will come out of this. I think not.

August 14, 2000. I get to work and Joshua is waiting for me. I've never seen him so well dressed. He's wearing a black shirt, black pants, and black shoes. Holy cow. Where's the funeral.

He calls me into one of the classrooms and fires my ass right away. He says he's very sad. He says he can't stand my attitude any longer. He says the former manager got her job back.

I can't believe this is happening. I'm appalled. In a desperate move, I try to be diplomatic and apologize. I tell him I only wanted what was best for the school. Too late.

He has some money in his hand and says it's the cash he owes me for the fourteen days I worked in August. Bullshit. He owes me much more than that. What about my percentage. What about my bonus. I tell him I will sue him. He laughs. Shit. There's no way I can sue him without written proof. I lower my head, get up, and leave.

Post Scriptum. After the fiasco with Joshua, I decide to give my old employers at the ESL school another try. I know Myrna's going to give me a hard time, but who knows, maybe I'll get lucky. It's been a while. I call them up and set up an interview.

I speak to the owners, one by one. I tell them I've learned my lesson. I tell them I can excel if they only allow me to return. I ask Wendy and Jade for help. They tell me they'd love to have me back, but the decision has to be unanimous. I speak to Fred and beg him for mercy. He tells me Joshua came by to bad-mouth me. Sneaky bastard. I apologize to Myrna for any harm I might have caused her. I can tell she's cracking up inside. *Payback is a bitch*, is what she's probably thinking. And she's the bitch. Then Fred tells me they've heard my plea and will call me if they need me.

Bullshit. That's just not gonna happen. They've had it with me for good. Now I can go home and cry some.

THIRTEEN

Pushed Out of the Nest

I haven't earned a red cent in over a month. My job's gone. My client's gone. I have no translations to work on. I'm behind on rent again and fear I'll be evicted. And there's nothing my fuck-buddy lady manager can do about it. I spend my days thinking hard of ways to make money. And when this fails, I invariably get high and experience some very bad feelings—intense fears and depressions that really knock my socks off. Ain't life grand.

Staring the Beast in the Face

One particular evening, I'm hanging out in the house. My son's asleep in his room. I get very high and am suddenly overcome by incredibly gloomy and heavy feelings. I feel like shit. My mind's plagued with thoughts about rejection, loss, powerlessness, and failure.

I would most certainly have slipped into one of those suicidal moods had it not been for my newly acquired skills. So, Instead of giving in to the depression, I decide to sit on my bed, close my eyes, and observe it directly.

Breathe. Breathe. At first, it's tough. I'm almost completely taken by this monster. But somewhere inside my system, there is this part of me that's detached and able to see the whole thing as if it were happening to another person. I fiercely cling onto that tiny point of awareness and start witnessing my own suffering.

My head hurts. A dense, cloudy, almost bloody sphere sits in my chest. It's alive. It's draining me of energy. It makes my body shiver with fear. It makes my breath slow and shallow. It's being fed by my thoughts of inadequacy, which go on and on inside my head. Life's so shitty. I'm lonely. I can't make money. I can't find a job. Nobody likes me. Nobody wants me. I don't have any money. What am I going to do. Everyone has rejected me. I'm such a dumb ass. I should have moved when I had the chance. I'm a piece of shit. I can't stop smoking. Why do I get high every day. I'm such a bad person. I'm not a good father. I'm too strict with my son. He's going to turn out full of traumas and it will be my fault. Life's so shitty…

The creepy thing is eating me alive. I have no alternative but to stay here for as long as it takes, focus on my breath, and look at this pattern until something happens.

After what seems to be an eternity, the entire thing starts to make no sense. Like my New Year's Eve rebirthing session at Ashlee's, suddenly the pain is just here. The thoughts are just here. The sphere is just here. I don't want to fight them. I don't want to make them go away. I don't care if they're here or not. I don't feel like paying attention to them.

And so the complex begins to dissolve before my very eyes. I realize I've been holding onto it with my attention. Then, for one moment, I'm able to let go and the whole thing's gone. I open my eyes and take a few deep breaths. Wow. It worked. I'm light as a feather. I'm relieved. I'm proud of myself. I need a nice, long, hot shower.

After my recent success I'm excited to work on myself some more. I pick up a book Shima has given me. It contains many pattern-processing techniques. I practice them all the time. I spend days writing and writing and writing and feeling and letting go. I fill several notebooks with silly thought patterns and verbal descriptions of emotions. Every night, I pray and ask Existence to end my harsh situation. Hey, at least I'm doing my bit.

And sure enough, things soon start to change. For the worse. Matilda's relationship with my cousin Chuck's neighbor Beatrice has been deteriorating by the day. Although fully in charge of the food in both resorts, Matilda constantly complains. She says she's being mistreated. She says she's being ripped off. No way.

Damn. I know my friends and family and they'd never do any of these things. Chuck and Beatrice might have their flaws, but they're both great people.

Anyway, one day I head over to the resort to hear the other side of the story. I tell Beatrice what's on Matilda's mind and she's appalled. She says Matilda really has nothing to complain about. Beatrice tells me she has even considered having Matilda as her business partner, granting her a share in the restaurant's earnings.

I think I know what's going on. Ding, ding, ding. Ladies and gentlemen, in the near corner, wearing a long white apron and weighing in at one hundred-twenty pounds of pure neurosis and victim consciousness, we have our challenger: Matilda. In the far corner, wearing a white T-shirt and jeans and weighing in at one hundred-twenty five pounds of serious problems in the past with employees who want to take advantage of her generosity is our defending champion: Beatrice. And I'm stuck as the fucking referee.

Showdown

Things get nasty very quickly. Matilda's now openly complaining at work. Beatrice is losing her temper. And I feel responsible for the situation. After all, I was the one who got Matilda the job in the first place. I try to intervene and fix things. I love Matilda as a mother but don't want to lose my friend either. I talk to Beatrice first. She's willing to find a solution to the unpleasant situation. She's willing to listen to what Matilda has to say. Fine.

I now talk to Matilda to sort things out. We're standing right outside of Beatrice's resort's kitchen. Matilda's acting very weird. She doesn't seem to be herself. She has even asked her husband to hang around and watch us from a distance, as if she needed some kind of protection.

I'm sick to my stomach. I've known this person all my life and now she needs a bodyguard. And what happened to all the times she was lovingly watching my son. I sure ain't getting no lovin' now. What the hell. I tell her husband to join us and be part of the conversation. I look Matilda in the eyes. She's completely out of her mind. Man, what is it with all these crazy-ass women in my life. She starts complaining and cussing. I tell her she's being ridiculous. I tell her no one's mistreating her or ripping her off. I ask her to calm down and listen. I try to make her see that she can solve things in a friendly way. I try and try and try. But all I'm doing is pissing her off more and more. She's completely blinded by her pattern. And her mind's made up. All the people at the resort are evil and want to crucify her.

Finally, she runs out of arguments and literally tells me to go fuck myself. I'm speechless. I've never seen her like this. Then, in a sudden move, Matilda turns her back, grabs her husband, and takes off. I just stand there for a while. I'm totally freaked out. I think I have just lost a friend.

Roberta has once again come to town for a rebirthing workshop. She has asked Virginia and me if we want to be her assistants. We agree. It'll be a good opportunity to see a few good friends.

Fifteen of us are in a room listening to Roberta. I'm looking around, checking out the participants and see a gorgeous blonde sitting next to Virginia. Uh-oh. Here I go again.

Virginia tells me that's her dermatologist friend, Jesse. She's a forty-one-year-old woman in the body of a twenty-year-old girl. Insane. I can't take my eyes off her. I must have her at all costs.

Too bad. Jesse leaves our group early. She has something to attend to. I barely get the chance to introduce myself to her. No problem. I'll get Virginia to help me out.

A Chapter Within a Chapter: Toys in the Attic

October 14, 2000. Virginia gives me the woman's phone number. I call Jesse and ask her out. The wench's trying not to show it, but she's interested in me as well. Ha, ha, ha. In the evening, we get together for drinks. Then we go back to her place for a special skin treatment...

Later, at home, I'm thinking Jesse's body isn't the only thing that turns me on. This woman's very intelligent, successful, and interesting. We have good conversations. Wow. This surely is a change from the silly girls I had been dating.

October 17, 2000. Jesse and I go out a few more times and soon a couple of factors lead me to suspect she's my new girlfriend. First, there's sort of an unspoken bond between us. We care about each other. We hold hands when we go out. We enjoy each other's company. She's surely more than just a fuck buddy. Second, there's someone else involved—a rival. Naturally.

It's early evening. Jesse and I are chatting on the street, right next to her building when a delivery guy comes by and hands her a huge bouquet of red roses. I learn the flowers are from an old geezer who's completely in love with her. The fucker then shows up from nowhere and starts kissing her ass right in front of me. I'm about to get jealous, but her indifference completely assures me I've nothing to worry about. After a little while, things get a bit awkward for Grandpa, who takes off. Jesse and I laugh about the entire thing and go up to her apartment for you-know-what.

October 20, 2000. We're chatting in Jesse's bedroom and I'm learning some more about my new girl. She's divorced and has two kids—a young son, who lives with her, and a teenaged daughter, who lives with her ex. Her office is downtown and she has many patients. In fact, she's well renowned in town. I feel embarrassed. I don't want to tell her about my shitty professional situation. But I have nothing to hide. Better tell her now and get it over with. So I dish out my usual brilliant prose, and to my surprise, she seems to admire my boldness.

Some more chatting and we're soon having sex again. Jesse is aggressive. I like that. She wants to be on top and in control all the time. And I don't care. It's part of my strategy. My power lies in pleasuring her by letting her think she has the power.

October 23, 2000. Jesse needs to go to Rio for a couple of days and invites me to come along. I tell her I can't because I have no money. She tells me not to worry. We'll be staying at a nice hotel and she has plenty of cash for the both of us. I feel sort of powerless and humiliated, but all that goes away as soon as I picture myself doing Jesse all night long in a soft hotel bed.

October 27, 2000. I leave my son with sweet cousin Ashlee for the weekend. He really enjoys staying with her and her two kids. He has loads of fun whenever he visits. I'm happy and relieved, especially because his out-to-lunch mother seldom comes to see him. She's too busy screwing up her own life.

It's early evening when Jesse and I arrive at the hotel. Great joint. I still feel a bit inferior and submissive because she's the one with the power and the money. Well, suck it up, my friend.

We get settled in our room and head up to the rooftop pool. I was hoping for some dirty nighttime underwater action, but we're far from being alone. No, siree. There are a bunch of obnoxious businessmen in the pool with drinks in hand and large pot bellies hanging over their worn-out shorts. Of course, they see Jesse in a bikini and freak out. I'm very jealous, but the situation doesn't seem to bother her.

Then some smart-mouthed dickhead makes a disrespectful remark about Jesse and I overhear it. I'm not afraid of these fucks. In fact, my jealousy is so strong I'm willing to pick a fight with five guys. And might even beat the living crap out of them. I ask them if there's a problem I can assist them with. Nobody says a word. And things get pretty quiet around the pool from then on.

After a while, we leave and go to the sauna. I try to get friendly but Jesse is afraid someone's going to walk in on us. I guess I'll have to be patient and wait until we're back in our room. So we just sit around and chat.

At one point, she invites me to spend the New Year at her parents' beach house. Her elderly folks will be away and we'll be able to enjoy some quality time together. Shit. How can I travel when I'm completely broke. I express my concerns and she gets pretty annoyed. She tells me we've already been through this. Her cash is our cash and I don't have to worry about a thing. I reluctantly agree, but can't help but feel like a damned gigolo.

October 29, 2000. Today I get a call from my gypsy momma Joyce. Her shaman friend's returning to town and she wants me to interpret at his workshops. Well, things have changed. I know she makes a ton of money during these events and I'm not willing to settle for crumbs. I feel I got ripped off last year and I won't let it happen again. Joyce has been taking advantage of me by sucking on my talents. Just like my mother.

I tell her that this year, I want to get paid professional interpreter fees. I tell her I want five percent of her profits. I can tell she's outraged. How dare I go against her, especially after all she has done for me. Hey, she was nice to me and threw me a surprise party and all, but I don't have to spend the rest of my life feeling grateful and trying to repay Joyce in some way. We have a pretty nasty argument and she ends up finding someone else. Fuck her. Although I need the money badly, I'm proud to have stood up for myself.

November 12, 2000. I've managed to scrounge up some money to attend the shaman's workshop as a participant. I think it'll do me an enormous amount of good. And I'm traveling to a different town, away from Joyce.

The time for my session has come. I'm terribly stirred. There is another guy doing the interpreting. The shaman works on my mother figure. He says nasty things about her. He says she's been trying to substitute me for my dad. Gross. The shaman does his thing and I feel liberated.

Then he moves on to my father image. He says my current image isn't working for me. Crap. I could have told him that. He tells me to simply let go and build a new father image within myself. Now how the hell am I supposed to do that. "Trust me," he says, "you'll do it."

After the session, I feel great. I've been purified. I'm filled with light. The shaman wants me to let his work sink in and tells me to sleep on it.

But instead of being a good boy and retreating into myself for the night, I get together with a few guys to party. I truly feel like a man. I feel empowered. I want to be with my buddies. I want to be part of a gang. So we drink, get high, talk about women, and laugh until dawn. Hope I haven't ruined my spiritual cleanse.

November 22, 2000. Things are going pretty well with Jesse. Today she has to go out of town on business and wants to take the bus. She asks me to take her car, drive her to the station, and pick her up in the evening when she gets back. No problem.

I get to her house a bit late, but there's still plenty of time to get to the bus station, which is only a couple of miles away. No big deal. Then we get into her car and she suddenly freaks out. I mean, completely.

The woman starts yelling at me out of the blue. She's mad beyond all reason because I was late and will make her miss her bus. I'm shocked. She has never behaved this way. She's acting very crazy. Her young son's also in the car and seems pretty scared. I try to calm her down but she's having a fit.

Naturally, we get to the bus station on time. She takes the bus and I drive back. I'm very confused. What is going on. Why has this woman gone bananas all of a sudden. Oh, Lord. Not again. I think of ditching her, but convince myself that one fit is not enough reason to give up the relationship. Holy hell. I think I've heard this one before…

In the early evening, Jesse is back with some news. Our romantic end-of-year getaway has turned into a gathering of friends. She tells me she has also invited Virginia and her daughter, who's also bringing a friend, to her parent's beach house. She's got to be kidding. What happened to our quality time together. I protest but she doesn't want to hear it. I think to myself, *how can she have changed so much in such a short time.* But as usual, we have great sex in the evening and I forget the entire thing. My pattern has literally grabbed me by the balls.

December 27, 2000. After the bus-station fiasco, we manage to get through the month without major incidents. The holidays have arrived and we're all heading for the beach. You guessed it. Our romantic getaway is a no-go. We'll have plenty of company. Jesse is starting to get on my nerves.

At the beach house, Jesse agrees to let me work on her energy to see if things improve a bit between us. We go to our room and I start fixing her energy centers. When I get to her heart, I feel a strange and sad energy. I channel it, cry for a while, and let everything run through me and down to the Earth.

After about one hour, I'm done with my treatment. Jesse feels very energized. She's very turned on. She starts grabbing me all over. She asks me what I have done to her. She tells me she wants me badly. I have no objection. She jumps on me and goes wild for a good half hour before she calms down. Hey. Maybe I've cured her aggressiveness. Not quite. As soon as we're done, "bad news Jesse" is back, shoving me away and storming out of the room.

December 30, 2000. I've pretty much had it with Jesse. I don't feel submissive or afraid she might reject me. I'm just plain mad. If I say anything at all, she tells me off immediately. If I try to be romantic, she yells at me. And what's worse, I don't even have any dope to help me cope with the situation.

By the end of the day, I decide I don't need this shit. That's it. I'm taking the bus home. I'd rather spend New Year's Eve alone than with this foolish bitch. But when I tell her I'm leaving, Jesse changes completely. Figures. Suddenly she's all smiles. Suddenly she's super-friendly. She begs me to stay. She apologizes for the way she has been treating me. I don't want to hear it. I just want her to take me to the bus station so I can get the hell out of here. She insists and asks me if we can talk it over at dinner. For some stupid reason, I agree.

We're sitting at a restaurant table and Jesse's telling me how much she likes me. All she wants is a chance to show me she can change. She's being very convincing. After a couple of kisses and a few beers, I sell myself cheap and end up accepting her apology.

December 31, 2000. We're at the beach. I'm enjoying the ocean, the warm weather, some fried fish, a beer, and my girlfriend's hot body. At some point I look around and realize all the other guys at the beach are checking her out as well. After all, she's awesome. I throw a jealousy fit, but nothing major.

Back at the house, I realize I overreacted and apologize. It's as if she had been waiting for a cue. In a burst of aggressiveness, Jesse uses my apology and turns things around. Now I'm the villain. Now I'm the crazy one.

I don't know what to say. I can't defend myself. I was wrong in throwing that fit. Jesse starts bullying me and soon things are worse than they were before last night's dinner. I think of leaving, but can no longer find a valid excuse for doing so.

Fireworks are blasting off into the clear night sky. People are drinking, singing, and flirting. The beach is all lit up. Beautiful women everywhere. Everyone's having a good time.

Not me. My strength's gone. My energy's gone. I feel bleak. I feel submissive. We head back to the house and I just go straight to bed. I feel like such a dumb ass. I'm such a dumb ass.

January 1, 2001. Jesse's in an unusually good mood and asks me if I want to go out with her. We drive off to town, where we have dinner and drinks. We then go to a motel for sex.

The motel room is incredible. Floor-to-ceiling mirrors surround a huge bed. The spacious bathroom is equipped with a sauna, a steam shower, and a bathtub with Jacuzzi facilities. The amenities even include a decent-sized swimming pool with a waterfall in an adjacent room.

But these paradisiacal elements simply aren't enough to make me feel at ease around Jesse. After spending time in the sauna, we're in bed fooling around. But then, just as she's ready to do her cowgirl thing, I can't get my egg roll up. I feel utterly powerless.

Surprisingly, Jesse tells me it's all good. She has run into this situation a couple of times before. I can't believe it. We're having a friendly chat in bed. I innocently suggest that her very aggressive behavior intimidates men and might cause them to fail, me included. Oh, *merde* (pardon my French). Why did I say that. She immediately gets very mad. She starts defending herself. She tells me I'm this and that. I decide to shut up and call it a night. We drive back to the house and go to sleep without uttering a word to each other.

January 2, 2001. After the previous night's catastrophe, I decide to do something to improve my sexual energy. I work on my energy centers. I pray and pray. I visualize myself full of power.

My efforts bear fruit. I get quite aroused and do Jesse in the shower. I feel a bit more empowered. But I still feel like crap. I don't want to be here at all. I don't want to be with someone who doesn't want me. I'm thinking about Virginia's daughter and her friend. My dirty mind's at it again. I'm thinking threesome. I wish Jesse and Virginia would go out for cigarettes or something and leave me alone in the house with these girls.

January 3, 2001. Jesse is jealous of the girls. Funny. She thinks they're checking me out. Well, fuck her. By now I don't care what she thinks anyway.

Jesse, the girls, and I drive to a deserted beach. We get to the beach and the three women take their tops off. I'm delighted. Am I glad saggy-tit Virginia decided to stay at the house. I'm thinking very naughty thoughts. I'd easily bang all three bitches at once on this beach. But I'm pretty sure Jesse would murder these girls before anything of the sort could happen. Anyway, I'm having a decent time. I flirt with Jesse. I flirt with the girls. And I spend all afternoon with a hard-on like you wouldn't believe.

January 5, 2001. A couple of days more and I'll be back home. I can't wait. My relationship sucks, there's no pot, and I can't even find my brand of cigarettes around this place.

Today Jesse, Virginia, and I are off to see Jesse's older brother, who lives in a local mental institution. No, I'm not kidding. Nor am I surprised when I hear that. But I feel bad for Jesse. I want to help. I figure she needs all the support she can get. I remind her I'm a psychologist and would also like to see her brother. But in a sudden burst of rage, she goes absolutely berserk and refuses. I try to insist on going inside with her, but she almost spanks me. What can I say. Fuck her. Again.

So Virginia and I remain outside, waiting for Jesse. And I'm telling myself this relationship is going nowhere. But my patterns have all settled in and won't let go. They're getting fed plenty.

January 8, 2001. I'm finally home and back to my senses. Although I'm still with Jesse, I've pretty much had it with her outrageous attitudes. Sex is great, but it's just not worth it. One more incident, one more issue, and I'll give her the boot for good.

At around noon, I call Jesse and she tells me to come over. Within a half hour, I'm at her place, ringing the doorbell. I ring and I ring. No answer. I ring again. Still no answer. I ask the custodian if he's seen her leave the building. Nope. She's definitely in. She might be taking a shower or something. I wait a while and ring again. No answer. I decide to call her from a pay phone. No answer. I try for about one hour and finally give up. That's it. As far as I'm concerned she can go and rot in hell.

I go home, roll me a nice hefty joint, and forget about Jesse. And she never calls me back either. Crazy fuck.

March 18, 2001. I haven't gotten laid in a while and am willing to screw anything that comes my way. So when Jesse and I meet on the street by chance, sex is all I have in mind. We cheerfully chat for a while and then set up a date for the evening.

At dinner, Jesse completely ignores the fact that our thing ended on such a bad note; she acts as if nothing bad has ever happened between us. I don't care. I'm over her.

But eventually we end up talking about our relationship. We start blaming each other for our split. Things are getting ugly. I soon tell her we should change the subject and finish our dinner. There's no way on Earth I'm going to miss out on this opportunity for sex.

After a few more beers, we leave and she drives me home. We get to my place. I invite her in for a nightcap. Yeah, right. Initially she says no, but it doesn't take much for her to consent and go up with me. We enter the apartment. She immediately pulls my pants down and proceeds to give me the best blowjob of my life. My tongue is dying for some action at this point, so we end up in a sixty-nine right on the floor. We then hop into bed, and she hops on me. Jesse is especially wild tonight. I guess she hasn't gotten laid in a while either.

After riding and riding and riding, she comes in an incredibly forceful, wet climax and with a look of triumph watches as I have a deep orgasm inside her.

Wow. What a trip. As our limp bodies lie in each other's arms, panting, I feel like saying something romantic, I feel like saying something nice. I tell her I really enjoy her company. I tell her I like her a lot. As usual, Jesse spoils the mood by being aggressive and saying something impolite. Whatever. I simply pretend I don't hear it. I'm fully satisfied and she can go away now. And never come back.

I've reached rock bottom. I don't have a girlfriend. I haven't had any work in a while. I barely have money to eat. I'm way behind on rent and will have to leave the apartment.

I'm fully aware that I must find a job if I'm going to keep up with my son's and my basic needs. So, in an(other) act of desperation, I decide to send out my résumé around town once again and see what happens.

Fortunately, my last-resort strategy works. I get a job as a teacher at one of the town's smaller ESL schools. The money sucks, but at least I can pay for transportation, food, and my son's education.

My aunt, Tammy's and Chuck's mother, feels sorry for us and offers us a room at Chuck's resort. That stinks. We're back in the countryside. But hey, better than nothing. At least I won't have to worry about rent. In fact, my financial worries have now been reduced to my long-time bank debt and the last few months of rent I could not pay at the apartment.

I head over to the bank and tell them I'll resume payments soon. Then I go to the apartment management company's office, tell them about my problem, and we settle on an agreement. Okay. Maybe I can sleep a little better now.

Oops. Not quite. A couple of weeks later, the stupid management company contacts me and says the apartment owner doesn't want to wait and has decided to sue my mom because she's listed as co-signer on my lease. Oh, shit. The last thing I want to do is involve her. This will be a pain in the ass.

I return to the management company's office and give them a whole lot of hell. I tell them there's no need for a lawsuit. We have an agreement. Furthermore, I've been dealing with them for years and have always paid on time. They tell me there's really nothing they can do about it. And there's nothing I can do about it either. Except beg around for some money, keep my fingers crossed and hope I'm able to fix this mess before my mother comes into the picture.

So off I go to humiliate myself. First, I travel to Rio to see Monica, my old sweetheart. She's happy to see me, but tells me she can't lend me any money. I then go to my father. As usual, he tells me he has no money whatsoever. I call my brother and he also says he has no money. I even go see Jesse in her office. She's thrilled to see me, but when I ask her for a loan, she just laughs in my face and says no. By the end of the day, I totally feel like shit. My efforts were useless.

Lawyer Mom

So my mother is forced to come to town for the back rent court hearing. Mom says she doesn't need a lawyer and will defend herself. She tells me she's read a few books and is ready for them. Yes, friend. Witness my mother's slightly unusual way of doing things. But despite her occasional loony behavior, she's a very intelligent woman and I can't wait to see how this comes out.

After waiting impatiently for hours, I see her coming out of the courthouse. She has a smile on her face. She's won. We can't believe it, but it's true. The dumb-ass, small-town lawyer wasn't able to make a case against us, because I had a written agreement with the management company. Yep, this time, I got it right. And my mother's now in the position of counter-suing for character defamation. But we decide not to do it. I just want to pay them back and get this over with. I contact the management company, tell them they're assholes, and set up a payment schedule.

Life is thankfully uneventful until late July, when I get a call from Shima. She wants me to interpret at her silent retreat. This time she wants to pay me even less for my time. Damn. She tells me I won't have to work much since it's a silent retreat. She tells me I'll greatly benefit from the work and implies I should be grateful.

I'm confused. I don't know what to think. I'm enraged because I feel I'm being taken advantage of, but at the same time I know she's right.

I do feel a little better when Shima asks me to translate that pattern-processing technique book I had been reading and is willing to pay me good money for it. Oh, well. I'm on vacation from work anyway and surely need the cash. I leave my son with sweet Ashlee and go.

The retreat ends up being crappy. I spend the entire time worrying about money. All I can think of is how Shima's ripping me off, how she's sucking on my energy, how I'm not being valued. Yuck. I'm immersed in my pattern and simply can't see beyond it.

A couple of months go by and I finish translating the book. I send it to Shima and hope to get paid as soon as possible. But I'm completely taken aback when she informs me I must demand payment from the publisher. What the heck. I thought I was dealing with her. I complain and remind her that wasn't our agreement. Useless. She gives me the publisher's phone number and tells me to contact them. Arrgh.

I spend weeks trying to get in touch with the stupid publishing company. Every time I call, I speak with a different person, who tells me to call some other day and speak with someone else. I'm being juggled around like a hot potato, which nobody wants to deal with. I'm pissed beyond belief.

Every once in a while clarity strikes and I can see that instead of forcing things with great stress and frustration, I should be working on releasing my pattern. But as soon as clarity comes, it goes and I'm back in my sick and repetitive slumber.

Eventually I give up trying and call Shima again. We have a heated argument and she finally agrees to take on responsibility for the payment of my fee. After all, she was the one who ordered the translation. But my ordeal isn't over just yet. Shima tells me to call Roberta, the rebirthing therapist, who will finally pay me. Or so she says.

I contact Roberta and she sends me a post-dated check for December. Fuckers. That's more than two months away. At least I'm done dealing with this bunch of low-lifes.

I need to work on my patterns very badly. I see no other way out. I pray hard for an improvement in my overall situation and soon get an answer.

Out of the blue, I get a call from Joyce. It's that time of the year. She wants me to interpret at the American shaman's workshop. She tells me she has no money and is willing to pay me very little. I hate Joyce. She's such a mischievous bitch. But this time I agree. Who knows. Maybe something good will come out of this.

I'm introspective at the shaman's workshop. I'm looking back at my life. I'm analyzing situations, relationships, and behaviors. I observe my ongoing struggle to overcome sick feelings and inhibitions. I can see how my self-esteem reflects my dependence on the female image. Lower self-esteem, steady relationships. Higher self-esteem, loose affairs and fuck buddies. What a mess.

But I feel detached from it all. I feel centered. There's something emerging within my system. It seems like a stronger, more stable personality. It shows itself for very brief periods, only to be once again overshadowed by the usual me, the old pothead and sex-addict character. But nevertheless it's here. It's here to stay. I know it. And it's becoming stronger by the day. Thank God. Boy, I've really come a long way.

Although my mind's not on women, some women at the workshop seem to have their mind on me. And thus I meet Stephanie. She lives in São Paulo, one of the largest and busiest cities in the world. She seems nice and mentally healthy. But we just chat a bit and exchange emails. I'm not in the mood for flirting.

Back from the workshop a few days later, I check my email. Stephanie has sent me a message. She wants me to come visit her. Wait up. Hold your horses. I've had it with bad relationships and won't have anything to do with this or any other woman before I get to know them. Let's keep this at the virtual level for now.

We exchange messages for a few weeks and everything's fine and dandy until one day, when she sends me a pretty nasty note. The woman's giving me shit about a joke I made on one of my emails. Hell, it was only a joke. And who does this bitch think she is anyway, telling me off when she doesn't even know me. She's clearly overreacting. Like I said before, I no longer need this crap in my life. I take a deep breath, write her back, and tell her to go away. But Stephanie comes to her senses and apologizes.

Reflection

Hmm, I'm beginning to see how this works. Stephanie's attitude largely depends on my own attitude. I think I've stumbled upon one of the major laws of human behavior. People act differently with different people. Maybe that's why I keep on getting the same response from all the women I relate to. My behavior is the common factor here. Once it changes, the response is bound to change. And so, for the time in my life, I've consciously understood the mechanism of my patterns. For the first time in my life, I feel I might have a choice.

FOURTEEN

Starting Over

The year 2001 is coming to an end and I'm on the verge of a breakdown. I'm at my weakest, yet something is pushing me forward. I've got to get away from this situation. I've got to get away from this place.

I decide to travel after the New Year festivities to find a place to live. This time it's for real. And I'm going to start by accepting Stephanie's invitation. Although I have no plans of moving to a big city, we've been on good terms for a while now, and I want to see what this woman's all about.

I begin a new series of active meditations to gather strength and energy for my move. In addition, I practice affirmations and visualizations on money, success, prosperity, and abundance. It's now or never. Do or die.

I spend Christmas at my father's and manage to borrow a bit of money for my trip. Before I leave, I sign up for a ten-day silent retreat, which is going to be held at my cousin's resort. It's free of charge, so I'll be okay. My son is spending his vacation at my mother's—perfect.

This retreat is different from the ones I'm used to attending. It's more of a solitary confinement kind of thing. I can stay in my room and meditate all day long. All by my lonesome. I meditate like never before, about fourteen hours every day. Pretty soon there's absolutely nothing on my mind. I feel a deep, inner peace. I feel empty and renewed.

Metamorphosis

I've noticed a cocoon just outside my room. Hmm. I understand it's a symbol of change, a sign of my metamorphosis. Every single day, I check on it and track its progress. Like me, the caterpillar's getting ready for a major rebirth.

Nature Speaks

After nine days of intense meditation, I'm just about ready to fly on out of here. I can see many things clearly. I'm indeed ready for change.

At about three in the morning on the last day of the retreat, something wakes me up. There seem to be insects on my bed. I turn the table lamp on and am startled to find hundreds, maybe thousands, of ants cruising up and down the wall right next to me and on my bed. Shit. One of my roommates is up as well and tells me this is a common local phenomenon where some species of ants periodically move their colony. And they have decided to do it tonight and across my fucking bed.

Big-time symbolism. It's high time I move my colony and get the hell out of here as well. I take a seat on the floor and watch as the ants do their thing. After a couple of hours, there isn't a single ant to be found anywhere and I can reclaim my sleeping quarters.

When I leave my room in the morning, I notice that the cocoon I'd been observing is hollow. The caterpillar's metamorphosis is finally complete. And so is mine.

I waste no time. By late afternoon, I'm at the bus station. On the bus, I'm thinking about São Paulo. So crowded, so polluted. I've gotten used to living in a small town surrounded by nature. There's no way I'm moving to a crappy metropolis...

Stephanie picks me up early the following day. Wow. She's cuter than I remember from the workshop. Still a brunette (you never know with women these days), bosomy body, mildly freckled skin, big dark eyes. And adorable little dimples on her cheeks when she smiles.

We drive to her place, which is in one of the most expensive neighborhoods in town. The woman's a struggling photographer, but her daddy is very wealthy and lavishly supports her lifestyle.

We spend most of the afternoon getting to know each other. We talk about our interests, our families, our future expectations.

Then she suddenly gets up, sits on my lap, and shoves her ample breasts in my face. We're not wasting any time here, now are we. We make out for a little while. She takes me by the hand and leads me to her bedroom. We remove each other's clothes and get down to business on her huge California king bed. Slow. Sensual. Passionate. We're certainly off to a good start.

And so my short visit turns into a ten-day romantic honeymoon. As for São Paulo, it's funny how I begin to see the city with different eyes. Such a vast universe, full of possibilities, many things to do and people to meet. My, I've been hiding in a hole for too long. I like this fast life. I like the lights. I might as well stay here for a while. Does my new girlfriend have anything to do with my sudden change of heart. You betcha.

My hopes of remaining in Stephanie's house without spending any money are gone when she invites me out to a live show. I was dreading this moment. I decide to once again be honest right off the bat and tell her I'm going through great changes, which include being temporarily broke. She doesn't seem to mind. She'll lend me the money and I can pay her back later. I'm relieved but I'm also annoyed. This gigolo thing's driving me crazy.

By the end of my stay, I'm having such a good time that I decide my search is over. This is the place for me. Yep. I think I've heard this all before. But I pretend I haven't. Stephanie's excited. I'm heading home and will return with my résumé and hopefully some money to rent a place of my own. Stephanie's house is nice and I can stay here for a while, but like I said, I ain't no gigolo.

Back in sweet cousin Ashlee's house, I'm preparing my move. I'm almost good to go, except for one major issue I still have to deal with. My son. It's simply not viable for him to continue staying at Ashlee's home. And he can't come to Stephanie's either.

Fortunately, he won't have to. His mom Kate's moving back to her hometown, which happens to be São Paulo. Perfect timing. I completely abhor the idea of seeing my son in his silly mother's custody, but on the other hand it might be good for him. They haven't seen each other for ages. Maybe I can let go of the tiring father-mother role and let his mom be a mom for a change.

Furthermore, he knows his daddy will see him every two weeks for sure and will snatch him back as soon as possible. I talk to Kate and she's delighted to have him stay with her for a while.

So I travel to São Paulo to find a job. It only takes me a few days to get a position as a teacher in a business ESL school just a few blocks from Stephanie's house. And what's more, they need a new service manager and I'll be promoted within a month. I couldn't be happier. All I need now is to find a place to live.

I visit my father, tell him of my plans, and ask him for some money. As usual, he dishes out the I-don't-have-any-cash routine, but I convince him to take out a bank loan on my behalf. I really don't need much money; just enough for a couple of months' rent. And with my new job, I'll pay him back soon.

Good Vibrations

Things are starting to look up for me. But the best news of all concerns my mother. She has decided to sell her apartment. The sale has earned her quite a lot of money and her life has changed completely. And so has our relationship. She's a much more pleasant person. She's out of her victim pattern. We become closer. We become friends. She offers to pay my old bank loan. Sure. After so many years of bitching and moaning in my ears, I guess we can call it even. I also settle my old rent dues and am finally debt-free.

My brother is managing Mom's finances. He wants to make her money last. We don't want to see her in poverty again. And that's a great idea, because she has already started living the good life. She takes trips, gives money away, and treats herself to fancy clothes. I sure hope she doesn't spend it all too quickly.

And so I rent a nice flat in São Paulo and finally move out of that stinky town for good. My boxes are still at Ashlee's, but that's not a problem. I'll be back to pick them up later. Also, I haven't been smoking pot for a while now and feel nice and clean.

Too Good to Be True

I'm spending the night at Stephanie's. We're having a good time munching on some cheese and drinking wine in front of the TV. We've just fooled around and are both relaxed. At least it seems this way. At some point we get into a discussion about recycling, which is what the TV show is about. Fine. I love a good debate.

But then, all of a sudden Stephanie starts overreacting. Our impersonal discussion turns into a heated argument. I try to cool things off, but she's on a roll. Pretty soon, she's attacking me as if I were the root cause of all the trash in the world. She's being rude. She's yelling at me for no reason whatsoever. I freak out. I thought I had had my share of this crap in my life.

I tell her I won't accept this kind of behavior. I ask her to be more polite. But she won't listen to me. Quite the contrary. Now she has forgotten all about the recycling issue and is accusing me of being a jerk. Now all she really wants is to pick a fight. She says I don't value her opinion. She says I don't listen to her. What the hell is this girl babbling about. She seems to be in another world. Goddamnit. Another crazy woman.

I try and try to reason with her, but it's useless. I'm terribly stressed out. It seems we are getting nowhere, no matter what I do. Maybe it's best if I leave.

I take off and walk around the block a few times. How could this have happened. We were doing great. And what exactly am I doing. Why can't I stay and find a plausible way out of this situation. I'm behaving like fucking crazy Cara.

I finally calm down and decide to come back. We still argue for a while, but soon get tired and go to sleep.

The following morning, things are much better between us. I feel as if I'm waking up from a bad dream. I want to forget the entire thing and concentrate on my new job.

As promised, I've been promoted to service manager at the ESL school, which means I'm fully in charge of the branch's academic resources. I have an administrative counterpart, the center director, who's in charge of sales and marketing.

I don't get along very well with my director. I think she's full of shit. But I put up with her because I've finally started to earn good money and really don't need financial trouble coming my way anytime soon.

All in all, though, I'm highly motivated and inspired in my brand new position. I have a few people working under me and that makes me feel worthy and responsible.

Sick Again

It's been a couple of months since my move and already things between Stephanie and me have become sort of stale. I'm talking about sex. She's full of traumas and I don't enjoy treating her as another patient, but that's basically what I end up doing. And to make matters worse, whenever I spend the night at her house, I'm forced to sleep in the guest room. Stephanie feels her personal space is being invaded if she shares her humongous bed with me. Weird, but true.

But other than that, our relationship is moving along smoothly. That is, except when she gets into her periodical mood swings.

And that's exactly what happens one evening when she freaks out on me once again. Our civilized conversation quickly turns into a series of personal attacks. I try to reason with her, but she just won't listen. She uses everything I say against me. After a few more useless attempts, I tell her I have a headache and retire to the guest room to recharge my batteries.

I'm lying in bed thinking about this odd situation. Although our relationship isn't ideal, Stephanie and I get along most of the time. Our last argument was about a month ago, when she went totally mad for no apparent reason. Exactly like today. What kind of weird pattern is this. Her fits seem to be linked to the time of the month. Unless…

Could this be an enhanced that-time-of-the-month symptom. It would explain her unusual behavior. I must perform some tests. Great. Just like the old days in college with the lab rats.

Let's see. If my theory is correct, I should be able to observe two events. First, she should have her period shortly. Second, her mood swings should reappear in about a month.

About a week later, I notice Stephanie has added tampons to her grocery list. My first hypothesis has been confirmed. All I need to do now is count the days until she blows up on me again.

Another month goes by and, bingo. Crazy-ass Steph's back like clockwork. But this time I'm prepared. Or so I think. I sit her down and tell her what's going on. Not a good idea. She's in the midst of her crisis and won't hear a single word I say. In fact, it only makes things worse. Then, in a flash of clarity, I come up with the perfect solution. Why hadn't I thought of this before. It's simple: when that time of the month comes, as soon as I realize she has started with the shit, I disappear for a couple of days and leave her to her own thing.

I have started an energetic revolution at my workplace. I'm like a freaking tornado. Things have changed completely and even our director has been fired. Her replacement is great. My new director's smart and playful and approves of my goals and ideas.

We quickly create a warm atmosphere and I'm happy to go to work every day, especially because there are plenty of hot female students around, and they are all of age. I work and flirt, flirt and work. I feel like I'm in a harem.

In the meantime, the cash my dad borrowed on my behalf is gone. This means that I can no longer afford living in my luxurious and expensive flat. Well, it was pretty much a façade, because I spend most of my evenings at Stephanie's anyway. Nevertheless, I need to find a place I can call my own. I don't think Stephanie's personal space would be able to cope with a tenant, at least not right now. So I rent a cheap and stinky extended-stay hotel room for the sake of political correctness.

But the situation makes me uneasy. I hate staying in my small hotel room. I find it very, very depressing. To top it all, I'm sick of not having my stuff with me. I want my clothes, my books, my tapes, my gadgets.

And so our relationship reaches a deadlock. What do I have to do to have her accept the fact that we are already living together. Hmm. Maybe I need to formally ask her out. Maybe I need to ask Stephanie's father for permission to date her or something. After all, she does seem to have old-fashioned values.

I pay a visit to my girlfriend's all-powerful father on his own terrain. He warmly greets me as I walk into his office. We talk for a while. He's delighted by the fact that I have come to ask for his blessing. And I'm amused. What a joke. I assure him I have the best intentions towards his daughter. He gives me his permission and we bid farewell. It's as simple as that.

Stephanie's anxiously waiting outside. I come out and tell her the good news. She's very excited. We go to her house and actually have good sex. Then she finally invites me to move in with her.

A few days later, I borrow her car, drive to Ashlee's and pick my stuff up. I then get back to Stephanie's house, unload my boxes, and pile them up under the staircase. You know, I really don't plan on living here for long.

Now that I'm relatively stress-free, I can focus on my goals. I want to rent my own place as soon as possible. After all, I see my son every two weeks and constantly assure him I'll take him back. And I have no intention of breaking my promise.

News of the brave young man who faced the powerful father figure soon spreads and everybody in Stephanie's large family wants to meet me. She's the third of six sisters, all of whom lead very successful lives. Her family's of Lebanese descent and loves to throw lavish parties, where everyone gets together, eats like pigs, and catches up on the latest gossip.

I'm first introduced to two of her younger siblings. Joan is a psychologist and nutritionist. She owns a restaurant. She's also hot as hell. Denise is the crazy one. She's very outgoing. She's an engineer and owns an entire apartment building. Denise quickly finds out I'm a psychologist and starts babbling about her love life. Hello. Some client potential here.

I'm introduced to the rest of Stephanie's family. Her oldest sister is married to a renowned surgeon. Another of her sisters manages a few of her daddy's farms. Finally there's her youngest sister, who's involved in real estate. And last but not least, I get to meet the matriarch. She seems to be one of those sophisticated ladies who has it all but still suffers from depression. Stephanie's parents are divorced and her mother lives in high style, all paid for by Daddy's alimony, of course. I have been dealing with high-society people all my life, and favorably impressing Stephanie's mother is a piece of cake.

One of the things that attracted me to Stephanie was her interest in esoteric matters. Hey, we met at a shamanic workshop. So it's no surprise to me when I find out she's in therapy with this weird, but cool, guy who deals with energy and stones. His work's pretty amazing and I eventually start seeing him once a month.

Another good thing about my new "therapist" is that he has pot and is happy to give me some. I haven't smoked in a while. Stephanie's not really into getting high, but she doesn't mind that I do. That's a big plus in our relationship.

My life's getting back on track once again. And as July is right around the corner, I've decided to further my development by attending Shima's annual retreat. The good news is that for the first time, I'll be joining the group as a paying participant. No more sour deals, no more hassle, no more stress—just good old meditation. I speak with corporate management at work and convince them to allow me take twenty days off. I tell them I'm going to an extremely important congress.

In a Flash

I'm very relaxed at the retreat. Although I still get stuck in a few sickly loops of thought, sometimes for days, I feel my patterns are loosening their grip on me. I feel clear. I feel present.

The two weeks fly by and before I know it, I'm back in São Paulo living the good life. And I'm not surprised to see that my recent meditation efforts have brought about some positive changes.

Steph's sister Denise wants me to be her therapist. She also wants me to conduct a therapy group consisting of her and three of her lady friends. And another of her friends has heard about me and also wants therapy. Damn. In less than a year, I go from poor struggling English teacher to school manager and highly sought-after therapist.

But I'm at war with a force that just won't allow me to have it all. As you might expect, as my finances improve, my love life deteriorates.

Stephanie hasn't been able to adapt to our new lifestyle. She still feels her personal space is being invaded. I'm still sleeping in her guest room. We seldom have sex. I'm no longer attracted to her. Our relationship has fallen into an unhealthy routine.

One day, Stephanie throws a party at her house. Her sister Joan's here and looks mighty nice. I can't stop staring at her. And she knows it. We play a dangerous flirting game all night long. Luckily, no one notices and nothing happens, but I fear next time I may not be able to control myself.

I really don't want any trouble, with Stephanie or anyone else. My life's evolving into something good, and there's no way in hell I'm going to let a stupid pattern ruin it.

November 2002

I've invited Denise to come to the shaman's workshop with me. I think it'll do her good. Stephanie doesn't want to go and doesn't care that I take her sister. Oh, well.

The shaman tours many cities, and I've chosen a location where I'll be as far away from Joyce as possible. No more translations or interpreting for me—at least when they involve Momma Joyce. I'm glad I have the money to pay for my trip and take part as a regular participant.

The workshop's pretty dense: many harsh stories, many sad situations, and many people suffering. And I'm still working on my mother. I tell the shaman our relationship has improved quite a bit. He tells me what I want to hear: that this will eventually be reflected on my relationship with other women. He does his usual stuff and I feel confident positive changes are bound to happen at some point in the near future.

Denise is working on her heavily distorted father image. As I watch her session, I begin to understand Stephanie's difficulties with men and sex. Her dad is constantly punishing his six daughters and his ex-wife for not having had a male heir to the throne. Of course, their individual reactions differ, but mostly have to do with rejection and fear of the male figures in their life.

As much as I now understand Stephanie's behavior towards me, I'm not sure I want to deal with certain attitudes anymore.

As with the other groups I attended in the past, I notice the first signs of change as soon as I get back. And they're at work. We get the news that our school has been sold, and word is around that the new owners will greatly improve things. Sweet. Maybe they'll acknowledge my hard work and promote me. I could surely use some acknowledgment right about now.

The ESL school's new owners soon take over and start interviewing everybody. They promise us many things. We'll have an entirely new structure. Things will change for the better. Even Mr. Skeptical here is optimistic after his interview with the general manager.

However, our initial expectations at work are shattered when the company's new owners quickly turn out to be complete assholes. All they care about is money. Never mind academic quality. They try to turn our schools into giant cash registers.

My director's fired. Her replacement is an emotionless robot with no mind of her own. She only does what she's told. We no longer have the cohesiveness we had before, and the work environment starts to deteriorate.

Things also change at home. Soon after the New Year, Steph tells me one of her friends is getting married and will move in with her husband. She'll vacate her fully furnished apartment and is looking for someone to rent it to. Unbelievable. I'll have my own place. Finally. I'll be able to unpack my stuff. Finally. My son will be able to come back home. And who knows, my relationship with Stephanie might even work out. I'll have my independence and she'll have her personal space back.

Sadly, my positive expectations are once again blown to bits. Instead of getting closer, Stephanie and I actually start drifting apart even more. My newly acquired freedom has brought about some unexpected and unwanted perks.

Now, every time I try to eff my girlfriend, she turns my advances into a quarrel. For some reason or other, she's trying to avoid sexual contact. It seems like some sort of bizarre defense mechanism. Maybe she thinks I've rejected her by moving out of her house. Maybe she thinks I no longer like her. Maybe she's trying to avoid getting hurt.

To tell you the truth, I don't know if I really care. Having my own place means I no longer have to take any shit from anyone, including Stephanie. So whenever she gives me crap I simply retreat to my headquarters and ignore her sorry ass.

And I have plenty to do in my new home. Kate has become my dope connection, so I have no problem smoking myself into a stupor whenever I feel like it. I also purchase a laptop and keep myself busy with a brand new hobby: surfing the Web.

July 2003

It's retreat time. Awesome. Away from the girlfriend, away from work. Two weeks completely immersed in peace. Two weeks completely immersed in nature. I purify my body, mind, and soul. I'm temporarily detached from my thoughts and patterns.

After the retreat, I'm psyched for some more big changes. I'm finally ready to support my son. I talk to Kate and she's happy to fork him over. Especially because she has just had a new child. What an irresponsible woman. Making babies all over the place.

My family members are also happy and relieved to see us reunited. I even manage to convince my father to take care of that loan he took out on my behalf. Super. This is the last time I ever ask him for money. It's about time.

I'm very excited to have my son back. And he's very excited to be back. He was away from me for over a year. But he's safe now. He gets a brand new place to stay. He gets new toys. He gets new clothes. He gets to eat well. He gets to go to a private school. We make arrangements with Kate and she promises to come pick him up on alternate weekends. Let's see if she keeps her promise.

I've noticed a few people at work are constantly on the computer. What's this all about. Excessive dedication, perhaps. I do some snooping around and find out they're all hooked on online chat rooms. Say what. I'm new to the Internet. I've never heard of this before. Although I don't think engaging on this sort of stuff at work is a good idea, I'm curious and will give it a try sometime.

Master Bates

I guess "sometime" has come sooner than I thought. I'm alone for the weekend. My son's spending some time with his mother. Stephanie's very busy with some photography event.

After a nice joint, I go online and decide to enter a chat room. At first I'm a bit shy, but I soon realize that my identity is safe behind the computer screen. Hey, this thing lets me to be anyone I want to be. I can create my very own persona. I can live out my fantasies and set inhibitions aside. And the best thing about it all is that everyone else is doing the same thing. Cool. Exciting. My very own make-believe world.

I soon start chatting with some girl. I tell her about myself. She tells me about herself. She tells me she's a model. Probably bullshit, but who cares. I can't see her anyway. (Remember, these are the old Internet days and webcams are a rarity.)

We start seducing each other. We start talking dirty. Then a very weird thing happens. We start having virtual sex. I tell her what I'm doing to her. She tells me what she's doing to me. Very strange indeed, but it's kind of hot. Then she asks me to keep writing while she masturbates. *I want to grab you. And turn you. And kiss you. And bite you. And do you.* Hey, I'm good at this. And I like it. Then it's her turn. *I want to suck you. And lick you. And sit on you.* And here I am, "taking matters into my own hands."

Then it's over. Wow. Amazing. Not the real thing, but close enough. I feel like having a cigarette. But the girl is still writing. She says she enjoyed our chat. She says she's in love with me. She wants me to send her a picture. Whoa, whoa, whoa. This is my fantasyland. There's no way I'll send someone I don't even know my picture or any real information about myself. Nooo way. And she might be a dog. And I have a girlfriend.

I freak out and leave the chat room. But I'll most probably be back. I might want to do this again some other time.

There's a growing feeling of unease throughout the ESL school. Our new management plan is going down the drain. Students are flocking out and enrolling in better schools. We're all scared and fear some of us will be laid off. I know I'll be one of those people, especially because I treat my new corporate boss like the fool that he is. Well, this is all his fault. He has managed to screw up the company in less than a year, and his bad academic practices have caught up with him. Dildo.

I constantly tell him off. I constantly outsmart him. I embarrass him in front of my colleagues. I'm acting the same way I did with my former boss Joshua. I can see that. But this time, instead of trying to fix things, I start looking for another job. I've had enough of people who don't value my skills. I can certainly get by as a therapist, but I don't want to simply get by. I need something else to supplement my income.

One day, I come across an online ad. A company needs translators for a long-term job and I think I might qualify. I give them a call and set up an interview.

At my interview, I find out the company needs independent translators to work on a lengthy lawsuit having to do erectile dysfunction pills. *Perfect,* I think to myself. *Here I am, once again working on powerlessness.* The company owner's very impressed with my résumé. He wants me to join his team. Not as an employee, though. I'm told I'll have to start my own business. There will be plenty of work. Plenty. Great. Bring it on.

I get my first translation a few days later. About one hundred pages of lawsuit bullshit. My team leader tells me that as soon as I'm done, he'll have more work for me. I feel I'm about to get my big break here. I work at night. I work on weekends. Hell, I even work while I'm at my shitty work. Fuck it.

I know my days are numbered at the ESL school, but now I don't really care. I get to work at nine and leave at five, sometimes four o'clock. My asshole boss wants us to work fifteen-hour days with no extra pay. Dream on, buddy. He demands full dedication from his employees, but isn't willing to offer anything in return.

It takes me less than a week to finish my first translation. I'm quick and accurate. I'm impressed with myself. I didn't know I could translate that kind of shit. I immediately get another job. This time the translation's around five hundred pages long. I'm delighted. I'm going to be rich.

About two weeks later, my jackass boss finally fires me. I'm a bit sad because of the friends at the ESL school, especially the woman friends, I'll be leaving behind, but overall I'm okay. I get paid a lot of money because my contract was terminated early. Ha, ha. I'm now my own boss. I get to make my own schedule. And since Steph and I barely see each other anymore, I can work on translations, spend more time with my son, and increase my therapy client base. Oh, and surf the World Wide Web.

Charming the Snake

Another one of those home-alone weekends. It's Friday evening. I get high and enter a chat room. By now I'm a seasoned chatter. I've been practicing. In no time at all, I'm juggling ten different girls. Nothing special is happening. I light up another cigarette.

Then a woman attracts my attention. She tells me her name's Julie. She tells me she's thirty-five. She tells me she has an incredibly hot body, and is an architect. For all I know, it's all bullshit, but then again, I don't care. We end up chatting for many hours and have virtual sex at the crack of dawn. At about eight o'clock in the morning, I finally turn off the computer and go to bed.

The following day, I blow Stephanie off and stay home to see if I can meet up with Julie again online. It doesn't take long before I find her. Tonight we have a more intimate chat. Julie says she's married, but her husband's never around. And when he is, he doesn't care much for her. The same old yadda yadda. A needy woman in search of excitement to help her cope with boring and lonely married life. Blarg. I've heard enough. Let's change the subject and get to some action.

We tease each other silly and are soon copulating virtually. Me this, you that, we this, we that. Then dirty Julie suggests we go beyond our comfort zone. She wants to hear my voice. She wants my phone number. She wants to have sex over the phone. Uh-oh. I'm hesitant, but by now I'm so horny that I give her my cell number. Hope I haven't made a mistake.

She calls me and we cut straight to the chase. She has a very sweet voice. We start talking dirty. Very dirty. We shoot seductive remarks back and forth. Julie's telling me about how she's touching herself while we speak. She tells me her legs are spread apart. She tells me she's not wearing anything under her tiny skirt. She tells me she wants me inside her. I tell her I'm touching myself. I tell her I'd do unimaginable things to her if she were here. I tell her exactly what she wants to hear. We moan and groan over the phone until we both reach intense orgasms.

Wow. This is hot. It's wonderfully naughty and new. We are both beat and say good night, but not before setting another date for the near future. I think Julie might be my first virtual fuck-buddy. And I wonder if this means I'm cheating on Stephanie.

Julie and I have sex over the phone almost every day for three weeks. Then, one Saturday evening, she tells me we won't be able to talk. She's going out with her husband. Fine.

I go online and meet another woman, Lauren. We spend the entire weekend doing all kinds of virtual sins. I mean, every trick in the book. By Monday morning, I've masturbated so much I couldn't produce a single sperm cell if my life depended on it.

Reflection

I feel weird. Without even noticing it, I have become addicted to these chat rooms. I rarely get out of the house. Why go out and struggle to get noticed in bars or parties when I can stay in, get high, order a pizza, and have sex with as many women as I can manage. And it's not only sex. It's virtual sex. It's clean, efficient, and safe. No STDs, no AIDS, no herpes, no babies. If a woman freaks out on me, freedom is just a click away. Lord Almighty. I'm definitely being seduced to the dark side.

But the new and healthy me isn't willing to compromise so easily. Although this solitary lifestyle is seemingly very attractive, deep down it enhances my feelings of anxiety and neediness. And I'm fully aware of that. I've had my fair share of the bad and the ugly. I'm ready for some good in my life.

So, after a few days of intense and productive introversion, I decide I want to clean up my act, one bitch at a time. I call Julie. I tell her I'm sick of virtual sex and want to meet her in person. As I expect, she freaks out and gives me the perfect excuse to break off our thing. No need to even bother about Lauren. She has no way of contacting me anyway. And as for Stephanie, I can no longer deal with her mood swings and rude attitudes. I've reached rock bottom. I'm ready to put a stop to that pronto.

Stephanie and I meet up at her house and I tell her we can no longer be together. We just don't get along. She can't believe I'm breaking up with her. She starts with her usual thing. She cries. She plays the victim. She begs for acknowledgement. She begs for love. No use. I won't give in.

Then she changes her tactics. She yells at me. She accuses me of being unfair. She tells me I'll regret my decision. Not this time, sweetheart. I'm immune to her rants. I remain calm and let her wind down. She eventually runs out of arguments and kicks me out of her house. Oh, well. Bye, bye, Stephanie.

FIFTEEN

Shin Aleph Hey

My company's blooming. I've managed to gain a couple of large clients who have kept me very busy with translations. And it's great timing, because unfortunately my work with the erectile-dysfunction-pill guy is over. No problem. It was a great start. This first job got me standing on my own two feet financially. It made me into a man. In a sense, the little magic pills worked wonders for me, too.

I Want It All, and I Want It Now

With my finances in order, I'm now completely obsessed with the idea of making my love life work. I finally see what a dork I've been all these years. I've let patterns manipulate me and dictate the rules in pretty much every relationship I've had.

But not anymore. I'll be the one making choices from now on. I'll be the one in charge of my own destiny. I'll be steering the course of my life. I'll be the master of my own fate. Damn. I'm amazed I'm even able to have these thoughts...

One day, I sit down at home and start imagining what my perfect woman would be like. I jot down a list of characteristics and post it on my wall. Then I close my eyes and picture my perfect girl. She's kind. She's understanding. She loves me to death. She's smart. She's successful. She's beautiful. She's hot.

I work on myself to accept the fact that I deserve to get what I want. But I don't want much. For once in my life, all I want is a relationship that simply works.

November 5, 2003
The Universe is conspiring in my favor. I get a promotional email from Joyce. Our friend the shaman will soon be around, and the theme of his work this year involves soul mates. What a coincidence. I have to attend one of his workshops and see what this is all about. I don't believe in that soul mate bullshit, but hey. I'll definitely go, if nothing else, for the sake of another cure.

November 14, 2003
The shaman now works with his partner, whom he calls "Soul Mate." Cute. The guy is a German seer who teaches Kabbalah, some hard-core mysticism.

During my session, I'm told I've been calling out for my soul mate and that she's near. Say what. Oh. I realize this possibly refers to my conscious decision to search for the perfect woman. If this is what they mean, then sure, I've surely been calling out for my soul mate.

Of the teachings introduced in the workshop, one catches my particular attention. It has to do with certain combinations of Hebrew letters that supposedly produce a number of magical formulas for various purposes. And one of these formulas is aimed at helping one find his or her soul mate.

You know, I'm an experienced bloke when it comes to spells and spirits and things of the sort. But I've never seen anything like this before and find it hard to believe that a simple combination of letters will lead me to my perfect woman. Well, if I don't try it out I'll never know, will I. And so I memorize the little formula and repeat it in my head over and over, and over, and over...

November 16, 2003
I'm thinking of ways to go about the search for my perfect girl. Strangely enough, I now find myself completely consumed by the soul mate idea. But I'm trying hard to be objective. What would Aristotle have done in a similar situation. I start sorting out possible soul mate candidates among the women I know.

First, the most peculiar thing happened to me during this workshop. I really can't explain why or how, but I fell madly in love with Paula, the woman sitting next to me. Just like that, out of the blue. Nothing really happened between us, but I can't stop thinking about her. I feel like a teenager. I close my eyes and see her shiny figure on a pedestal sending me warm rays of love and desire. She's definitely candidate number one.

Then there's Nicole, the girl I met during my chakra training back in the late nineties. Even though we never got to spend any time together, we've had strong feelings towards each other ever since and have kept in touch over the Internet. Clearly soul mate material and most certainly candidate number two.

Finally, candidate number three's got to be my old girlfriend, Monica, whom I've never really been able to let go of. We still speak occasionally and I think that flame may still be there. Okay. Now I've got my list. I can start checking them out, one by one.

Open Heart

I'm lying in bed, my eyes closed. My body feels light as a feather. My breath is slow and relaxed. I can see Paula's image before me, glowing with beauty; immaculate, pure, unreachable. I examine my emotions. Deep infatuation, admiration, a mix of excitement and bewilderment, longing. I'm a medieval troubadour and she's my muse. How peculiar is that.

Then everything expands and for a moment I experience a most wonderful and unexpected feeling. It flows from my chest area. My heart's opening. I feel humble. I feel grateful. Thank you, thank you, thank you, thank you.

I'm now fully aware that Paula's just a projection of my own inner female side. She's the one I'm really singing odes of love to. She's the one I'm really longing for. She's the one. She's eternally here. She's eternally mine.

Then the entire thing vanishes just as quickly as it had come. And I'm left with an incredibly sweet taste of paradise. Wow. Wow. That was one hell of a trip. It really blew me away. And the funny thing is, my feelings for Paula are gone. Candidate number one's out of the picture.

November 25, 2003
I now want to focus on Nicole. I feel there's a lot of potential here. I send her an email and tell her we absolutely have to meet in person. Enough of this virtual shit. She promptly replies and agrees. She tells me she's coming to town for a workshop in December. Perhaps we can spend some alone time somewhere. Great. I'll make the arrangements and prepare for the very special occasion. I have a good feeling about this.

In the afternoon, I get a call from my friend the shaman himself. He wants me to interpret at his workshop at a nearby beach resort. I gladly agree. And since I need the cure more than I need the money this time, I tell him I'll be happy to exchange my fee for another session.

November 29, 2003
During my session at the workshop, the shaman dissolves a longstanding attachment I had to my son's mother, Kate. I'm told she had been riding my ass for many lives. Something about Karma. But it's all over now. They have released me from her bondage.

After my session, I tell everyone about my girl Nicole and our curious story. My fellow participants agree she must be my soul mate. I'm very excited. And I repeat the soul mate formula over and over again like a madman.

December 1, 2003
Oh, yeah. I get a phone call from my soul mate. She'll be arriving in four days. Everything's ready for our big weekend. I've booked the best suite at a wonderful resort in the mountains. It'll be our love nest. I'm fired up. I'm horny. I'm hungry for love.

December 5, 2003
I've come to the airport to meet my soul mate. Her plane has arrived. My heart beats faster. She'll be coming out of the restricted area any minute now. Wait. There she is.

And what a disappointment. As soon as I see her, my feeling of exhilaration turns into disbelief, denial, and rejection. My dick goes completely limp. I don't know why. I just can't explain it; somehow I know she's not the one. A voice inside me screams she's not the one. Shit. My feelings are so strong I want to call the whole thing off and send her away.

This can't be right. She's my soul mate. I'm sure of it. Maybe I'm just scared. Maybe my feelings will change. Well, now that we got this far it makes no sense not seeing this through to the end.

December 6, 2003

It's no use. We've been together for a couple of days and my feelings of rejection have only gotten worse. The woman's not what I had imagined her to be. She doesn't utter a word all weekend long. The strong sexual attraction I felt before is gone. We do have sex, but it sucks.

I'm very confused. I can't get this soul mate idea off my mind. It has turned into an insatiable monster with a life of its own. And it's frantically signaling in Nicole's direction. But what can I do. I want to puke when I see the damned woman.

December 7, 2003

The weekend's finally over. I want to get the hell away from this woman as quickly as possible. We drive to her workshop. I drop Nicole off and disappear from sight like a polished stone dropped in the deep blue sea.

But Nicole hasn't given up. I get home and see she has sent me a huge flower arrangement. Man. Maybe I was mistaken after all. Maybe she's my soul mate and I just couldn't see it. It *has* to be her. I may be missing out on the greatest opportunity of my life. I'm so stupid.

Hold on. God, I'm once again compromising. How can this woman be my soul mate if I can't stand her. How can this woman be my soul mate if she doesn't turn me on. How can this woman be my soul mate if we can't even communicate properly. It's obvious she's not the one. Confusion, confusion, confusion.

December 10, 2003

I feel exhausted. I'm too entangled in this mess to find a way out. This sick anxiety has created an unfortunate situation, and my neediness pattern is taking full advantage of it. This entire thing is bogus. And there's only one thing to do. Out of sheer despair, I sit on my couch, close my eyes, and pray hard for some clarity.

And clarity comes. I know what I need to do. I must remove all the pending relationships from my life and make room for my soul mate. I realize I can't remember the last time I had no pending affair with a woman in one way or another. There has always been a gal there, taking up space. Even when physically alone, my thoughts were polluted with all sorts of desires for women.

So that's it. I'll forget all about the candidate approach and pursue a clean-up campaign.

December 11, 2003

I begin to sweep my life clean of evil, so that good may come in. I send emails to both Nicole and Monica. I tell them our thing was great while it lasted, but it's time for me to move on. Monica is busy with her own life and understands my move. Sweet. We're now simply friends. Nicole writes back and wants to give our relationship another chance, but I ignore her plea. I don't even reply. I've said enough.

It's time to rid myself of Kate. The energetic work was done during my shamanic session. Our only connection involves the fact that she's my dope connection. Oh, and she's the mother of my child, but that's his problem, not mine. He lives with me and she can no longer blackmail my ass for anything. So I just stop buying pot from her. I can get it somewhere else. Phew. That's enough for one day.

December 12, 2003

I feel delusional. Soul mate, soul mate, soul mate. My common sense has vanished. I've now decided to rely on child intuition. I tell my nine-year-old son we're playing a little game. I tell him a new woman's coming into our lives. I ask him to close his eyes and describe her to me. My son giggles and plays along. He sees a blonde woman who has two children.

His answer totally surprises me. Where the heck did he come up with that. Where the heck did that come from. I don't know anyone who fits that description. At least not yet. Hmm. I'll make sure to be on the lookout.

Late at night, I'm surfing the Web and enter a chat room. I'm not in the mood for sex. I want to find someone nice I can talk to for a while. After a few fruitless attempts, I finally start chatting with a decent human being. We introduce ourselves and dish out the usual information. Me, six-foot-two, two-hundred-ten-pound, dark-haired male, unmarried, one child. She, five-foot-three, one-hundred-thirty-pound, blonde female, divorced, two children. A little on the chubby side, but I really don't care. Not tonight. *Wait.* Did she say blonde and two kids. I'll be damned.

We go on talking and I can barely hold my excitement. Damn. My kid hit the spot dead on. Could she really be my soul mate. What an amazing and fortuitous way to meet.

She eventually sends me her photo. I'm even more turned on. She looks gorgeous. I absolutely have to check this woman out in person and see if she's for real. She agrees to meet me and we set up a date at a local restaurant.

By the time I turn my computer off, the soul mate formula's once again continuously banging in my head. Wow. This thing really works. Let me check my perfect woman list. Blonde, check. Two kids, check. Cute, check. Hot (probably), check. Nice and gentle, check. Lives close by, check. Intelligent, check. Sounds pretty good to me.

December 13, 2003

Something special's about to happen. I can feel it in my gut. Pure excitement. But that's not the only thing rattling my insides. I'm afraid of another disillusion. The fear makes me lazy. I want to go but I don't want to go. Maybe I should forget the entire thing and stay home. That would be a no-painer, guaranteed.

A short battle between the forces of good and evil takes place. Good wins. I shake off my laziness and get out of the house.

I arrive at the joint before my soul mate. I get a table and look around. Many couples are kissing, cuddling, and having a good time. Tons of questions pop up in my mind. I wonder what she looks like in person, if we'll get along, if she's really my soul mate.

My racing thoughts come to a sudden halt as I recognize the woman walking into the joint. Oh, my. Worst-case scenario. I'm trying hard not to puke. I want to hide under the table. I have the exact same feeling I had when I saw Nicole at the airport. She's overweight. Her mouth's crooked. Not at all like the picture she sent me.

This can only be a test. It has got to be a test. I know. Maybe life's telling me not to be prejudiced. Maybe it's time for me to open my eyes and see the person's interior before I judge the exterior. Bullshit. Who am I kidding. I'm not that evolved.

The girl takes a seat and we talk for a while. She tells me she has recently been to a fortune-teller, who told her she was about to meet the man of her dreams. I listen in awe as she describes my exact characteristics.

I'm really confused. On the one hand, she's nice and we do get along well. The fact that my son described her before we even met is hard to ignore. And she also got a pretty good description of me. But on the other hand, I find her physically appalling. And let's not forget that nauseating feeling screaming bloody murder.

I hate to admit it, but she's not the one. I feel like I'm looking at a distorted image of my soul mate.

We talk some more and have a few more drinks. It's getting late and she has to leave. We say our goodbyes and agree to meet again some other time. Not a chance in hell.

December 16, 2003

I'm truly depressed. I'm crushed by grief. I'm on the verge of a breakdown. I've had as much as I can handle. I've been trying to control what can't be controlled and predict what can't be predicted. So of course life has been playing dirty tricks on me and I'm getting badly burned.

Poor me. I'm such a victim. This must be the work of some sadistic god who gets his kicks from making people's lives so miserable they wish they were dead. Shit. I wish I were dead.

But then, as I'm about to seriously freak out, the unexpected happens. Something inside me shatters and tears break free. I feel strangely serene. The soul mate quest isn't so important anymore.

In fact, I couldn't care less about the whole thing. I just want to carry on with my life. I still hope for the best, but as the old song goes, *que sera sera, whatever will be, will be.* In other words, Fuck it.

December 20, 2003
I'm going out on a date. No one special. Just another woman I met at the shaman's workshop. I have no expectations. And that's great, because things end up being pretty boring. The girl seems to have no interest in me whatsoever. And I don't have the hots for her either. We have lunch at a nice place near my home. We barely talk to each other, but for some odd reason, make plans to meet again early next year. Who knows, it might at least be worth some good horizontal mambo.

Bachelor Party

I'm spending New Year's Eve at my cousin Chuck's therapeutic resort. I figured it would be healthy for me to get away from home and forget my worries for a while.

As usual, he has invited plenty of women to his party. I'm not in the mood for romance, but if I happen to meet a libidinous nymph, I definitely won't kick her out of bed.

Most chicks are after Chuck, the ace therapist. Unfortunately for them, his girlfriend is with him. I guess I'm the second best thing around. I'm okay being second choice, as long as the bitch doesn't yell out my cousin's name while we're getting busy.

At some point, a few people decide to organize a talent show. I take the guitar and play some Elvis. Wow. Everyone's thrilled. I win the talent show. I've become an instant celebrity.

After my performance, a woman named Joy approaches me. Nice name. She's pretty hot and also pretty drunk. She thinks I'm a rock star. Her wish is my command. I'm a rock star.

We dance. We make out. We are all over each other. Then we leave the party and walk down to a nearby creek in the property. Hmm. Sex by the river. Kinky. But as soon as we start fooling around, I realize I don't have any condoms. And I'm too drunk to go find some. Joy gets pissed and wants to go back to the party. Whatever.

A few hours later, we try again. This time I've brought plenty of condoms along, but now Joy refuses to lie on the lawn. It's cold. It's wet. There might be bugs, and we don't want bugs crawling up her butt crack now, do we. Goddamned fussy lady. Sex is once again a no-go and we return to the party.

It's almost dawn. Still no sex. Enough. I lose my patience. I grab Joy by the arm and take her to one of the empty bungalows. She's got nothing to complain about. Not this time. We jump into bed and finally go all the way. What a bundle of Joy.

The next day, the stupid woman acts as if she doesn't know me. I think maybe I was her second choice. So what. We both got what we wanted. And she wasn't that good anyway.

January 10, 2004
I'm at home getting ready for my second date with that woman I met at the shaman's workshop. Yawn. Boring. I don't really feel like going. Not at all. We didn't get along on our first date, so why should we get along now. Oh, well. I might as well get rid of this last pending thing. No more soul mate story on my mind. Thank God. There's a good soccer game on TV. I might even be back in time to watch the second half.

I get to her apartment and she lets me in. I like the energy of her place. Bright. Cozy. I take a seat on the sofa next to her and we start talking. I'm surprised. This woman's completely different from the one I went out with a couple of weeks ago. She's gorgeous. But I don't care what she looks like. She's smart. She's witty. She's interesting. But it doesn't make a difference. I just feel totally comfortable around her. No fancy feelings, just comfortable. We spend all afternoon chatting and in the evening we make beautiful love.

January 11, 2004
I'm strangely mellow. The sun shines bright. Birds sing their delicate melodies. Ain't life sweet. Ah, so this is what it feels like to have a lifelong yearning fulfilled. Not at all what I had expected. No fireworks. No balloon drop. No confetti. Just a deep certainty

that I've found what I had been looking for. I look back into the past few months and can't help but laugh. God indeed works in mysterious ways…

I don't think I've ever felt quite like this before. But I don't care. I have no expectations of my new lady or our relationship. I don't care if she's my soul mate. I don't care if our love will last forever. All I can say is I'm happy I found a way into her life.

hiatus…

POSTSCRIPT

Fast-Forward

Fall 2010

So here I am. Still working on myself. Getting better by the day. And I'm on a lifelong roll, baby. You know, that date in early 2004 was a true milestone for me. And that's why I chose to end my account at that point. It's not that the date was so wondrously fabulous it totally changed my life. My life had been totally changing for quite some time, thank you very much. But at that point I felt different. I felt a major shift had taken place.

Well, the way I see it, inner work is like learning the guitar. You practice, practice, and practice but don't see any real progress. Then you get tired and set the guitar aside for a few days. When you decide to pick it up again, voila! Major improvement. And that's exactly what happened at that point. A perception. A major de-patterning perception. And just to let you know that this was not just time out for a breather before the sex, drugs, and booze kicked in again, here's a progress report...

It's been seven years since I stopped having sex and started making love. Much has happened. But my beloved and I still enjoy each other's company. We still understand each other. We still respect each other. We still cherish each other. I know our relationship isn't picture-perfect, but what we have is most certainly good enough for me.

In 2006, we moved permanently to the U.S., and I'm pleased to say the better part of me has been getting stronger by the day.

I'm a changed man. Although I still indulge in an occasional cigarette, I feel I've had enough drugs and unhealthy sex for this lifetime (I must confess I still listen to plenty of rock and roll). The closest I get to any kind of booze is the brandy in the Bach flower remedies I take every once in a blue moon.

I'm well on my way into building a new father image within. I can't help but also notice daily improvements in dealing with my son and with my green friend, money.

I no longer blame my parents (or anyone else for that matter) for my misfortunes, personality quirks, or unwanted habits. I've learned to take full responsibility for my own behavior. I'm fully aware that people do the best they can with what they've got, and writing this book has helped me a great deal in changing my old attitudes. It was a catharsis, after all.

The relationship with my brother is much improved. Even though we really don't have that much in common, we keep in touch for the sake of blood ties. After all we've been through, I'm not complaining. And, hey, we are even Facebook buddies.

My boy's mother, Kate, was never able to fix her life, and an unfortunate course of events led to her death in 2005. But things turned out well. Better than we could have ever expected. M'lady adopted the boy in 2006 and is now officially his mother.

As for all the other women, affairs, sickly masturbation needs, and hard-ass father figures: gone with the wind. Also gone with the wind is the full-time dependence on self-destructive patterns. My old neurotic anxiety has been replaced by a sweet optimism, a sweet trust, a long-forgotten feeling that has resurfaced and reassures me my actions are perfect as they are and everything is going to be all right. Many times now I'm on what I like to call conscious automatic—*wu wei*, as they say in Taoism—action without action. And my story invents itself as it goes along.

Oops, almost forgot. I have a little something else I want to share. After years of groping in the dark, I have finally found out that the secret to a happier life is to let it happen. The secret to a happier life is to become empty. The secret to a happier life is to simply relax. Sounds simple enough. Right, easier said than done. But here's a clue.

You see, the thing is, it's no use blaming other people for the bad things in your life. In my case, it was only when I looked at my repetitive patterns and felt them through, again and again and again and again, that my surroundings changed like magic. They changed to adapt to the changes in my inner world. And I was left empty. Ah, sweet emptiness. So in a sense, I had to work my ass off to see that there was absolutely no need to work my ass off.

And speaking of blaming others, I'm also exhilarated to say that the years have utterly transformed my view of the opposite sex. Nonetheless, here I stand, truly sorry that you, dear reader, had to withstand my petty chauvinistic rants, but also immensely grateful for your witnessing of my full-blown catharsis, a necessary evil toward a much more realistic mindset.

Now, how exactly did I get from point A to point B? Well, I'll tell you this. Think mind and body techniques—exercise, visualizations, affirmations, and meditation, among other things. Yep. Eclectic, "irregular," but effective nonetheless. They have helped me and could surely help you. But, before you get all excited and run off looking for more details on my healing journey, ask yourself how serious you really are about change. Ask yourself how serious you really are about facing yourself. Not for your parents. Not for your partner. Not for your kids. Not for the human race. *But for your own sake.*

Finally, I have some good news and some bad news. I know. You want to hear the bad news first. Here it is. The healing journey does take some time. And it is tough in the beginning. Don't expect major changes in the blink of an eye. Despite what others may tell you, there are no quick fixes here. As the cover text aptly states: my self-destructive patterns didn't develop overnight, and my solutions didn't either.

But the good news is that the healing journey takes far less time than it took to create the damned patterns. Indeed, it does get easier as you go along, and the result is truly transforming. That's a promise. And it's up to you how deep, how fast, and how far you want to go.

And in the end...well, in the end, like the Zen master said, mountains are again mountains, rivers are again rivers. (Bet you thought I was going to quote the Beatles. Gotcha.) Or as my father, the prominent psychiatrist, so faithfully and simply once put it, people change, but not really. Hmm. A tough Zen *koan.* Let me explain. As my patterns dissolve, I change. I feel expanded, I feel free, I feel whole. I change, but not really. Somehow I'm still me. Go figure.

ABOUT THE AUTHOR

Having formally plunged into the depths of scientific and psychological abstractions, Ron Wyn has got both sides of the brain covered. Primarily a man of thought, his systematic mind insisted on a skeptical approach to life, a because-I-have-seen-I-believe *modus operandi*, but his troubled relationships ended up leading him to a path of action that opened his heart up to new and exciting inner experiences.

Ron has been working with teaching, counseling, translation, writing, and music for over twenty-five years. Since 1998 his interests have expanded to include alternative treatments and therapies such as rebirthing, Applied Kinesiology, Reiki, Yoga Nidra, shamanism, Kabbalah, and meditation, all of which provided the perfect foundation for a remarkably effective set of tools that fully addresses healing in mind, body, and soul.

Ron Wyn currently lives and works in the United States. His main focus in life is to embrace his True Self through the silent blossoming of awareness.

Ron is also available for speaking engagements and private coaching and can be contacted at ron@irregulartherapy.com.

For more information on *irregular therapy*™, articles, books, audio, and other products and services, please visit

www.irregulartherapy.com

BEAUTY, BALANCE, BEING

our three-fold mission:

Beauty—to color the world with meaningful and inspirational words, music, and insight while helping people feel better about themselves.

Balance—to help disseminate powerful body and mind practices while effectively bringing out a wealth of down-to-earth knowledge in simple and understandable terms, in a way applicable to practical solutions.

Being—to demystify spirituality while guiding and supporting fellow humans on their journey to reconnect and realign with their true nature, in their own words.

For more information visit

www.irregulartherapy.com

www.ingramcontent.com/pod-product-compliance
Lightning Source LLC
Chambersburg PA
CBHW021048090426
42738CB00006B/241
9780983281047